Veiled Courage

also by Cheryl Benard

Turning On the Girls

Moghul Buffet

The Government of God

Veiled Courage

INSIDE THE AFGHAN WOMEN'S RESISTANCE

Cheryl Benard

in cooperation with Edit Schlaffer

DISCARD

Broadway Books ~ New York

Acknowledgments

This book came into being under extraordinary circumstances, and many people helped make that possible. I want to thank our very own "male supporters," Dr. Zal Khalilzad, Alexander, Max, Nicholas von Gersdorff, Dr. Ulrich Kropiunigg, Dr. Abdul Ahad, Wahid Monawar and Joe Regal, for translations, technical support, Web design, organization of RAWA events, exercises of "people politics" and other crucial contributions. I also want to thank Kris Puopolo for a high-intensity writing and editing experience I don't think either one of us will soon forget.

For more information about RAWA and ways to participate in their work, go to www.rawa.org. To support a more equitable representation of women in diplomacy, international relations and development aid, or to share your own ideas for people politics, contact www.women-without-borders.org.

Contents

Veiled Courage

CHAPTER I

Men, Boys
and Dust

M en, boys and dust. That was my initial impression when I first went to the Afghan border area in 1982, an expert in project design sent to assess the efficiency with which aid was being delivered to Afghan refugees by the international community. I had lived, traveled and studied in other countries, including Islamic ones, but even there, my contacts had been limited to people like me—modern, educated, urban people. This was not the group that populated the border area or lived in the refugee camps.

Reviewing the aid projects consisted of two activities. I toured the camps, visited the health clinics and distribution centers and surveyed the other services Western agencies were providing. I took part in the meetings where these agencies discussed how things were going and decided what to do next.

The camps were in desolate areas half an hour to an hour from the nearest Pakistani town. You took an unpaved road into what seemed like nowhere and bounced along until the drab silhouette of tents or mud huts appeared before you. Your driver stopped at a polite distance, and you got out. Within seconds, a crowd of men and boys materialized, apparently out of nowhere. They must have seen you coming, then emerged from their dwellings and approached, but it never seemed that way. They always seemed to just appear, and in large numbers, too.

They would form a circle around you and stare at you intently, though not threateningly. There were no women in their midst, never, and no girls. Their society was highly segregated, you knew that much already, and here you could plainly see it for yourself. However, they seemed to take your presence completely in stride. After a while, children would be dispatched to run into the camp and fetch a person of authority. If someone had some knowledge of English, that person would also arrive. The reason for your visit would be elicited through a combination of the driver's explanations and your own communication with the powers that be.

In the tedium of camp life, your arrival was a major ceremonial occasion. If the camp featured a school, the children would be exhibited, the little girls peeping out from their many-layered wrappings while the boys were made to perform their military drills for you. Tea would be brought. Chairs would be fetched, two or three of them, whatever number the camp owned, and set up right there on the middle of the plain, and you would be urged to sit down while the important people of the camp—the elders, the schoolteacher, the person who spoke some English—drank tea with you, sitting on chairs if there were enough, or squatting on the ground if there weren't. Everyone else would remain standing in a circle, still watching and staring. You would feel a little bit like the French kings, who took their meals in public while select groups of their subjects paraded past the table to watch them eat.

Your gender never seemed to make the slightest bit of difference. These tribal Afghan men were completely willing to negotiate, debate, interact with you in a neutral and solemn manner. Even their body language indicated that they weren't perceiving you as female. They neither kept an awkward distance nor did they seek an uncomfortable proximity. For photo opportunities, they would stand shoulder to shoulder with you, fixing the camera with a grimly somber gaze. You could feel like "one of the guys."

I also took part in the meetings where the resident Western helpers discussed their work. There were quite a few women among the aid workers, but as an issue, Afghan women went as unremarked in these meetings as they were physically invisible in the camps. Occasionally, someone would bring up the horrific mortality rates for women and newborns during childbirth, as well as for children under the age of five. Someone who had just compiled clinic statistics would mention the extremely high rates of domestic violence, the many women whose arm had been broken, who had been severely beaten by a husband or a male in-law or whose life-threatening health problem had been neglected until the matter was hopeless, even though the free clinic was a stone's throw away and the men of that family visited the clinic constantly to complain of a headache or to demand vitamins.

The outcome of these discussions was always the same. There was nothing you could do about it, the aid workers regretfully concluded. You weren't here to interfere in people's cultural traditions. The Pashtuns were just like that. You couldn't change them. It was pointless to offer services that would benefit the women, because the Afghans just didn't want that. They were used to things being this way. Even the women themselves didn't expect anything different.

I found these discussions deeply depressing, of course, but was inclined at first to accept the premise. It was obvious that the Afghans lived in an age, if not a universe, quite different from our own. Their men indeed made a very resolute impression and did not at first sight appear to be a group you could easily sway or mold. Collectively, their reputation was this: an intractable, archaic people, stubborn, violent, with a history of overthrowing any ruler who tried to reform their backward social ways and of defeating any foreigner who tried to change them. Even their own kings were not able to move them forward by more than a cautious millimeter or so without risking assassination or at best deposition. They rose up when you tried to free their women from the veil. Talk of educating their girls, and they would rebel. After hearing enough of these cautionary tales, the term *they* might start nagging at you a little. "They" were the Afghan men, clearly. Weren't the Afghan women part of the national "they"? Did they have opinions, too? It seemed not. "They don't question their lot," you would be told. "They feel safe within the family," some would offer consolingly. "They can't imagine a different life."

I couldn't argue with any of that. The statistics were appalling, mortality rates astronomically high, literacy rates appallingly low, but in the end they were just that—numbers. It was hard to get any real sense of Afghan women. You never met them, they didn't talk to you, you barely saw them. They were little more than a defensive motion in the distance—a covering hastily drawn around themselves and a glimpse of fabric as they disappeared into the recesses of a tent at the first sight of strangers. At your approach, the women vanished with the same immediate magic that made the men suddenly appear. Maybe the women really did accept things as they were. Maybe it really would take a very, very long time to gradually change things. Maybe you really couldn't apply your own standards and had to leave it up to them to transform their own society in due course. Maybe they really were so shy and traditional that the idea of visiting a clinic, of going to a school, of leaving their tents was anathema to them.

Then, on a later trip, I was told that there was a hospital for Afghan women, a small one, on the outskirts of Peshawar, run by an idealistic group of Afghan doctors— and that I might find it an interesting place to visit.

It wasn't part of my official program, so I took a scooter taxi, tunneling down a series of increasingly narrow streets and alleys until I reached the flat brown building, encircled by a mud wall, that held this clinic. There was one ward, a large room consisting of about thirty beds. The doctor led me in and took me from bed to bed. I started at the first one and made my way around the room, talking to each occupant while he translated or added his own explanation. The visit lasted for perhaps an hour, but it seemed like forever, in the way of tragedies and accidents and other terrible, unmeasurable moments. It is no exaggeration to say that when I emerged from that room, I was not the same person who had gone in.

The women in that ward were simple, ordinary refugee women. They came from villages or very small towns. Even before becoming refugees, they had been poor. They had no education. They had no notion of an outside world where life might be different. They were being treated for various ailments, but in the end, their gender was their ailment.

In the first bed, a skinny fourteen-year-old girl lay rolled into her sheets in a state of almost catatonic unresponsiveness, eyes closed, not speaking even in reply to the doctor's gentle greeting. Her family had brought her to be treated for mental illness, the doctor explained with regret. They had recently married her to a man in his seventies, a wealthy and influential personage by their standards. In their version of things, something had started mysteriously to go wrong with her mind as soon as the marriage was agreed upon—a case of demon possession, her family supposed. When, after repeated beatings, she still failed to cooperate gracefully with her new husband's sexual demands, he had angrily returned her to her family and ordered them to fix this problem. They had taken the girl to a mullah, who had tried to expel the demon through prayers and by writing Quranic passages on little pieces of paper that had to be dissolved in water and then drunk, but this had brought no improvement, so the mullah had abandoned his diagnosis of demon possession and decided that the girl was sick. The family had brought her to the clinic, to be treated for insanity.

"We'll keep her here for as long as we can," the doctor said. "Then we'll prescribe tranquilizers. There's nothing else we can do. She has no choice. She has nowhere else to go. She just has to come to terms with this."

The second woman had a baby in the bed with her, a tiny thing with a shock of dark hair, hooked under her arm like a doll; the mother seemed listless, barely more responsive than the girl we had just visited.

What was wrong with her? Or was it the baby that was ill?

There was nothing wrong with either one of them, the doctor said. A normal birth, a healthy baby. They should have gone home a week ago, but no one had come to pick them up. The doctor shrugged, patted the woman's arm and said something consoling to her, but she didn't answer. The baby was a girl, he explained, and this had made her husband and his family very angry. To show their disapproval, they were refusing to collect her. They would come eventually, they always did; this was just a disciplinary measure, to frighten her into thinking she had been abandoned, so that she would try harder to meet their expectations in the future.

The woman in the next bed looked really ill, haggard and very pale. She had a visitor. An elderly woman was perched right up on the bed beside her, sitting on her heels like a little sparrow, clutching the younger woman's hand tightly and stroking her cheek, looking sad and worried: her mother. This young woman had suffered a miscarriage, the doctor explained, her sixth or seventh one in a row. He had sat down with the husband and explained to him very carefully that there was no reason why he and his wife should not one day have a successful pregnancy and healthy children. But first, his wife's body needed a chance to rest. There was no point in relentlessly trying for one pregnancy after another. It was not only pointless but also dangerous. His wife was already weak and anemic; if the next miscarriage brought any complications, she might die.

The husband had listened with little interest. "Then he said, 'It is the woman's job, intended by God, to give children. If she dies, that is God's will, and I will marry another woman,'" the doctor related, his voice somewhere between indignation and despair. Sometimes he thought of dispensing birth control secretly, but women had so little privacy in these traditional families, and if anyone found out, it would be the end of him.

I continued the circuit. Looking back, I don't remember a single woman whose problem was primarily medical. The doctor knew that; for most of his patients, dispensing tranquilizers was the best he could do.

As we progressed deeper into the ward, the women became more vocal, on each other's behalf if not on their own. The next patient had been brought in for "mental disturbances" caused by the fact that her eight-year-old son had been taken away by her husband to participate in the "holy war." This happened a lot, the doctor explained, and the mothers often took it very badly. Some became hysterical and could not be calmed down. They would cry for days and even become violent, throwing themselves against walls in their grief. Many of these boys died; what did they know about being a warrior? This woman's story caused a number of the other women to sit upright in their beds and start speaking in agitated voices. I had been led to believe that the Afghans were universally behind the "freedom fighters," ready to pay any price to punish the Soviets. These women had a different view. To them, martyrdom was not heroic and the sacrifice of children was not gladly given. They wanted their young sons alive and accused the rebel leaders of being tyrants, unscrupulous and corrupt. I had been led to believe that Afghan women had no views or, if they did, that they followed those of their men exactly. This was my first indication that such was not the case.

I met women who were not ill at all, not the least little bit; having been widowed or rejected by an angry husband, they just had nowhere else to go, and the doctor was allowing them this bed as their only refuge. I met women who needed physical therapy because they had been confined to dark tents for so long that their bones and muscles and skin had been damaged. Convicts get an hour in the prison yard, to exercise and see the light of day; I met women who had not been allowed out of their tents for years, except under cover of darkness. I met women who had been forcibly married, women who had been arbitrarily divorced, women whose sons had been turned into child soldiers and their daughters into child brides through the whim of their husbands, women who were crippled because after a severe beating medical treatment had been withheld. Some had been made apathetic by despair, but not one of them welcomed her abuse as being in line with her religion or her culture, and several of them were very angry. You could go to a conference on women in Islam in Washington, D.C., or Berlin or Los Angeles and hear Muslim women militantly defend all sorts of inequities on the grounds that the Prophet or their national tradition or the Quran wanted it so, but you didn't hear anything like that in this ward. This was more like Gulag Archipelago, like visiting the political prisoners of a merciless military dictatorship. It was one thing to realize abstractly that these women's lives were sad, telling myself that they weren't really like me and didn't expect anything different and therefore didn't really mind. It was another to come face-to-face with an entire roomful of their helpless, hopeless misery. And if these thirty women minded, perhaps they all did.

These women were not resigned, they hadn't grown indifferent to the deaths of their children, they didn't accept loveless arranged marriages as a given, they didn't feel secure in the arms of an extended family, they weren't content in deep traditionalism. It was obvious that I had fallen prey to a comfortable deception.

"These are the lucky ones," the doctor remarked. "Their families are modern enough to allow them medical treatment. Have you heard the Afghan saying? A woman should only leave her house twice: once at her wedding, to go to the household of her husband, and once when she dies, to be taken to the graveyard."

This new and awful knowledge left me with nowhere to go, with no discernible assignment. The international organizations were not going to rock the boat just for the sake of Afghan women. They had no champion, and they themselves were in no position to fight. Was the doctor's approach the best one could hope for? Did we need to mobilize the pharmaceutical companies and organize a giant shipment of Xanax to be dropped over Afghanistan like food packets, to anesthetize Afghan women to their lot?

"There's this school . . . ," a young Afghan woman whispered to me timidly, having heard from the doctor that these matters were of interest to me.

Another scooter taxi, this time into a lower-middle-class residential area. A glance to the right and to the left, then a quick dash inside. No, it wasn't illegal here in Pakistan, but still, a girls' school—that was a very controversial thing, and it was better not to attract notice. I found myself inside a normal home. In the shaded courtyard, surrounded by plants and vines, twenty girls sat in rows, their eyes bright and lively and darkened with kohl, their books open before them. A motherly, businesslike teacher turned to greet me.

That was how I found RAWA.

I didn't know, at that moment, exactly what it was that I had found, or what it would come to mean to me. I didn't know yet that besides running schools and clinics, RAWA was also a political movement, determined to offer Afghan women more than sedatives to palliate the injustices of their lives. I didn't know that the Taliban would come and establish a reign of terror far worse than that of the fundamentalists who currently held sway, or that RAWA would become the only group, male or female, to organize an underground resistance against them. And I certainly did not anticipate the grip RAWA would claim on my heart, the painful disillusionment I would suffer on their behalf as world politics showed its worst and most cynical face, the long-standing partnership that would extend from fundraising events in Vienna to conference halls in Bonn to interviews conducted practically under the rain of American bombs falling on Kabul. And I did not know that, for the small help I was able to give them, a determination to carry on under all and any odds would be their gift to me.

CHAPTER 2

The Petal and the Rock: Meena

T he story of Meena, the legendary founder of the Revolutionary Association of the Women of Afghanistan, begins in the early 1970s. On university campuses the world over, turmoil was rife. The world's youth was filled with energy, idealism and the determination to make the world a better, fairer place. They formed groups, movements and organizations; they distributed leaflets, chanted slogans, organized demonstrations, rebelled against the older generation and their antiquated values.

The winds of change were powerful enough to sweep all the way to far-off, remote Afghanistan. Even in Afghanistan, students traveled, spent semesters abroad with relatives or on exchange scholarships. They went to the Soviet Union, to France, to the United States, and when they returned they brought exciting and incendiary ideas with them, tales of freedom, progress, equality and revolution. Even the girls traveled. The government sent a clutch of them to modern, exciting, progressive Turkey to study nursing. Others went abroad with their parents or their brothers.

Western movies arrived on the cinema screens of Jalalabad and Mazar-i-Sharif, bringing glimpses of alien and wonderful worlds, worlds where men—and women, too— lived lives of unimaginable freedom. Sitting there in the darkness while these panoramic visions filled their minds,

Afghanistan's young people did not aspire to the full measure of such liberation, but they longed for just a little slice of it.

Wouldn't it be wonderful to marry for love? To meet someone you liked and got along with, then to get to know him, to fall in love and marry—instead of being handed over on your wedding day to a total stranger selected by your parents, someone whose looks you might find repellent and who might turn out to be mean.

An unhappy marriage with an incompatible partner was worse for the woman than the man, but young men had their romantic dreams, too. They didn't much like it, either, to have a bride picked out by their family according to the last generation's criteria, then foisted on them sight unseen. It would be much more wonderful to fall in love, to spend your life with someone who liked you and with whom you had things in common, someone who could be a friend and a partner.

And young Afghan girls wanted to go to university. A few years of glamorous and exciting student life, then a career and their own money—that was clearly better than the conventional life plan, which foresaw being a quiet, obedient, self-effacing daughter-in-law in the household of a husband's extended family.

And even the most cursory glimpse of an outside world revealed this much: that Afghanistan, compared with nearly anywhere else, was extremely, heartbreakingly backward. Conditions that before had seemed natural or at any rate inevitable came into question when you compared them with the larger world.

As always, change came rapidly in the cities, more slowly in towns and hardly at all in rural villages. In places such as

Kabul, young people seemed ready to abandon centuries of tradition without so much as a backward glance.

Western clothes and music were adopted with enthusiasm. Girls wore miniskirts, hung out with their girlfriends in giggling groups, and took the long way home from school, carefully choosing a detour that would route them past the local boys' school. Their mothers, as girls, had still worn the veil and meekly gone as brides to an unknown husband's house at the age of twelve.

Kabul's young women studied medicine, journalism and law. When they graduated, they took jobs in offices, ministries, brand-new clinics. Their mothers were illiterate but were a welcome and valuable part of the modern new dual-career household, which needed them as baby-sitters.

Afghan pop stars such as Ahmad Zaher sang about love and justice and were mobbed by hysterical teenagers, just like the Beatles in Liverpool.

And an earnest young woman named Meena was preparing to graduate from high school.

Born in 1957 to a middle-class family, Meena had always been a star pupil, bright, serious, inquisitive. That had landed her a place in the desirable Malalai High School for Girls. Meena enjoyed literature, liked to read biographies of famous women such as Joan of Arc and was interested in philosophy, but the big issues of the day fascinated her the most. Several of her teachers were social activists. In their lectures, they spoke to the girls about democracy, class struggle, the politics of poverty, the role of political parties and movements and the responsibility of intellectuals. And it wasn't just talk. One of her teachers was threatened by the secret police. A famous social critic and poet, Saidal

Sukhandan, was assassinated by fundamentalists. Politics was serious business, and the stakes were high.

Meena was accepted at the highly regarded Shariat University, which had formerly been an institute for Islamic law but was now just an ordinary university, considered one of the country's most prestigious places of learning. There is a photograph of her from those days: slender, pretty, terribly young, wearing a thin sweater and looking composed and hopeful. It's my favorite picture of her.

It was almost inevitable, in Afghanistan, that university students became radicalized. The country's poverty was so extreme, social conditions were so desperate, the political system was so patently corrupt, the elites were so manifestly overadvantaged. Outside of the big cities, hardly anyone could read or write; girls were still married off at or before puberty; infant mortality was astronomically high, and children died in huge numbers of illnesses easily prevented by better hygiene, cleaner water and vaccinations or easily cured by modern medicine. How could these conditions be rectified, the country modernized, democracy introduced? Kabul's students debated these questions passionately with each other and with their professors. They demanded reforms and progress. They organized demonstrations to push for change.

The monarchy was sympathetic to such views and goals but slow to implement them. The king, his family and his entourage preferred the spas of Europe to the depressing conditions at home. Their distance from the common people was symbolized by the fact that most of them did not even speak the country's dominant language, Pashtu, conversing instead in cultured Persian or French.

Meena was immediately attracted by the student movement, but a number of things bothered her about it. Women
had hardly any role to play, and their specific situation was
not addressed. Nor did it seem sufficiently mainstream and
democratic, with its tendency to splinter into innumerable
factions to debate the finer points of leftist ideology. Also,
they didn't seem sufficiently concerned about fundamentalism. Already, a young engineering student named Gulbuddin Hekmatyar had rallied like-minded fundamentalists and
was targeting female students and demanding their removal
from campus, throwing acid on them to protest their shame-
less modern dress.

What was really needed, Meena thought, was a broad,
genuinely democratic movement. Maybe it should be organized in the form of an independent women's organization.
That was probably the only way that women could determine the issues that were important to them and plan their
own political activities. In traditional Afghanistan, women
working with other women was also a much more acceptable and familiar way of doing things.

In 1976, at age nineteen, Meena married Faiz Ahmad,
the head of a leftist organization. Starting with the no-
nonsense ceremony they chose in place of the elaborate,
days-long rituals customary in Afghanistan, the marriage
was an intellectual partnership, though not always a political one. Meena and Faiz didn't always agree, but Meena had
apparently chosen her partner with care. Unlike many men,
many Afghans and many leftists, Faiz was able to tolerate
dissent, even in his own household.

From Meena herself, we have this description of the
"politics" of her marriage: "I never felt any kind of obstacles from him regarding my mission. I have to say, he is my

strong partner. When I first consulted him about the establishment of a woman's organization, he immediately saw the merit of the idea and advised me to concentrate all my energies on it and not to be distracted by other things or even by housework.

"He asked me how I viewed the relationship between my new women's organization and the liberation movement in general, and I explained to him that we needed to separate this issue from our personal life. We could love each other, but I wanted the left-wing organization he was leading to be completely separate from the democratic organization I was planning to establish.

"When I showed him the draft of our organization's principles, those of RAWA, he commented on some of the points. He also liked to joke, so he said, 'I just hope you women won't become completely independent of us.'

"If I had married a traditional, reactionary or unpolitical man, I would have faced a lot of difficulties. And my husband also said that if he had married a backward and reactionary wife, it would have been a big problem for him. Both he and his organization welcomed the creation of RAWA, not just out of respect for me, but because they shared our principles. Of course, some people couldn't fathom that, they couldn't believe that a married woman could really establish an independent woman's organization that wasn't just a shadow of her husband's organization. But other than this, there was nothing about my marriage that I ever regretted."*

The last two sentences of this statement have to be seen in the Afghan context. Meena's organization was extremely dif-

---

* "Life Sketch of Martyred Meena," RAWA. I have lightly edited the English translation of this document.

ferent in style and in ideology from that of her husband, but
to a traditional Afghan mind-set, this is almost impossible to
credit. Not only for the rest of her political career and her life
but to this very day, many Afghans assume that RAWA can
be nothing other than the women's auxiliary to Faiz's organization. This persistent assumption was annoying in the
extreme. It was difficult to persuade people to look at and
judge the organization on its own merits and to try to believe
that women could be independent actors. Though neither
Faiz nor his organization could be blamed for that, it was the
one regrettable thing about Meena's marriage.

By the end of the 1970s, enlightened modern parents in
Kabul were just beginning to take the radical step of allowing young engaged couples—accompanied by a chaperone,
of course—to date once or twice before their wedding. And
some young wives were working, with the blessing of their
husband and his family. But an arrangement such as
Meena's, where the woman struck out completely on her
own in a high-profile political way, was unheard of.

Meena soon became aware that her personal life was
falling under intense scrutiny not just by critics but, more
important, by a generation of young women looking for
new role models, for someone to test the boundaries on
their behalf.

Could a woman really form her own organization, take
political action independently from the leadership of men?
Well, maybe—but surely only while she was a student, not
as a married woman. Obviously, no husband would tolerate
a wife who took public stands separate and different from
his, would he? And his family wouldn't tolerate such an
independent daughter-in-law, would they? Many interested

eyes observed Meena's marriage, waiting for her female destiny to catch up with her. Pregnant, aha! That, definitely, would put an end to things. Motherhood made women sedentary and domestic, everybody knew that.

Since Meena's high school days, Afghanistan had undergone dramatic changes. The monarchy had been overthrown, the replacement government had also been toppled, and now a highly unpopular Communist regime was barely hanging on to power.

During her first pregnancy, Russian troops arrived to occupy Afghanistan, hoping to prevent the overthrow of their protégés. Surely, everyone concluded, Meena would not be able to continue her work under such circumstances, but would be forced to withdraw and behave cautiously at least for a while.

From her own remarks, it is clear that Meena was strongly mindful both of the political necessities of the situation and of her own role as a pioneer and role model: "It is considered a very unusual event in our country that a pregnant woman should work and, even more, that she should be involved in political activities. Apart from the absolute need of the circumstances, which required constant effort on the part of every politically committed person, I also wanted to prove in practice that pregnancy shouldn't paralyze women or provide them with a pretext, and I wanted to remove the misconception of men who think that women are incapable of any activity during pregnancy."

Indeed, I've encountered women who were girls during those years and who still remembered being inspired and emboldened by the example of this woman who could not be stopped, not even by biology.

Still, for regime opponents and for intellectuals generally, life was becoming very dangerous. Anyone even vaguely suspected of opposing the regime was rounded up and jailed. Many were summarily executed or disappeared, their fate never known. Faiz, too, was arrested. Shortly thereafter, Meena gave birth to their first child, a daughter. When she learned that her own name was also on a list of suspects, she was forced to leave her newborn with friends, to keep the child safe, and flee.

It was a desperate time. Separated from her baby, barely recovered from the birth, grieving over the reported deaths of several friends, fearful for her husband, she was obliged to stay constantly on the run.

Should she leave the country, abandon her activism?

Facing an entirely new level of danger and political gravity, Meena made a fateful decision. Women were not taken seriously as a political force, she concluded, because they were not willing to take the same risks or to show the same resolve as men. When things got serious, they drew back while the men stepped forward. Men shaped history and ruled the world because they stayed on target and fought things through. It was time for women to do the same—but using the nonviolent, democratic means that Meena and RAWA stood for.

The moment was ripe for such an experiment. Kabul's resistance to the Soviet-backed regime was nearly broken. Almost all middle-class or intellectual men had been killed, jailed, forcibly drafted into the army or driven into exile. If there was to be any further opposition, it was up to the women.

Teachers and university students were the educated and politicized class in this society, and schools and universities were the only real sites of political discussion and of convocation. There is one method common to pacifists and to women when they are the carriers of political protest—they emphasize their status as an unarmed, nonviolent civil force. In South America, demonstrations against military dictatorships are often led by middle-aged or older women and mothers. Against the declining Soviet army, older Soviet peasant women confronted young soldiers in a show of maternal authority. In Israel and the Balkans, women in black symbolize the moral reprimand of grief and loss.*

The message is always the same: "We are here not to fight, but to articulate the will of the people and to appeal to the country's conscience." In Afghanistan, unarmed young girls in their school uniforms and young female university students became the messengers of choice. What developed in Kabul was a new and effective method of political agitation: schoolgirls' demonstrations. Asifa, a longtime RAWA member, remembers, "Our work was mostly oriented toward the girls and women in school and university. We were distributing leaflets, called *shabnamahs* or night letters because we had to spread them during the hours of darkness, and from week to week we were reaching a wider and wider audience. However, the most important work RAWA did at that time was organizing the schoolgirls in demonstrations. In these demonstrations women would express their position against the Khalq and Parcham, the two pro-

* See Ayala Emmett, *Our Sisters' Promised Land: Women, Politics and Israeli-Palestinian Coexistence* (Ann Arbor: University of Michigan Press, 1996); Cynthia Enloe, *The Morning After: Sexual Politics at the End of the Cold War* (Berkeley: University of Calif. Press, 1993); Sarah Radcliffe and Sallie Westwood, eds., *Viva: Women and Popular Protest in Latin America* (London: Routledge, 1996).

Soviet factions whose fight against each other and against the people was tearing the country apart, and against the Russians. We used to say poetry against them."

The demonstrations started out small in 1978, flagged altogether during the first school break, then gathered steam and began to grow steadily until, by the end of 1979, they had become a genuine mass movement. In April 1980, RAWA helped organize what looked to be a very major rally. Announced in advance by *shabnamahs,* the theme of the march was "Our Girls Against the Red Dragon." Thousands of girls turned out; there was an accompanying poem with the same theme, which they chanted in lieu of slogans—"saying poetry against them," as RAWA calls it.

Unfortunately, their opponents did not take the same lyrical approach. Soldiers fired on the demonstration, and two young girls were killed.

Asifa continues, "One of the incidents that is unforgettable is when Nahid from the Rabia Balkhi School and another girl, Wajiha from the Lycée Amenah, were both killed. This became a grave situation in Kabul, and everybody was talking about these two girls and was enraged that the soldiers had simply killed them. Even the kindergarten children refused to listen to the Russian stories that were being read to them in school after that." The first issue of *Payam-e-Zan* (Women's Message), RAWA's new political magazine, had a photograph of Nahid on its cover.

One would expect the population to have been intimidated by such a show of brutal force, and parents to have forbidden their daughters any further political participation. But as Asifa related, the overall response instead was a wave of public outrage. Not only did girls continue to march, but RAWA members began to travel to other provinces to expand the group's activities. This was a true innovation. As a RAWA brochure notes, "In Afghan history there was no previous example where girls were able to travel around the country, going to different cities for the purpose of political activities."

Men were increasingly joining armed resistance groups against the Soviet occupation, groups that later became known as the mujahideen or, as they were referred to in the American press, "freedom fighters." These groups fought from the Afghan mountains or from their bases in neighboring Pakistan. Urban civil resistance became the domain of women. As the brochure goes on to state, "In the villages [the Russians] were targeted by the bullets of men, but in the cities they were surrounded by the anger of women."

That anger manifested itself in demonstrations, in the distribution of protest leaflets, in the wave of hostility and lack of cooperation that met the occupying soldiers, and in the support, supplies and information smuggled out to the fighters. All of these activities were rigorously sanctioned by the government, which, aware of its tenuous grasp on power, was nervous and thus especially prone to violence. Arbitrary arrests and killings increased as the government felt its hold slip. People were persecuted for minor political activities, for expressing the wrong opinion or even in complete error because they had fallen under suspicion for no good reason at all. This was the atmosphere that marked this middle period of Meena's activism, during which she moved from being a campus activist to being a serious political agitator and organizer. Asifa, who today is a member of

RAWA's inner leadership and who was my collaborator in overseeing the interviews for this book, met Meena during this period of her life.

Asifa was twelve years old when Meena and her husband moved into the house across the street. As far as anyone knew, Meena was a housewife named Laila. She was sometimes gone during the day or even for several days, absences for which she proffered banal reasons: visits to relatives, errands. Still, Asifa remembers, for some reason "we never looked at her as a usual neighbor. Instead, all of us were proud to talk to her for a few minutes and to be able to do something for her. I still don't know what made her so interesting and what gave her that charisma, that we were so attracted to her."

Something was different about this new neighbor, and young Asifa was fascinated by her. A neighborly friendship developed—not an unusual occurrence in Afghanistan, where people rely on their neighbors, helping each other in countless ways. But there was a difference. When Asifa's life started falling apart, others turned away, while Meena remained a steadfast friend.

"This was the time of Nur Taraki and Hafizullah Amin.* My father, who was an army officer and who did not have any association with any political group, was put in jail, and we were very upset and worried. Shortly after that, my aunt's husband was also put in jail. Everyone started avoiding us, including our close friends and relatives; they cut off their relationship with us because at the time of the Khalq party, if you went to the house of someone who had politi-

* Rival members of the Afghan pro-Soviet regime.

cal prisoners, they would be under surveillance and suspicion, and it could then involve you too.

"The best friend and only friend at the time of those dark days was Meena. She was like a mother to us."

But things were about to take a turn for the worse. When Asifa was thirteen, her father was killed by the pro-Soviet regime. Other male relatives were in prison. Civil unrest had reached a point where people did not feel safe going out on the streets. Meena's way of explaining this violent new world to a terrified, disoriented young girl is noteworthy.

"One night Meena came to our house. She talked with me and she asked me, 'What is your feeling about politics?' I responded, 'What is that anyway, politics?'

"She smiled at my question. Then she said, 'Politics is a wild animal with three horns and two tails and six feet that lives deep in a forest.' I laughed also, but Meena became serious and explained that politics can mean different things, but that to her, political activity meant to work for the people of our country, especially the situation of women.

"It was this year, 1978, that a revolt started against the government in different parts of the city, Kabul. The most important incident was around Chindawal on the third of Hoot [March]. That was the time that everybody was being followed and suspected, and people were afraid of their own shadow. When these incidents were happening, Meena was explaining the chaotic situation to me—what was Khalq and Parcham, who are those people who, under the name of wanting to help the working-class proletariat and socialism and equality, in fact have other agendas. This was the first time that I understood the meaning of a political party, and how to distinguish between working for your country and betraying your country."

By now, the situation in the neighborhood had changed. Meena no longer lived there openly; that would have been too dangerous. She had gone underground and was staying in changing locations, but her former neighborhood, where people were loyal to her, was still a safe haven. Asifa's family was typical in this regard. With the men having been killed or arrested, theirs was now a household of women. The grandmother, a pious elderly lady but one who had experienced the first wave of Afghanistan's historic monarchist reform and regarded herself as a pioneer of women's emancipation, had only a vaguely humanist interest in politics. But she loved Meena and praised her for offering up her entire life to the service of her country. Asifa's mother admired Meena wholeheartedly, while Asifa thought that "there was no one else like her in our country, that she resembled those brave heroines in the movies and that it was amazing to know someone like this."

Asifa's active partnership with Meena began abruptly and dramatically, as she remembers. "It was the twenty-fifth of April 1979. The situation was so bad that people were almost trampling each other in the street to safely reach their home. It was nine o'clock when Meena knocked on our door; she was wearing a burqa to hide herself, but her demeanor was calm and thereby she made us calm, too. And she said that everything was okay but that she was going out again because somebody was waiting for her outside. She asked me and my mother to come into the room, and she pulled a bundle of *shabnamahs* out and said, 'The day after tomorrow, we will demonstrate and we will be arrested. But tomorrow we distribute this, and you should join us.' She looked at my mother and me and asked, 'Can you do it?'

"My mother said laughingly, 'Why not? You can do it and we cannot? Is our life and livelihood better than yours?' I was very proud and happy at this response of my mother. Then Meena asked us to take the papers and distribute them from house to house. She also gave us a packet of dried pepper and said that if we got caught, we should throw it in the eyes of the police and we might have a chance to run away and not get arrested. But if we were careful, nobody should see us. Then she left and we started reading those *shabnamahs* and subsequently my mother and my grandmother and I cried to think of Meena and her condition, being so calm though she was involved in this risky endeavor. My grandmother went to pray an extra prayer for her.* She read a few *rakat* and subsequently prayed for her. And she did not sleep, but started reading the Quran and was holding the Quran to her tearful eyes. And she called Meena's name out loud as she did this, and prayed for her safety and long life.

"The next day, the twenty-sixth of April, my mother and I in the darkness of the night went to the *hammam*, because going to the public bathhouse was a usual thing that would not arouse suspicion, and on the way we distributed the *shabnamahs*. We made sure that we got to the *hammam* before dawn, to bathe and come back home. So the twenty-

---

* Islam requires five daily prayers and provides a format for each of them. However, if one has a particular worry or request or to lend greater power to the prayer, one can add extra prayers and dedicate them to a person or an issue.

sixth of April 1979 was my first day as a political activist, and it still is going on."

In the charged, chilling atmosphere of a beleaguered Kabul, it is amazing that Meena still found moments of humor, ways to keep an ironic perspective on her situation and its risks. There are two stories that illustrate that.

When Asifa entered into RAWA's political work in earnest, one of her assignments was to help provide cover for Meena's clandestine work by accompanying her and lending the outing the appearance of a family trip. One such trip took them to Badakhshan, where Meena needed to hold some political meetings. On the journey, the brother of a RAWA member went along. He, Meena and the teenage Asifa gave the appearance of being an ordinary family group. However, the man could not accompany them on the way back, so the two women were alone. Asifa had a tendency to become sick during travel, a problem that was particularly pronounced on this trip. This gave Meena the idea to introduce Asifa as her daughter, who had a stomach ailment and was being taken to Kabul for medical treatment. "When we got back we were laughing so hard about that. Meena said that I was the best companion imaginable for any underground political activist, because with my talent for throwing up and having stomach problems, I provided the perfect cover and no one would ever become suspicious."

A second incident falls into the category of gallows humor. One evening Meena arrived secretly at Asifa's house but had to be turned away at the door because the family had company. They promised to get rid of their guests as quickly as possible and asked Meena to come back in an hour. It was winter, and Meena, who always suffered from poor health and didn't cope well with the cold, spent the hour walking briskly around the market to keep warm.

"Shortly after her return, there came some quiet knocks on our door, and Meena hid in another room, not to be seen. It was our next-door neighbor. She asked if we knew what was going on outside. She was very nervous and frightened and she told us that the whole neighborhood was surrounded by soldiers, and that something must be going on. Immediately, we feared that they might be searching for Meena. Meena berated herself, saying that it had perhaps been a mistake to walk around the market, even though she had worn her burqa and hadn't noticed anyone following her. Then she told us that she would leave now so that they shouldn't find her in our house if they came to search. We didn't want her to go. It was much too dangerous to go outside when soldiers were everywhere. My mother even tried forcibly to hold her back. Meena was sweet. She said, 'Forgive me for not accepting your advice this time.' And she said, 'No matter what happens, you and the others should continue our work.' Then she put on her burqa and went out. As she opened the door you could hear the noise of many people running and shouting, but we couldn't make out what they were saying.

"I will not forget that night as long as I live. To think of her stepping out into the unknown like that, it was terrible. Around midnight the noises got louder again. This time my mother went out to see what was happening. And she heard from the neighbors that Fathana, the wife of the head of KHAD, the Afghan secret police, had wanted to run away to Pakistan with her lover and that Naguib had found out about it and had surrounded the house that his wife was hiding in, which just happened to be in our neighborhood. The next time we saw Meena, she laughed and said, 'May God keep them busy with each other's strange affairs. Then they won't have the time to come after us.'"

Not all difficult situations resolved themselves so easily, and by the 1980s, the situation had become untenable. Meena and the bulk of RAWA's membership were forced to flee to the border areas of Pakistan and Iran, where millions of their countryfolk were settling into camps and shanty-towns.

Some RAWA members came from wealthy backgrounds or had relatives in the West; they had the option of emigration. Others were forced to seek shelter in the slums and camps along with everyone else. It seemed likely that RAWA would now disintegrate. Instead, rallied by Meena, they regrouped.

First, RAWA members made a commitment not to emigrate. Already, most of the educated and modern elements of the Afghan population had left, starting new lives in Europe, Canada or the United States. RAWA members resolved to stay in their country. Second, they took stock. Their only resource was that they had education and professional training. Their nurses and doctors could provide health care; their teachers could organize schools and literacy programs.

Even as Meena was starting to set up headquarters in Pakistan, her longtime enemy and nemesis, Gulbuddin Hekmatyar, was doing the same. He was an important man now, running Peshawar like his personal fiefdom, using his new status as a U.S.-backed "freedom fighter" to expand his fundamentalist influence.

The Cold War was still in full swing, and the United States was determined to thwart the Soviet Union wherever possible. Obviously, a country such as Afghanistan could never defeat invading Soviet troops, American strategists believed, but by backing their Afghan opponents, one could at least make the Russians work hard for their victory. Since the object was to create the maximum amount of trouble for the Soviets, it made sense to back the fiercest, most ruthless groups and fighters. There seemed to be no point in supporting the moderate, modern, democratic Afghans who also opposed the Soviets—those kinds of people would surely be too civilized to throw themselves headlong into what the Americans had decided was a doomed venture. No, for that one needed the crazies, and Hekmatyar definitely fit the bill.

Awash in dollars, Stinger missiles and other signs of U.S. affection, he and a collection of other fundamentalist warlords formed personal armies and soon developed a significant power base. Once the Soviets were gone, they intended to rule Afghanistan according to values completely inimical to those of their Western backers. The Western governments, if they even thought about this, weren't worried. They were sure the Soviets were there to stay. Meena made a different assessment, and she was very worried indeed. The outlines of this new societal development were shaping up ominously: Educated Afghans were leaving for the international diaspora. Progressive and moderate political forces were being deprived of Western support and were fading into irrelevance. Instead, the most backward and extremist elements of the political spectrum were being nourished and enhanced. From an Afghan point of view, that left only two likely outcomes, and neither of them was attractive. One was that the United States was correct in its assessment and it was impossible for Afghans to defeat the Soviet Union. In that case, the current regime would stay, and thousands of Afghans were losing their lives and contributing to the devastation of their country for nothing. Or the United States was wrong, and the Soviets and their regime could be expelled. If so, the spoils would go to the victors, which meant that the radical fundamentalists would be installed in power.

Meena knew that the ruling pro-Soviet regime, while brutal, was weak and felt insecure, and she believed that the Soviet Union could be defeated. That left the fundamentalists and their daily expansion of power and wealth as her main worry. Pakistan, especially the border area, provided a hospitable environment for them. The refugees, dislocated, politically ignorant and dependent on others for their daily survival, were vulnerable to their influence. The Pakistani government, its powerful secret police (ISI), and the Americans were pumping money to the fundamentalists. The prospects were ominous. Where to start in any effort to form a bulwark against them?

Meena believed that women—educated women—were the first and most natural opponents of fundamentalism. They had the most to lose, and their values were the most naturally inimical to this brand of extremism. The key was to increase their numbers. And the path to that was education. Women or men who had some understanding of the broader world would not fall prey so easily to the fundamentalists' narrow, ignorant vision. Education was essential.

It was also something RAWA could provide. Its member-ship included a large number of teachers, professors, uni-versity students and other educated people. To operate schools was a doable prospect.

The refugees had no money, however, so these schools needed to be free. How to fund them? Meena appears to have possessed an almost American sense of entrepreneur-ship and drive. Her colleagues from those days recollect her motto: "Staring at others and waiting for them to help isn't the best approach." Instead, she came up with ideas for income-generating projects to support the organization and its projects and to provide an improved livelihood for refugee women.

Of necessity, the scope of RAWA's activities remained small. It was extremely frustrating for Meena to watch as radical fundamentalists were showered with Western fund-ing while moderates such as herself were hard pressed to scrape together even the smallest sums.

Any politically knowledgeable Afghan could foresee the tragic outcome of this very shortsighted American strategy: They were pouring money into groups that hated the West and everything it stood for. Meanwhile, she and her com-panions were trying to fund an antifundamentalist move-ment by weaving carpets, raising chickens and sewing little mirrors onto ornamental cushions.

"She used to say that if RAWA had even one-hundredth of what each one of those fundamentalist parties was receiv-ing from America, we could set up tens of schools, courses and hospitals, and even universities. But since everyone was pouring deluges of money into the pockets of the funda-mentalists, RAWA couldn't do all that."

34 ~ *Cheryl Benard*

Still, considering their limited means, RAWA did a lot. They were successful in their plan to set up schools, including high schools for boys and girls. These, the Watan Schools, today enjoy a superior reputation as excellent academic institutions. They organized literacy classes. They opened orphanages and dormitories. They printed textbooks. They conducted nursing courses and first-aid classes.

By this time, the turmoil in Afghanistan had given rise to one of the world's largest refugee crises—and it was clear to the experts that the crisis would not end quickly. NGOs,* international organizations and a variety of humanitarian aid groups began to set up pharmacies, clinics, even teahouses for the entertainment of bored refugee men. Nobody thought to build schools for the children, and no one paid attention to the refugee women, secluded and isolated in their tents and compounds. This, as we know today, was a fateful mistake. Pakistani fundamentalists would soon step into the vacuum, enrolling Afghan boys in their fanatic madrassas and turning them into "religious students": Taliban. It is to Meena's enduring credit that she recognized the role education could play as a force for the prevention of violence and extremism.

Her flight to Pakistan had two compensating features for her. Since her work was more overt than it had been in Afghanistan, it began to attract more notice and to have a greater impact. She was invited to Europe on a speaking tour that brought her to the attention of Western media and some European politicians who also had begun to be wary of the Islamic "freedom fighters." And in Pakistan, Meena

* Nongovernmental organizations.

was able to enjoy at least fragments of a more normal private life. In 1984, Meena gave birth to twins, a boy and a girl. However, these moments of personal happiness were of short duration. In 1986, while she was in Quetta and her husband had gone to Peshawar, Meena learned that Faiz had been abducted and killed by Gulbuddin Hekmatyar's henchmen; in fact, the report was that Hekmatyar had personally tortured him to death. Once again, this time under especially cruel circumstances, Meena felt the weight of everyone's expectant eyes on her: If she broke down now, so would her organization. She forced herself to carry on, to make the rounds of schools and projects and camps, to spend time with the children in the orphanages and make things seem as normal as they could.

The following spring, Meena's enemies caught up with her as well. She disappeared, along with two of her aides. There was no message, no sign of her. While her friends undertook a frantic search, opponents started spreading the rumor that she had taken RAWA's money and escaped to Europe. Some time later, two men were arrested in a different matter by the Pakistani police. During interrogation, they confessed to the murder of Meena and her assistants and revealed the location of the bodies. The men were connected to KHAD. When Meena's body was recovered, its condition revealed that before being killed, she had been tortured. Yet there had been no consequences for any of her organization's other members, no raids against their secret locations. Clearly, she had somehow found the final strength to resist, refusing to betray any of their secrets.

For RAWA, this was a major and traumatic blow. In the initial period following Meena's disappearance and the subsequent information about her death, the organization fell into panic and disarray. The more sensitive locations were shut down, members moved their residences constantly and—to the later great regret of those who made the decision—a large number of important documents pertaining to RAWA's earlier history, including many of Meena's letters, were burned. In addition, every RAWA member was faced with the chilling new knowledge of just how dangerous her work was. To go on now meant coming to terms with a situation of imminent mortal danger. They chose to continue.

Political killings are not a rare event in Afghanistan. Most of us will remember that Abdul Haq, a political and tribal leader, was ambushed and killed by the Taliban in the fall of 2001. Hamid Karzai, interim president of Afghanistan, lost his father to a political assassination in Pakistan. As in some other Third World settings, Afghan politics are played as a high-stakes game, rivals eliminated in the crudest possible way. Over the past decades, numerous intellectuals, activists and public figures of all kinds have been murdered or "disappeared," either by their opponents or by the state. Many were mourned and considered martyrs, but in Meena's case it has gone beyond that—she has been transmuted into a legend, into the kind of heroine rare in the political history of women.

She clearly possessed a charismatic personality, that much is clear from all accounts. The dictionary defines charisma as containing "grace, beauty and kindness," as making up a "special quality of leadership that captures the popular imagination and inspires allegiance and devotion," and as comprising "a special charm or allure that inspires fascination or devotion."* All of these elements are reflected in the descriptions, anecdotes and recollections of those who knew her—in fact, it is striking that the narrators of these stories often use those exact terms, giving you a whole new level of respect for Webster's. When Meena spoke to you, these witnesses say, you felt enfolded by her warmth. You immediately realized that this was not an ordinary person, that you were dealing with someone very exceptional. People felt moved to help her, to be near her. Even her ordinary residential neighborhood was overcome by the sense that someone extraordinary had come to live in their midst. You remembered her smile, her voice, her way of putting things. You couldn't explain it exactly, but she had something that drew you to her.

A number of photographs survive. They show a woman with strong, classic features and dark, thoughtful eyes, a woman of resolve and practicality. When she looks into the distance, her expression is not dreamy but clear; you sense that she is seeing a vivid, concrete future and is determined to help bring it about. Obviously, she was earnest, intelligent, strong. From the stories we learn that she was also warm, emotionally responsive and gifted in the art of motivating others. The following story, told by an older lady, is typical of the kind of ordinary, everyday event that nonetheless left a deep impression on her companions.

"Once Meena came to my house for lunch. She was exhausted; it was one of the hottest days in Kabul. Seeing her so tired, I rushed to the kitchen, and was surprised to see her follow me, insisting upon helping. While having her

* *Webster's New World Dictionary,* third college edition.

lunch, she told me that some families had just arrived in Kabul from other provinces, to get medical treatment. They had been provided with housing but needed dishes and other household items. I eagerly started assembling things and told her to take anything that she found useful for those families. I called my daughter to come and help her carry the things. She was thrilled and tears rolled down her cheeks, which induced me also to weep. 'What a pity that I am old,' I told her as I embraced and kissed her, 'and have lost the ability to work with you.' But she said no, that if they didn't have the sympathy of women like me, they would not be able to carry on their struggle."

That was a flattering and politic thing to say—but it also happened to be true. The broad base of support from ordinary people such as this elderly woman was RAWA's only guarantee of safety during times of persecution.

This ability to get support from unlikely quarters was characteristic of Meena. Pious, elderly women became sympathetic to what in the final analysis was a radical, leftist, feminist movement. And men, apparently, were inspired to support its feminist agenda by Meena's ability to persuade them. "It happened often that Meena came into direct arguments with men, defending the necessity of women's struggle. Usually, she was able to turn their opinion around. Then, after she had given these men a belief in women's power, she would joke, 'If RAWA wasn't a women's organization, then certainly we would have many men members.'"

It was important to Meena to maintain coherence between her values and the way she conducted her life. Unlike many political philosophers and leaders whose private lives contradict their supposed principles, who are corrupt or have affairs with subordinates or abuse their privileges or become consumed by their own ego and importance, Meena was meticulous in her efforts to practice what she preached. Asifa remembers, "In Pakistan, for some time I and a few others shared a house with Meena, and there I learned a few things about her character. She had so many responsibilities that we did not want to include her in the housekeeping. One day, we were sitting there making a plan of who would do what, and Meena happened to come by. When she saw what we were doing and that everyone had a specific task except for her, she said, 'Cleaning the bathrooms will be my job.' We were all surprised, but she explained that she wasn't doing it to be self-sacrificing, but out of practical considerations. Since she had to leave the house early each day, and wasn't home to do other things, cleaning the bathrooms in the morning was the most realistic job for her to take on. All of us, with one voice, protested against this, but she said, 'You might as well give up, I'm not changing my mind. Everyone has to do their part.'

"Of course, after this conversation several of us, including some of the men, rushed to get up before her every morning, to prevent her from cleaning the bathrooms, but she did not accept this. So we made a new plan, which divided the work by days instead of specific tasks. When Meena saw this new list and noticed that her name again wasn't on it, she said decisively, 'This schedule is going to change. My day is Friday.' And that's how it was from then on. In addition to cooking, she would also clean. But we found a way to cheat a little—we would make things so clean on Thursday that on Friday there wasn't much left for her to do. She was a good cook, though, and quick. Meena worked so hard that it upset us to see her working in the house as well. We used to urge her to go and spend some time with her husband instead, whenever he was in town, and with her family."

Perhaps the most noteworthy thing about Meena is the unambivalent admiration and loyalty she inspired in the women who worked with her, and in those who continue to follow her today. Her name is still the rallying cry for the organization she founded, her face its flag. "Meena's blood flows through the veins of each and every RAWA member and her memory and her thinking is the moving spirit of RAWA," one official biography states. "Have you heard about Meena?" RAWA members will soon ask the foreign visitor. "Will you put a photograph of Meena in your book?" RAWA women asked when they learned of this project. In a sense, she is the symbol of their collective identity. To an organization whose members, for their safety, routinely change their address and their name, the constancy of Meena is a fixed point.

Meena's personal style in matters large and small permeates the organization. Her habit of showing gratitude even for small acts of support has become part of RAWA's "corporate style"; donors and helpers don't expect or demand gratitude, but the charm of this habit is nonetheless undeniable—it's nice to be thanked and to feel that your contribution is valued. Warmth, emotion and appreciation are not the usual currency of political organizations immersed in matters of grim severity—but they pay off.

The same style marks RAWA's interaction with the refugees, as one young woman remembers. "I was thirteen when my father was killed at the hands of the pro-Soviet Afghan secret police, KHAD. My mother, my two sisters, my little brother and I fled to Pakistan. Already in Kabul I had heard the name RAWA on the radio, and in Pakistan, my sister showed me a copy of their magazine, *Payam-e-Zan*. I immediately wrote to RAWA, and after a few days they got in touch with us. On our first encounter, which consisted of two women coming to see us, the feeling was so warm and friendly that we thought we had known them for years. It was during the third or fourth meeting that my sister expressed her wish to work with RAWA, while I became a student at their Watan middle school."

A murdered father, a family in upheaval, an uncertain future, a sparse refugee camp run by a cold, alien bureaucracy—and then two women appear. They are strangers, but they approach you with concern and warmth. They are women, like you, and refugees, like you, yet they have mastered their situation and are even in a position to help others. If they could survive and prosper, maybe you can, too.

The girl in the above story graduated from RAWA's schools and today oversees the running of two of them, besides being a leading member of the education and cultural committees.

"We have an expression in Persian," Asifa told me. "It says, 'Human beings are more fragile than the petal of a flower, but at the same time they are stronger than a rock.'"

It seems an apt epitaph for Meena—whose name, by the way, means "love." Her life was ended by two executioners sent by the secret police, but her thoughts and example endure and have only begun to unfold their potential.

To the Fundamentalists
You can dim the light of the candles whose glow warms
  my eyes

You can freeze the kisses on my lips
You can fill the air with curses
Or with the terrible silence of my grief
You can steal my sister's smile
You can put up a thousand walls
You can do all that
And I, I can fight.

—*From a RAWA brochure*

CHAPTER 3

The Work of RAWA

I don't think you can imagine how deeply it has been implanted in us to believe that we are only half as valuable and half as smart as our brothers, only half as brave as a man," Tameena notes ruefully.

For many women, RAWA is first and foremost a glimpse of a universe where this hitherto unshakable natural law might not necessarily be true. They describe this moment as a radical turning point in their lives, a revision of their entire prior view of the world and their place in it.

For many of them, their first contact with RAWA is through a teacher who cares about them enthusiastically and ungrudgingly, who is educated and brave and warm and articulate in her explanations of the role women can play in society and on behalf of other women. Or RAWA is a magazine, *Payam-e-Zan*, nuanced, erudite, read and studied and respected not just by women but by men, too. And RAWA is that group of self-confident, purposeful young women wearing white jackets with *RAWA* stenciled on the back, striding through the camps with something to give—distributing blankets and food, fearless in their encounters with international organizations and camp leaders, resourceful and independent. For many Afghan women, RAWA is the first hint that the things they have thus far been told about women and their limits and frailties and incapacities are, plainly and simply, not true.

This chapter provides an overview of the most important aspects of RAWA's work, which includes consciousness raising, therapy, education, information and social services. The overarching purpose of its work is to awaken and mobilize civil society, to break the terrible circle of violence and warlordism that has eaten up Afghanistan for almost half a century.

At RAWA's core is the executive committee, with eleven elected members. Each of the members of this inner leadership circle is also the head of one of RAWA's committees: the educational committee, the publications committee, the foreign affairs committee and so on. Members with guiding responsibilities in these committees form a second leadership circle. Issues related to the individual committees are debated in regular meetings. At greater intervals, assemblies are held to discuss matters relevant to the direction of the organization as a whole. Given the irregular political circumstances, there are no formal rules about quora. If it is safe to come and you can make it, you participate.

Membership, likewise, is in tiers. There are approximately two thousand full-fledged members, who pledge to work directly with the organization and not to emigrate. Then there are many people with looser affiliations to RAWA—people who teach in their schools but do not belong to the organization, people who support its program and help occasionally but have not joined, women who would like to join but can't participate actively because of family constraints, a large number of male supporters. All of these people can attend the meetings, participate in the debates and offer suggestions but not vote. Finally, there are the thousands of foreign sympathizers worldwide.

CONSCIOUSNESS RAISING

"How did you first learn about RAWA?" That was one of the standard questions in the interviews for this book, and it usually elicited one of three answers. Some people had been university students in Afghanistan in the years before the Soviet invasion and had come into contact with RAWA then. Some came into contact with RAWA through its network of schools and social services. And many knew about RAWA from its magazine, *Payam-e-Zan*.

If you go to Borders or Barnes & Noble, you will find an entire wall covered with any imaginable sort of magazine, row upon overlapping row. It's not like that in Afghanistan. In the barren landscape of nearly nonexistent social debate, *Payam-e-Zan* was striking, noteworthy and unique. For years it was the only magazine that provided independent, intellectual discussions of current events, and as such it was read by men and women alike. That women were its creators was, of course, especially remarkable.

For many of the men and women we interviewed, discovering *Payam-e-Zan* for the first time had been an event of significance. They remembered and could relate the exact circumstances: They found it in the box of papers a friend left behind when she fled to Iran; their older sister brought it home from college one day; a little boy sold it to them during a demonstration. Many had immediately felt compelled to contact RAWA through its magazine, and lengthy correspondences often ensued. One of the organization's young male supporters describes the process that turned him from a scoffer into a fan. Mohammad Hassan spent his childhood and youth in a refugee camp in Iran, attending a fundamentalist school. When he ran across a copy of *Payam-e-Zan* at a friend's house, he was astonished. Independent, politically active Afghan women—that was something new. Their response to his somewhat aggressive overture surprised him even more: "Their address was in the magazine, so I decided to write to them. To be honest with you, my letter was pretty impertinent. I asked a million questions, and some of them were intended purely as provocation. But in their answering letter, they responded thoroughly and patiently to each and every one of the points I had made. That reaction alone already brought me closer to them. It was so different from what I was accustomed to in my school. With those *jihadis,* you weren't allowed to ask questions. Right away they would say, 'What kind of a question is that? Are you an unbeliever? You'd better stop trying to be disruptive.' And they would get angry. But RAWA didn't seem to be angry about my questions at all. On the contrary, they told me that if I had any more questions, I should ask them."

RAWA's political culture—their willingness to discuss things, to listen to opposing points of view, to persuade through arguments instead of brute force—is different and noteworthy; many Afghans, used to the opposite, find it very attractive. To conduct a lengthy political correspondence with each interested individual is a painstaking, not very efficient but very democratic way to work. It's also a RAWA trademark.

The website, a kind of international equivalent of *Payam-e-Zan*, uses the same approach. The typical course of events is identical to the one described above. Somebody sees the website more or less by coincidence, feels curious about it and sends an e-mail. A correspondence develops. Through a series of exchanges, the person can determine whether he or she shares RAWA's values and goals. If so, the person often feels inspired to support the group in some way. RAWA never asks for anything, which is wise on two levels. First, people themselves are the best judge of what they can do and want to do for RAWA. From their forwarded correspondence, for example, I suspect that RAWA to this day does not know that "German supporter Nina Hagen" happens to be a major European pop icon—though they'll find out shortly, when she hosts a huge rock concert on their behalf. Second, their restraint seems to inspire huge bursts of participatory energy. Not being pressed or asked for anything specific seems to make people more creative. Our intern fell in love with RAWA's songs and remixed them into a CD to aid their hospital project. Motherly Austrian ladies, hearing about the cold Afghan winter on CNN's military coverage, sent a shipment of special ski underwear made out of silk and cashmere, so RAWA activists inside Afghanistan wouldn't "catch a chill under their thin burqas."

Many RAWA members confessed that selling *Payam-e-Zan* and other RAWA publications on the streets is the hardest part of their activism. It is interesting and a good way to open a dialogue with a great variety of people, but it's scary, too. Inside Afghanistan under Taliban rule, though, such public discussions were not only scary but impossible. Publications could only be distributed very cautiously, to known supporters.

INFORMATION

RAWA's efforts to make contact with the broader Afghan public inside Afghanistan has two goals: to gather information about events in different regions of the country and to gauge public attitudes. How do ordinary people evaluate the situation? What outcome do they hope for? What solutions do they envision?

RAWA keeps its finger on the pulse of Afghan public opinion through interviews and by forming contacts. Their most productive method is to simply sit with people and to talk. What we might call "undercover chatting" became an important tool for gathering intelligence and spreading news.

This is accomplished by sending small groups, usually two women and one man, out to talk with neighbors. These people link the interviewers with friends and relatives, and the network widens. Once inside a house, either the RAWA women talk to the women alone or, depending on the attitudes and habits of the family in question, there might be a mixed gathering.

This method of undercover chatting strikes me as interesting not only because it's new but because it's clearly populist and woman-friendly. On this level, even someone who considers herself apolitical can be enticed into formulating her views and opinions, where a more formal forum would probably intimidate her.

ACTION AS THERAPY

Many of the women, children and youths that RAWA comes into contact with have suffered extreme personal blows and are clearly traumatized. Beyond that, many RAWA members themselves come from tragic circumstances. Some of them were salvaged from a hopeless situation by RAWA and were later inspired to join the organization and participate in its work. In some ways, RAWA functions as a self-help group, and its work is a kind of therapy.

Few organizations take the designation "grassroots" as seriously as RAWA does. Others may stand up for the underdogs, but RAWA actively cultivates them, educates them, sees their potential. Distraught young girls, abandoned women, widows, elderly ladies—these people are completely invisible to other political movements, except maybe as recipients of their charity. RAWA—well, if the word hadn't become such a cliché, one would say that RAWA empowers them. RAWA activists come in all sizes, shapes and ages, which not only is very democratic but also turns out to be a phenomenal asset. That introspective, shy, elderly widow? No one pays any attention to her, least of all the Taliban. No one would ever suspect her of being a RAWA sympathizer—so there's probably no safer place in all of Afghanistan for RAWA underground activists to spend the night than at her home.

Many women who later became RAWA supporters, members, activists or even leaders first met that organization in their own hour of need. Someone from RAWA listened to them, helped them, befriended them. The concrete help was useful—the money, the clothes, the food, the medical help, the school slot, the job—but what they remembered most later was the time and personal attention. Often, the RAWA mentor came from a background similar to that of her new protégé and could serve as living proof that something she no longer thought possible just might be true: She, too, might get through this and go on to have an effective and fulfilling new life.

"I decided that I wanted to be exactly like her"—to forget one's own grief by helping others was a therapeutic approach that manifestly worked.

LITERACY AND EDUCATION

Education is at the heart of RAWA's efforts. "Education is our weapon," they say, and it's not just a slogan. The organization maintains dozens of schools and sponsors many literacy courses, both inside Afghanistan and in Pakistan among the refugees. Under the Taliban, and in fundamentalist-dominated regions of Pakistan, the schools can't officially be identified as RAWA schools—only the parents, teachers and older pupils know of the affiliation. Others, such as the highly regarded Watan Schools, are known under the RAWA name.

Almost every member of the organization is involved in the educational effort in some way. Even the underground members inside Afghanistan normally taught a literacy class or ran a secret girls' school on the side. The publications committee prints the schoolbooks, the cultural committee organizes school plays and music performances, and the income-generating projects provide funds for literacy or other classes for the women who work there. This keeps them grounded in the daily life of the population. "My school is like a miniature version of the Afghan people" is how one director puts it. Through her conferences with the students' mothers, she is constantly in touch with the problems and worries of the refugees.

RAWA's main educational problem lies in meeting the demand. Sometimes a traditionally minded parent has to be persuaded of the benefits of education, particularly for a daughter, but the more common case is the reverse: far too many applicants for too few spaces. Part of it is the result of example. The refugee experience brought villagers into urban settings and exposed them to new things. In Pakistan, Afghan refugees can see for themselves that women who have an education and skills can hold a well-paying job. Add to that the backlash caused by the Taliban's extremism, and you get a population much more open to modern ways.

What impressed me most about RAWA's schools was how teachers and principals had independently developed their own modern pedagogy. Following a talk she gave to a major educational institution in Washington, D.C., RAWA's Tameena was startled to learn that there was a whole professional terminology for the things they were doing. Through trial, error and ingenuity, RAWA had happened on many of the same modern teaching methods found in the West. For example, RAWA had decided that rote learning, a staple of the Afghan traditional education system, was not a good idea, and had decided to simply abandon it, shifting to a style that encouraged problem solving and critical thinking. They invited the children to work in teams, not just in the classroom but in the dormitories, too. They taught them life skills, self-esteem and competency—they just didn't call it that. They noticed that traumatized children responded especially to art and drama, and so they encouraged the children to write and perform plays, to compose poetry, to paint. Tameena was amazed to learn that, through happenstance, their pedadgogy was pretty much state-of-the-art, and that a whole body of theory existed to support methods they had thought were experimental.

Many of RAWA's "pupils" are illiterate adult women. Working with them presents special challenges. When they begin their course, many of them are filled with trepidation. Will they be able to learn? Aren't they too old to be going to school? Won't they just make fools of themselves? Many arrive with the gentle ridicule of friends, neighbors and relatives in their ears: "You're going to school? At your age?"

Others are so preoccupied by worries and by multiple traumatic events that they can barely concentrate. But their classmates are in a similar situation, and they give each other support and encouragement. Very quickly, the women find themselves applying their new learning in everyday situations. It's called a literacy course, but it's really more accurate to think of it as elementary school for adults, with some health education thrown in. Math skills help them feel confident that they aren't being cheated in the market or when selling their handicrafts. And then there is the brand-new experience of success. To receive praise from the teacher, to read a magazine passage all alone for the first time, to actually write a letter to a relative in a distant town—the women describe these as truly life-altering moments.

Women attend the literacy classes for the obvious reason: because they want to learn how to read. What interests them initially is that the class is nearby, is free and is taught and attended only by women—three things that make their attendance acceptable to husbands and family. The fact that a women's organization autonomously organized such an effort soon impresses them, as does their teacher. Thoughts and questions that have long preoccupied them gradually begin to take form as they find themselves in the company of other intellectually curious women.

Sabera, an activist who also teaches literacy classes, is constantly surprised at the eagerness with which ordinary, traditional Afghan women jump into political discussions. As she explains, adult literacy classes for women easily segue into broader issues. "After mutual trust is established, we usually tell our students about RAWA and its activities. And these women whose primary objective is to learn literacy, when they hear this, they also become attracted to the political issues.

"When we speak to them, their view is that Afghan women have been quiet for too long in the face of much oppression. And they say that they do not want to remain the prisoners of lunatic elements like the Taliban or the *jihadis* any longer. Rather, they would like to get organized."

RAWA's most impressive educational effort, however, are the elementary and middle schools. These schools, as portrayed by one of the teachers, are organized as follows: "Our school is conducted in both of Afghanistan's official languages, Persian and Pashtu. And we've recently introduced English, starting from first grade. That's something very unusual, and we're proud to offer it. School starts at seven-forty-five and finishes at noon.

"My particular school is located in a refugee neighborhood. Most of the families have been in Pakistan for five or six years. Typically the parents don't have work, though some of them find odd jobs in the bazaar. In contrast, almost all of the children work. Their task is to sort through the garbage in search of paper, which can be bundled and sold. They also try to find food, spoiled fruit and vegetables that have been thrown out. They take those home for the family to eat. Our families live in the greatest poverty you can imagine.

"Our biggest problem is the number of children who want to attend. At present, my school can only accommodate a hundred children. If at all possible, next year we want to add one more class at each grade level. Every year, as soon as registration starts, we have five hundred children signed up. It is very painful for us to have to choose. We try to determine which ones are the neediest, because those are the ones who have no chance to find a different school. The other schools charge tuition, but ours is free. The school situation in Pakistan is very unequal. You can get a world-class education here, with libraries and computers and everything, but it costs five thousand rupees' tuition. The cheaper the school is, the worse the teachers. In free schools, the teachers still carry sticks and beat the children. How well your children are treated depends on what you can pay.

"Many of the parents are illiterate. When the children go to the garbage dump to work, their parents help them. I suppose this is the opposite of what is usual; usually it is the parents who work and the children who help them.

"The other thing that refugee fathers can do, they can sit on a certain street corner that is the known place for those who are looking for work. These are handyman sorts of jobs: painting, or helping in a store, or repairing something. Usually the men have to wait for several days before someone finally hires them.

"But we also have some highly educated people. They have no more chance than anyone else, because they aren't allowed a work permit in Pakistan. One such family that I know supports itself by baking cookies and selling them on the street. Back at home the father used to be a high-ranking government official."

As we can testify, RAWA's "alumni," both male and female, are the best evidence for the quality of their work. Not only do they speak in the warmest possible tones about their teachers and their classroom memories, they are almost implausibly well educated, articulate, self-confident, even urbane. All of them love to discuss politics and earnestly profess democratic values. Many have an artistic bent. You will have trouble believing that the classroom these people graduated from was just a cordoned-off rooftop in Islamabad or a rented room in a Quetta slum.

Shahla, who is herself the product of a RAWA school, adds the following observations: "From a social point of view, we try to give the children at least a little hint of a childhood. Many Afghan adults are so disturbed by all the years of war and their life as refugees that they have no tolerance for the noisiness of children. When I walk through one of our schools and see the children laughing and jumping, boys and girls together, then I think, 'This is really worth the effort.'

"It's a wonderful thing for these children to be in a school where they can be certain that no one will hit them, where a nurse comes regularly to do checkups, where on special occasions they receive colored pencils and can paint posters and use their imaginations."

Inside Afghanistan during the Taliban years, RAWA's educational work was enormously difficult and dangerous. Any carelessness could jeopardize not only the RAWA organizer but the parents, the children, the neighbors, the women attending literacy courses, the men who volunteered to act the part of *mahram* (the male family member required to accompany any women who left her house)—a whole chain of people would be at risk. Despite the precautions, incidents occurred.

"The Taliban would conduct raids, especially in Kabul—not so much in other areas. They would burst into houses without warning. If they found secular books, anything but the Quran, they would beat the adults, and sometimes the children, too, and they would rip the books apart. On those occasions they didn't even suspect that classes were being taught; they just thought the parents were teaching their children on their own. If they had guessed that they had found a secret school, everyone would have been arrested. Therefore we strictly avoided any indication that RAWA was behind these home schools, and the Taliban never guessed."

Not that the work is easy, even in Pakistan. One big problem is that Afghans haven't had a functioning educational system for decades. As a result, there is no correlation between someone's chronological age and his or her level of schooling. Instead, there are people with no formal schooling at all, people with a few years of elementary school and then years of nothing, people who have attended only Quranic schools, people whose parents tried to teach them at home, and a few people with a "normal" education. Devising a curriculum under such circumstances is extremely challenging. And RAWA confronts other difficulties as well, as this teacher explains: "In the past we did have a normal school system in Afghanistan, comprising twelve years. Now everything is in chaos. In some of our schools we can use a conventional curriculum and something approaching the customary number of years, but that's really the exception. Recently, for example, we were able to open a middle school like that, in Islamabad, where we had a lot of urban families with partially schooled children. But in most places, regardless of the pupils' ages, we have to start from the very beginning. If the young people have never been in any sort of school at all, then we really have to begin at a primary school and sometimes even a preprimary level.

"At the moment we have more than ten schools in Pakistan, which have three hundred children each, so that's about three thousand refugee children that we are teaching.

In Afghanistan it's harder to give a correct number, because the situation is more fluid—the schools are more numerous but much smaller, with usually just a handful of pupils. Often the school has to change location on short notice or even shut down for a while.

"In Pakistan anyone who wants to can open up a private school. You don't need a license or anything. It's considered quite normal for somebody to just start a school in their own home. That makes it easy for us, because we can do the same.

"We teach all the usual subjects, math and history and languages. We have religion, too—that's necessary because the parents expect it. One difference is that in middle school, we offer political science as an elective.

"I have the impression that our children are much more excited about going to school than children in other countries are. They think of it as a special privilege. Going to school, being with other children, getting books and pencils—all of that is like a dream for them. Then, if it actually comes true, they are very happy and excited."

By most accounts, the Taliban caused an ironic backlash in hypertraditional Afghanistan—they changed people's minds about education, especially girls' education. Where the reformers failed, the extremists succeeded: Most Afghans today are proponents of education for girls. Still there are barriers, as RAWA regularly discovers. A teacher notes, "Recently I visited a different teacher's classroom and one of the girls was crying. She said, 'My mother wants to take me out of school so I can work. She wants me to clean the house and wash clothes for a Pakistani family, but I don't want to. I want to stay in school and finish my education.'

"But then she calmed herself down, and when she had stopped crying, she said, 'It's all right, though, because I know my family doesn't have any other choice. My father is sick and old, my sister is too young, my mother has to take care of them, so I guess I'm the only person who can work.' Then she said that if she ever got the chance, she would like to come back to us and finish her schooling. It was a sad moment.

"It's quite common, though, for girls to be taken out of school when they are fourteen or fifteen. A lot of parents don't want them to go out of the house anymore then. To get the girls into school, we sometimes have to persuade the parents first. We visit the families, we explain to them that schooling will be good for their daughters. Usually the mother agrees and is even happy about the idea, but the father is less so. . . .

"Another time one of the other teachers told me that a certain girl was not attending her classes regularly enough. So I went to talk to that girl, and she said, 'It's because my younger brother sometimes won't allow me to come.' As it happened, I knew that family, so I said, 'But he's younger than you, he's just a child.' The girl was around twelve or thirteen, and her brother was only nine or ten. She replied, 'My mother agreed that I could go to school as long as I did the housework first, but she also said that it depends on my brother. She said, "The one who makes the decisions in this household is your brother."'

"With many families it's still like that. Already when the child is born, if it's a boy, it has more rights and gets more attention, more care, more love and more to eat. So of course the young people grow up with this attitude, that as a boy you are more powerful and more important, and more necessary to your family.

"And it's also widespread for people to think that it's smarter to invest in a boy, because a girl will just get married and join a different family, while the boy will support them in their old age."

WORK AGAINST VIOLENCE

Afghan women have spent decades in a situation of permanent threat and violence, on a variety of levels.

The images coming out of Kabul in the days following its "liberation" were revealing. Men were dancing in the streets and on the backs of pickup trucks, playing music, standing in festive lines at the barbershop to have their formerly mandatory beards removed to general applause.

The women held back. Western journalists were waiting for them to throw off their burqas with the same cheerful abandon that their men were displaying, waiting for the photo op of the Great Burqa Removal, but it didn't happen. There were hardly any women to be seen at all. Once in a while you could spy one in the distance, still wrapped in her burqa, hovering cautiously on the edge of a crowd.

It was obvious that for the women, neither the heavily armed Northern Alliance soldiers nor the streets full of jubilantly celebrating men were an inviting environment. They were still waiting to see what would happen next.

Political violence is not the only level of violence Afghan women have had to contend with. Sexual violence was a particular problem during the 1992–1996 period, when the various factions of the Northern Alliance ruled. During that time, many women were kidnapped and raped. Few of them sought help; rather, they tried to keep the experience a secret from everyone, even their closest friends and family. Those who became pregnant tried to run away to the Pakistani border to have their babies secretly and leave them behind. For a few years, hospitals in that region served on the side as adoption agencies.

The high incidence of rape during Northern Alliance rule served as an indirect method of social control. Strict and direct prohibitions against women's freedom of movement, as later practiced by the Taliban, were not necessary. Women felt sufficiently terrorized to restrict themselves. Theoretically, girls were allowed to go to school and women to work. But most young women were afraid to be out on the streets, because rape was so common. As ABC correspondent Jim Wooten reported from Kabul in January 2002, Afghan women continued to wear the burqa in that city even after the removal of the Taliban because they well remembered the excesses of the Northern Alliance and didn't yet trust the situation.

The only really effective instrument against Northern Alliance abuses during their period of governance would have been world public opinion, but in those years the world was indifferent to Afghanistan. Besides, the effective use of world public opinion would have required one other condition, which was also not present in Afghanistan: the willingness of women to speak out. Opinion turned against the Serbs in the Bosnian conflict because Bosnian women were prepared to testify to their abuses. "Afghan women have yet to become less inhibited, to speak up for themselves, not to be silently suffering victims," Shahla notes.

And that's not true just of rape. The extreme atmosphere of shame and secrecy surrounding anything sexual makes Afghan women very vulnerable. They are easily intimidated and driven out of public spaces. The aggressor doesn't have to fear any reprisals; embarrassment will keep his victim from ever speaking up, let alone defending herself.

Even without my specifically asking about it, violence in marriage emerged as another widespread problem. Afghan traditional society is tolerant of male violence against weaker family members—children, daughters-in-law, wives. Children are often struck in public by men, even by random men not related to them. It is known that family violence increases significantly in refugee settings. Stress, crowded conditions, enforced proximity and separation from the extended family, who often act as mediators, all contribute to that outcome.

SOCIAL SERVICES

Many women are at the end of their rope when they first encounter RAWA. They are traumatized by terrible experiences, alone, disoriented and desperate. In the traditional world they come from, some man would have been responsible for them, and they were raised to depend on that entirely.

"Social security" in Afghanistan has for centuries been organized through a complex system of responsibilities based on family and clan. Women are necessary to this system; in fact, they are the fabric that holds it together, by providing the linkages and interlinkages of marriage that connect families to each other. But they are rarely permitted to take an active role, or even to have a voice in decisions that will most intimately affect their lives. They are expected to marry whatever person is chosen for them, and then to deliver children to their new family. In exchange, theoretically at least, they can expect to be cared and provided for throughout their lives. Their grandfather and father are responsible for them initially, and then their father-in-law and their husband. If they both die and there is no grown son to take charge of things, then the brother-in-law inherits the responsibility for the widow. The practice of levirate marriage is still alive in rural areas of Afghanistan, obliging a man to marry his brother's widow.

Even modern urban families adhere to remnants of this practice. Forty-year-old Aziza, for example, who emigrated to Germany with her family, told us the story of her brother-in-law's murder in Peshawar. He was survived by his widow, two daughters and a son. In the course of the first distraught telephone conversation between Germany and Pakistan, Aziza heard her husband instruct the new widow in a very authoritative tone of voice that she was henceforth to regard him as her husband and to worry about nothing. "It's very strange to hear your husband say that to another woman," Aziza remembers. "I have to admit, it really startled me."

Her husband, a completely modern and secular—and monogamous—Afghan engineer, had intended only to console the distraught woman and to reassure her that she was not alone but could count on his full support for herself and the children. He did not literally intend to install her as his second wife in the apartment in Bielefeld. He was trying to say that he intended to honor his traditional obligation to her.

For most of the women who come to RAWA, the network of traditional obligations has broken down. There is no brother-in-law, or he is a refugee in a faraway camp in Iran and in no position to help them even if they could find him. In addition, the long years of war and flight appear to have undermined many traditional linkages, a fact many Afghans deplore as they relate shocking stories of things that would have been unthinkable in the old days: an uncle refusing to take a niece and nephew into his home, a father selling his children, old people abandoned and left to fend for themselves. In an intact village community, no one could have acted thus without suffering vast general disapproval. Today, that control is gone.

It is no coincidence that so many of RAWA's newer members are widows and orphaned girls. Abandoned by their clan and their relatives, they turn to RAWA as their new family. And RAWA offers them more than charity; it gives them a whole new way of looking at themselves as women, and a new concept of female solidarity.

These women describe their first meeting with a RAWA representative as unforgettable. Here comes a woman from a background similar to their own, a refugee like themselves, and yet she is completely different: proud, self-assured, educated and in command of independent resources. This woman can support herself; she is not dependent on the charity of men. And she seems to believe firmly that every woman can do the same, and is prepared to help them along the way. Again and again, refugee women echo the same phrase: "And I decided that I wanted to become just like her."

LEADERSHIP

One striking feature of RAWA's work is the enduring leadership role they assign to their founder, Meena. She left no "book" behind, no *Das Kapital* or *Thoughts of Chairman Mao*. There are poems and some writings, but most significantly, there is the example of her life. Meena is a vivid presence in RAWA. The women speak of her, remember her, cherish her picture, refer to her, motivate themselves by imagining how she might have reacted and how she definitely would have persevered.

Meena's iconic role is interesting when we reflect on the respective roles played by famous men, versus famous women, in history. One reason for the overwhelmingly male character of history is that men make it a habit to plant themselves solidly in time and space, to put down their markers, to engrave their names on all available surfaces. By this method, they even manage to co-opt the fruits of typically female endeavors. The woman's investment in terms of the sheer physical effort of pregnancy and birth, as well as her input of time and care and thought from infancy to adulthood, is in almost all instances vastly greater than the man's—yet children bear their father's name.

Men build statues and monuments and triumphal arches to themselves, chisel themselves in granite, aspire to spend eternity sitting on a horse and being photographed by tourists. Even the most progressive among them, those who allegedly believe in collectivities and equality and the masses, are still compelled to stamp their ideas with their name: Marxism, Leninism, Maoism.

The common goal of "making a name for themselves" unites men so clearly that it becomes a shared enterprise, and history becomes a progression of great men, a sequence of male names and accomplishments, something for any man to take pride in. It would be wrong to underestimate the significance of this. People's aspirations are formed by their idea of what is possible, and that in turn is derived from examples. What others to whom you can compare yourself have accomplished, moves into your own realm of possibilities. We will see clearly in a later chapter how illiterate women or disoriented young refugee girls latched onto a RAWA teacher or activist, studied her, admired her and aspired to be "exactly like her." Women don't have to be timid, ignorant and passive; they can be fearless, bold, builders of things, movers of events. If on top of that they are kind, care about you, and insist that you are capable of the same level of accomplishment, you may begin to reassess your goals and your original image of yourself. For girls and women in a traditional Afghan setting, that image and those goals are brutally fixed during childhood at the lowest possible settings. It is impressive to see how RAWA manages, for all whom it comes in contact with, to turn up the dial.

Men's dominant place in history and politics has two contributing factors. The first we have already touched upon: the male propensity to turn other men into heroes, to celebrate their leadership and fame and immortality. Men also base their claim to power on the fact that they are more engaged than women in the affairs of the world. They play the greater role, take the greater risks. When something important is at stake, they put their lives on the line. Therefore, they say, they deserve a larger portion of the spoils at the end of the conflict.

RAWA departs from the usual approach of women's movements on both accounts. Its members encourage the fame and heroism of women, but more controversially, they also make a conscious decision to participate in politics "all the way," up to and including the sacrifice of life.

This is not to say that women have never been willing to

risk their lives for a political purpose. In the context of military combat, in the antifascist resistance, and even in radical terrorist groups such as the Red Brigades, they have. Leila Khaled attained fame as a Palestinian airplane hijacker. Other women have consciously risked execution as spies. However, none of these women ever risked her life for herself as a woman, for women's human rights. Women's efforts on behalf of their own political rights can seem, in contrast, somewhat paltry. They will chain themselves to the gates of parliament in pursuit of women's right to vote, or march in demonstrations, or engage in flashy public relations stunts, but that is usually the extent of it. The result is clearly mirrored in their image—even the suffragettes, who fought long and hard, are remembered as somewhat droll figures.

RAWA is the first women's organization whose members are willing to risk their lives explicitly for the issue of women's rights. Whatever we may think of that, the results of this earnestness are incontrovertible. There are people who hate RAWA, malign its members and spread rumors about them, but the organization is never ridiculed or made light of.

History, of course, has its share of heroines—its small share. Most of them have not been women who led other women. Most heroines can more correctly be described as martyrs. Joan of Arc is a classic heroine, but she was a leader of men, not women; she did not care about women's issues and strove for an androgynous image. Anne Frank is a kind of heroine, but a passive one. Her battle was spiritual and psychological. She struggled to endure inhuman conditions but not to change them. Undoubtedly there were women who fought and died for their rights, but they lacked the other prerequisite—other women who were determined to keep their memory alive.

Although she has been dead for almost fifteen years, Meena is a tangible presence in RAWA. Her picture, splashed across banners, accompanies their demonstrations. Her poetry is featured in their brochures. "We honor Meena and celebrate her" is how one activist sums it up. "When I am working, I feel her presence behind me, like my shadow," another says. Meena has become a legend, a tragic heroine, a mythical figure.

Women's groups aren't usually good at uniting behind a leader. Their inclination to form factions and to turn on each other is a frequently lamented fact in many of their leaders' biographies.* One sometimes gains the impression that feminists aren't comfortable with the idea of a leader at all but rather would like the world to just be one big committee.

Years ago, when I first became interested in RAWA, Meena was the first thing that struck me about them—that this was a group of women capable of wholeheartedly, unreservedly admiring another woman, acknowledging her gifts and benefiting from her talent. Their willingness to seek the help of others, including strangers from different countries and cultures, instead of hunkering down into cultural defensiveness—that was the second thing I noticed about them. Their "men's auxiliary" was the third. Men's movements, clubs and associations never hesitate to let women work for them in subsidiary, helping positions. In fact, we could

---

* See Betty Friedan, *Life So Far* (New York: Touchstone Books, 2001) and Christina Hoff Sommers, *Who Stole Feminism?* (New York: Simon and Schuster, 1995).

argue that the entire world functions as a kind of huge men's club, assisted by a helpful women's auxiliary that minds the children, types the papers, washes the dishes and generally makes men's productivity possible. Feminist groups tend to disdain the help of men, but not RAWA. They use all resources to good effect.

Acknowledge the unique contributions of others without rivalry or ambivalence, accept help, define your principles inclusively: These elements of RAWA's very successful formula are worth studying and possibly even copying by other women's movements, including those who work in modern democratic settings in the West.

CHAPTER 4

"I Can Be a Sword": Life in the Underground

I n sharp contrast to the work RAWA conducted publicly among refugees in Pakistan was the clandestine work that brought them into daily mortal danger. Smuggling endangered families to safety. Getting the survivors of massacres out of the killing zone and onto neutral ground. Secretly photographing Taliban beatings, torture and executions to provide documentation and evidence and persuade the outside world to finally act. Warning political activists that questions are being asked about them and that the Taliban may be on their trail. Quickly closing down a secret school and shepherding children and teachers to safety before the Taliban patrol can arrive. Subverting the news blackout by gathering information from different provinces and passing it along.

These were the reasons why the Taliban put RAWA's members on their death list.

In the past, whenever I thought about "resistance fighters" or "working in the underground," it was in abstract terms, and I was filled with a general though vague sense of admiration. Saving Jews from the Nazis, smuggling slaves from the pre–Civil War South to the freedom of the North, demonstrating against vicious South American dictator-

ships—these were noble enterprises that clearly were performed by wonderful and exceptional people.

Then one day, when I was visiting Vienna, Austria, I happened across a tiny municipal museum dedicated to the
local history of one of the city's districts, the ninth. There
were a number of interesting displays illustrating the enormous changes this neighborhood had undergone since Vienna evolved from a medieval town into a big modern city.
And there was a section devoted to the World War II era and
the antifascist resistance. It listed the names and briefly
related the stories of the sons and daughters of the ninth district who had been executed by the Nazis in connection with
their underground work against Hitler and the NSDAP
(*Nationalsozialistische Arbeiterpartei*). I looked at their
sepia photographs and read their brief biographies, and
what I felt was not only sadness but a sobering shock of
enlightenment. What caught me unawares and made a
strong impression on me was the curious ordinariness of the
people and lives I had before me. If evil is banal, as Hannah
Arendt claims, then so, apparently, is courage.

Here were schoolgirls and students, housewives and rail-
road workers, secretaries and salesmen—completely and
totally average people, leading completely unspectacular
lives, who had somehow decided one day that an insane and
genocidal fascist dictatorship was just not something they,
personally, were going to put up with. That instead they,
Liselotte and Stefan and Sigrid and Theodor, were going to
do something about it. Their normalness impressed me—
and made me uncomfortable. Because now, of course, I had
to take a whole new look at myself.

What would I have done?

It's easy to tell yourself that you're no hero, never

claimed to be, and that therefore no one can fairly expect you to act like one. But these people, very obviously, weren't heroes, either. They were just average normal people, yet when fate presented them with a stark moral choice, they rose to the occasion.

After World War II, Nechama Tec went to Poland and sought out people who had been active in the underground.* She, too, found that as a rule, they were ordinary people. Most of them had not previously even been interested in politics. Some were simple farmers, others were educated city dwellers; they ranged from very young to very old. There were men, but there were also a lot of women. One of the most impressive feats of heroism had been accomplished by a farm woman who had to keep her work secret not only from the Nazis but also from her domineering husband. By focusing her activities during the hours he spent drinking with friends in the local pub, she was able to rescue twenty-five Jews, hiding them, provisioning them and finally smuggling them to safety.

RAWA gives us the unique opportunity to observe in real time, not through the distance of a past event but in the actual unfolding of our own contemporary history, how ordinary people are transformed into resistance fighters. That those ordinary people are women, fighting against a totally misogynist regime of fundamentalists, only makes their example all the more remarkable.

When I think about RAWA's women, engaging in forbidden activities right under the noses—and, more to the point, under the guns—of the Taliban, all of my earlier questions

---

* Nechama Tec, *When Light Pierced the Darkness* (New York: Oxford University Press, 1986).

come back to plague me with double force. How exactly does one end up in the underground, anyway? What possesses a person to make a decision as consequential as that, to face such risks? And once you are actually in the underground, how do you deal with your fear? After all, it isn't just a matter of experiencing one courageous moment, of surviving one close call or one dangerous encounter. Somehow you have to find a way to live with the constant possibility of discovery, the constant knowledge that you might be caught and killed.

THE FEAR FACTOR

Almost all of the RAWA underground activists interviewed for this book admitted to feeling fear. Regimes such as that of the Taliban rule through terror and intimidation, committing acts of great cruelty and then advertising them. Opposing them was no joke.

Latifa relates a recent example to illustrate the atmosphere created by their reign of terror. In October 2001, in Darlaman, two young men died under mysterious circumstances during their first night in a Taliban jail, where they were being held on vague charges. The population of this town was so intimidated by the Taliban that they were afraid even to bury their dead, and the young men's own families felt forced to deny them. "The next day when people gathered to look at their dead bodies, a Talib soldier sitting in a Toyota pickup truck spoke in Pashtu and asked tauntingly: 'Where are the relatives of these criminals?' No one answered; who would have dared to?"

Under the Taliban, prisoners were flogged, stoned and executed in public; after punitive amputations, the severed hands and feet of the victims were nailed to walls or paraded through the streets in wheelbarrows. Such acts were calculated to frighten the population into submission. Activists in the resistance were frightened, too; they just didn't submit. Heli, a particularly resolved and courageous woman, confesses, "I feel afraid at times. I think that's normal. In the current conditions in our country—in which there is no legal government, and its rulers don't follow any outside laws or principles, and the only logic they obey is the power of the gun—once in a while one naturally gets scared. Especially when I hear the noise of the cars belonging to the Department of Vice and Virtue, I start to tremble, because they are very heartless and without culture, and brutal and ruthless."

And it's one thing to contemplate discovery and accept the possibility of death; it's more burdensome still to have the possible details of such an end in one's mind, to consider the accompanying circumstances.

Fariha, a young activist who hopes that there will be peace one day so that she might be able to fulfill her dream of writing short stories for children, explains, "When I have an assignment inside Afghanistan, I get frightened every now and then, especially when I see one of the Datsun automobiles used by the Taliban. I'm not so much afraid of them killing me and my blood being spilled on the ground. What I am more frightened of is that I might be arrested first and taken away by them. Unfortunately, we have had several such cases, maybe a dozen. And the Taliban committed a lot of crimes against these women before killing them."

Even short of death, a simple confrontation with the Taliban is no laughing matter. Women were supposed to remain in their houses, unseen; even taking the greatest possible precautions, their frequent outings alone exposed RAWA members disproportionately to the risk of attracting the notice and ire of the Taliban. Once noticed, any pretext was enough for a violent encounter. As Heli says, "Besides hitting you with whips, which, as I know from some of my friends, leaves marks on you that don't fade for months, also there is the fact that they humiliate you, and that is even worse than the physical abuse."

Twenty-four-year-old Roya can attest to that much from personal experience. "Today in Afghanistan, being a woman is a crime, and we are under constant scrutiny. Sometimes I have the fear of what could happen if the Taliban captures me.

"The last time I was in Kabul on a mission, I was in a store. The weather was extremely hot, I just couldn't tolerate my burqa anymore, so I lifted it up for just a moment, to breathe. Suddenly I saw the shopkeeper looking frightened. He told me to put it back on because there was a Talib just around the corner. But it was too late; already I saw him rushing toward me. The expression on the Talib's face and his profanity were more painful than the actual lashing."

We might expect such an encounter to weaken her resolve. However, the insults and violence, far from intimidating her, clarified Roya's sense of purpose. She says: "For me, this was a moment of connection with the other women in Afghanistan, and with their exposure to these barbaric acts. I love life—it's not that I'm eager to experience danger or to be killed—but I also want to live a humane life. When I see women like me experiencing humiliation and insult at the hands of the Taliban, my own safety becomes meaningless, and I feel that I could sacrifice my life to free these women, and it will be a point of redemption and honor."

THE NATURE OF UNDERGROUND WORK

In Hollywood's rendition of the underground, a group of lean and determined men—plus one glamorous woman to provide a love interest or to die tragically—put on dark clothes and stocking masks and slink through the night like cat burglars to blow up a bridge right under a Nazi convoy.

This, however, is not the typical scenario, nor does it do justice to the essence of underground work. The distinguishing feature of such an undertaking is its staggering odds. Underground work pits a murderous, highly disciplined military or paramilitary force, backed by a secret police and possessed of total and unchecked power, against a few frail civilians. In the case of Afghanistan, it pitted heavily indoctrinated, well-armed, pitiless male fanatics who hated women against unarmed, untrained female civilians who were additionally hampered in their ability to act by cultural constraints, family obligations and a slew of rules restricting their behavior and movements, plus a lifelong indoctrination process aimed at telling them how inferior and incompetent they were.

If you are dealing with a normal sort of political opponent, you have an array of options, from the ballot box to critical journalism to demonstrations and rallies. Your opponent will try to defeat you, but he has to follow certain rules and laws that restrain his powers. None of this holds true when you are dealing with a totalitarian system. In addition, such systems aim to control not only the political realm but every aspect of life, imposing a multitude of rules and using surveillance to ensure everyone's adherence to them. The Nazis had the Gestapo. Iran had SAVAK. The Soviet Union had the KGB. And the Taliban had their "religious police" or, to use their actual and Kafkaesque name, their Ministry for the Discouragement of Vice and the Encouragement of Virtue.

In an environment like that, the smallest action carries danger. Leaving the lights on in your house in the evening because a messenger is unexpectedly passing through and you have to write up the report that she must carry with her is enough to attract the notice of a Taliban spy and lead to your capture. Carrying a letter, dropping off a note of warning, being caught with a camera—these are the tiny acts that make up the daily process of resistance. One word, one note, one little piece of paper can save a life, but if a mistake is made or luck is not with you, it can also mean a death sentence.

The odds, as I've just said, are not good. On the other hand, as RAWA's example shows, underground fighters have unexpected resources and allies. One surprising aspect is the extent to which clandestine underground activities are aided and abetted by the community. And that's a good thing, because you can't possibly be clandestine enough that no one else will figure out what you are up to. Neighbors will suspect, relatives will know, and very often you will depend on the goodwill or sympathy of other people to be able to function. Their help will draw them in and endanger them, and they will choose to accept that risk. Like a pebble thrown into a lake, each resistance fighter will generate concentric circles of courage as friends, family and random others decide to help her.

"Civil society" has become a modern catchphrase, but as our examples will show, it is a living, breathing entity, and the courage of civilians is greatly underrated by historians.

The entire neighborhood proudly sheltered Meena in the full knowledge of her illegal activism. Everyone went along with the fiction that she was Laila, a harmless local housewife. Without the network of ordinary ladies, grandmothers and admiring teenage boys who kept her secrets, watched over her, knocked on her door to warn of approaching dangers and helped her in a thousand tiny ways, she wouldn't have survived for a week.

Heli's father, whom we will meet in this chapter, was extremely alarmed when he first learned of his daughter's involvement in a forbidden resistance group, so much so that he plotted to immobilize her by pushing her into an arranged marriage. When he understood the degree of her commitment, however, he overcame his fear for her and even participated in some of her missions.

As for those of us who let small obstacles stand in the way of things our conscience tells us we really ought to be doing, we might consider the case of Sohaila, also discussed later in this chapter. Like the peasant woman in Nechama Tec's study who had to work her underground activities around the absences of a tyrannical husband, Sohaila doesn't let her multiple domestic burdens stop her from playing her part.

Generally, there are three roads that lead into the underground. Its activists are composed of volunteers, recruits and spontaneous joiners. *Volunteers* are drawn to the organization by its boldness, which matches their own deep inner wish to act. They might not know the exact details of what they are getting into, but they seek RAWA out because they sense the strength of its commitment. The prospect of finally having a chance to act, and like-minded partners, and a mission, fills them with happiness. As Mahboba relates, she was so thrilled when the local clandestine RAWA representative finally made contact with her that her mother suspected her of having secretly met a man and fallen in love.

Recruits are identified by activists as persons who might be interested in joining them. There is a certain missionary aspect involved. The activist believes that her political work has made a great difference in her life and wants to share it. Sabera's befriending and ultimate recruitment of an isolated, traumatized widow provides an example of this.

Spontaneous joiners find themselves in the unexpected situation of making a sudden choice. Sheer coincidence places them in a situation of potential involvement—they overhear something or are in a sudden position to help or warn or hide someone. Should they help, betray or just look away? In one way or another, a moment of decision comes, and the individual irrevocably steps across a boundary. "Tomorrow we distribute this," said Meena to her neighbor, an ordinary middle-aged woman whose husband, father-in-law and brother-in-law had been arrested and then murdered by the regime. "This" was the forbidden flyer RAWA was planning to hand out secretly during the night. "You should join us," she said. "Can you do it?" And the woman replied, "Why not?"

Heli

Heli is a vibrant, self-confident young woman in her twenties who chose to go right to the heart of RAWA's most dangerous clandestine activities.

"In 1993, I came to Pakistan for medical treatment, to have a throat operation. One day in Islamabad, I was just coming out of the clinic when I saw a crowd of women marching down the street. I thought they must be Pakistani women, demonstrating about something, but then I heard the slogan they were chanting:

Darker than the seventh of Saur
Eighth of Saur
Day of oppression, day of abuses
Everyone hates you
Eighth of Saur.*

"Obviously, they had to be Afghans, because the date they were reviling was one noteworthy only in Afghan history.

"I was amazed that someone would call out such a bold slogan, especially women, especially in this part of Pakistan, where fundamentalism was very powerful. When I first came to Islamabad, my aunt's family prepared to go out to the store, and they all put their burqas on. I was surprised and asked them why they did that. I had thought that Pakistan was more progressive and freer than that. But my nephew smiled sadly and explained that in this district, fundamentalists dominated. And that because of them, men and women were afraid of their own shadows.

"Now here were these women, and apparently they were not afraid at all. I stopped to watch their demonstration.

* Saur is a month in the Afghan calendar during which the 1978 pro-Soviet coup d'état took place.

Some little boys were running alongside the demonstrators, selling a magazine called *Payam-e-Zan,* so I bought a few copies and I started to read them. The only thing I didn't like were their criticisms of poets and writers who were supporting the jihad. At that time, I still thought that these people were probably just patriots, and one should be kind to them.

"I started a correspondence with RAWA that continued for several months, and finally in my last letter I told them that I and my family had to go back to Afghanistan now, but that I really wanted to meet them before I left.

"A few days later, a middle-aged woman came to our neighborhood and asked questions about me; the neighbors told us. Today I know that it was out of caution, to see if I really was who I had said. Then they phoned me and we talked a few times, and finally we arranged to meet in a restaurant in Peshawar. I had believed that RAWA's activities were limited to Pakistan and so I didn't think I could do anything with them, since I was going back to Kabul. However, the woman who met me said to me that our work is really inside Afghanistan, and we had a long conversation about it. She asked a lot of questions about me and my family, and I answered all of them.

"We agreed that I would make contact with one of their members in Kabul. And these repeated contacts ultimately led to my work in the underground.

"There was a lot that needed to be done. Even just keeping our schools and education programs going was quite tricky. Our classes could not take place anywhere that there might be concentrations of Taliban or groups of their supporters. If we heard about them moving into an area, then we had to relocate our schools. Literacy courses, even in-home courses for girls—this was all forbidden. However, we were determined not to stop these courses. In addition, we were struggling to help people in the war areas. Even if we were not able to help them a lot, our basic point was not to leave them alone. Some of us would always make our way to such an area to talk to the people, offer whatever help we could, and let them know that they were not forgotten. Because of this, people know us, and they know that we do not care about ethnic differences. So when people from minority areas need to flee, they know that we will try to take them. Recently I had the responsibility for moving eight families to Pakistan, and I accomplished that.

"Before starting this work, I didn't know much about photography, but because of the importance of document-ing things, I became appointed to take pictures and films in three specific areas of the city. This was an interesting assignment, since I know that RAWA's role in exposing the crimes of the extremists gets a great deal of attention. Lastly, I teach one home-school class and two courses on literacy for women.

"I have two sisters who are older than I am and who are busy with their own lives. My brother is a student and lives with my uncle in Pakistan. My father used to be a govern-ment employee, an office worker, but since his place of birth is Shamali, a minority area, when the Taliban came they dis-missed him.* This was not only a disaster for our family financially, but also had a bad effect on my father emotion-

---

* The Taliban favored their own ethnic group, the Pashtuns or Pathans, over everyone else.

ally and physically. The only thing left for him to do was to start selling vegetables, pulling a cart and doing other hard physical work, which was difficult for him.

"While I was growing up, there was one sentence that my father always used to repeat. He would always say that he felt sorry for us, his children, because we had been born into such bad times and had never seen anything good in life—no school, no education, no peace, not even the simple joy of going to picnics. Unfortunately, he was powerless to change any of this. But to make it up to us, he intended to do the only thing he could, which was to leave us our freedom. He promised never to interfere in our lives at all, but to let us do whatever we liked. We were to choose whom we wanted to marry, and make all the decisions concerning ourselves in complete freedom. That was what my father always used to say.

"Therefore, after I got to know RAWA, I discussed it openly with my father and told him that I had decided to become politically active. He said, 'I remember what I promised you, and I intend to honor it, but you need to think this over carefully, and take your time with this decision.' But I told him that I wasn't acting on impulse. So he didn't raise any further objections, but let me be. However, soon thereafter something happened that showed me he had not really accepted it at all.

"My aunt had a son, and one day they sent a message asking for me in marriage. Now, in the case of my two older sisters, my father had not interfered or tried to arrange anything, a fact he made much of. But now, suddenly, he started putting a lot of pressure on me, and saying how happy it would make him if I married this boy. And I realized that he was disturbed by my political activities and wanted to marry me off, thinking that I would have to settle down then. I firmly rejected the proposal and told my father not to interfere again in these matters of my life.

"Some time after that, I had to go somewhere, and none of the men who usually helped us with this were available to accompany me as my *mahram*. With no further questions, my father volunteered to go with me. Then I knew that he had truly accepted my decision at last.

"My mother is illiterate, an uneducated woman, but nevertheless she is my mother and stands by me. When I am not home, she makes excuses about where I am to the neighbors. One day, the car of Vice and Virtue pulled up in front of our house. My mother became extremely agitated. She came running into the room, crying, 'They've come for you!' I tried to calm her down, telling her that nothing untoward had happened, so why should they come after me? Nevertheless, to be honest with you, I was worried, too. My mother handed me a big tarp to put over me, and pushed me out of the house to go and hide in the chicken coop. I spent an hour there, until finally my mother came and said that the car was gone. But we still didn't know why the car had come in the first place. So it seemed odd to me that my mother was now quite relaxed, announcing that she didn't care if they came again, because it would be all right now. I didn't know what she meant. Then I went to the storage room where I kept all my RAWA papers, and I saw that they were gone. I asked her, 'What did you do with all of my things?' and she told me that she had taken them and thrown them all in the bread oven and burned them. And if the police came again, they wouldn't find anything. I was very upset and demanded of her, 'How could you do that?' And she replied, 'Which do you suppose is more important to me, your life or some scraps of paper?'"

Sohaila

Sohaila was recruited into RAWA by her teacher. She is a kind of Cinderella figure: Before she can get on with her political work, she has to cook, clean, do the laundry and appease an irritable aunt.

For Sohaila, political activism has been a form of therapy, a way to put her own tragedy in perspective by focusing on the plight of others. It has also enabled her to transform her personal grief into action, by taking up arms against the fundamentalists and the political order that killed her mother.

"Unfortunately, I was the eldest child in my family. This turned out not to be a lucky thing for me. At first, things were good. With my parents and my five sisters and one brother, I lived in the province of Ghoorband. With our small plot of land, we led a comfortable and relatively worry-free life. My father worked in an office; he had finished twelfth grade and could have gone on to university, but his family didn't have the financial means for that. My mother was a charming and beautiful woman; everyone loved her.

"For a while, I went to school, but then in 1995 all schools and offices were closed, due to the civil war. Gulbuddin was fighting against the ruling government, and neither side had any mercy or concern for innocent and poor people.

"It was the first day of Eid, and both sides had declared a cease-fire. Everyone took advantage of this welcome opportunity. Some went to visit their relatives in nearby towns to see if they were all right; others rushed out to replenish their food supply. My father went shopping for groceries, and my mother was in the front yard by the well, preparing a bath for my sisters. I was upstairs, just looking down onto the street and all the activities, when I suddenly heard my mother scream, 'Sohaila, get down!' Then I heard a very loud noise, like a bomb or a missile. I rushed downstairs hoping everyone would be okay, and ran out into the garden. I remember that when I got there, everyone was standing in place like statues, or like they were frozen or something. But from the corner of my eyes I caught a glimpse of a big dark hole in the middle of the yard. And I saw my mother's veil lying there at the edge of it, and in another place her shoes. I started shouting for her, 'Mother, Mother,' but there was no answer, and the next thing that happened was I fainted.

"When I became conscious again, I was in bed, and my aunt was sitting next to me, trying to pamper me, kissing my cheeks and stroking my hair. I asked her about the others, and she said that everyone was fine, and I should just rest. Then at night my uncle came, and they packed my things and put me in a car and took me with them to their house. It was a long trip, about thirteen hours, but they gave me Valium for most of it, so that I would sleep but also so that I would appear sick, because that made it easier to pass the checkpoints.

"I felt very confused when I got to their house. I could only remember bits and pieces of what had happened, and I spent most of my time crying. Whenever I asked about my mother, my aunt told me that she would come to join me soon, in about fifteen days. To distract me, she brought me some novels to read. I hadn't gone to school for very long, just a few years, but my father had helped me to continue learning, and he had always admonished me to work with my sisters and brother, so that none of us would lose the little bit of learning that we had. Therefore, I could read quite well.

"One day my aunt told me that one of the neighbors was teaching a literacy class, and that I could join it if I wished. I thought it might be a way to occupy my days, so I agreed.

"Right from the first moment, I liked my teacher and my classmates. When class was finished, my teacher asked me to stay behind, because she wanted to talk to me. She asked me about my educational background and spoke to me in a very gentle and kind way. Today I realize that she already knew, from my aunt, that my mother was dead, because the rocket had killed her. But on that day she didn't mention this, but just asked me what I was doing with my time, and I told her about the novels. She asked me what I thought of those books, and I told her that I neither liked them nor disliked them. They just helped me get through the day. So she said that if I agreed with her, then I should stop reading such books, because books were a wonderful thing, but only if they were good books, books that did not decrease the level of seriousness in one's mind. She said it would be her recommendation that I pursue a serious life, being altruistic and thinking about the future of my people and my country. Her words had an enormous impact on me. They resonated in my mind constantly.

"A few weeks later, my grandparents arrived, along with my brother and my sisters. My mother, of course, was not with them. And this was the day when they told me about her death. Before that, whenever I asked my aunt about her, she would tell me that my mother would be coming any day now, maybe tomorrow or the day after. But now they told me that she was gone and that it was my job to take her place and be responsible for these six younger children.

"After I learned of my mother's death, I became especially close to my teacher. We spent many hours talking. Sometimes she could even make me laugh, and our bond became very strong. After a while our discussions started to shift to politics, and she became my political mentor. Eventually I joined RAWA.

"My father remarried almost immediately after my mother's death. My stepmother was not an evil person, but before the marriage, her family had imposed the condition that she should not be expected to live with her stepchildren, and my father had agreed. Therefore it fell to my grandparents and my uncles to take us in. They all lived together. My grandfather is the oldest man in the family, and he has a bad temper. My grandmother is old and sick. My aunt is not happy about us staying with them permanently, and most of the time she displays it with her bad mood. My other uncle is single. He's nice, and when he comes home from his store, he tries to spend some time with us.

"My days are always the same. I get up early and make breakfast, then I clean the house and prepare the dough for bread, followed by the laundry. In the beginning, my aunt used to cook, but when my sisters and brother came, she said she was unable to cook for such a large army, and it should be my job. The room they gave us to stay in is also used as the kitchen, which is actually a good thing because the heat from the cooking makes the room somewhat warm. We had electricity until the bombing started, but since then our life has become very primitive. The winter has not even started yet, but since our room is on the shady side of the courtyard, we can already feel the bitter cold.

"My aunt is the only one who knows about my work for RAWA. Because of her intervention, I am allowed to go outside the house. None of the other grandchildren are permitted to do that. If anyone else in the family knew, they would definitely try to prevent me.

"I go around collecting news; I have a regular circuit that I am responsible for. Then I write things down and pass them along. Also, I supervise some literacy classes.

"Recently I got into a conversation with the woman who has the bakery where I take my dough. The way it happened was, another woman came in and addressed her as 'dear teacher.' I was surprised when I heard that, and asked why she was given that title—wasn't she a baker? And she said no, she used to be a teacher—in fact, she used to be the principal of a school. And her husband used to be a teacher, too, she said. Then she waved me behind the counter and had me follow her to the back, into a dark room, with only a little bit of light coming in through a tiny cracked window. There was a mattress in one corner, and on it I saw a man missing two limbs. And she told me her story. When the Taliban came, all the teachers were dismissed, and they were left with no income. Her husband found work as a laborer. One day, although they finished the work, they were not given their compensation, and he became very depressed. While walking home, he decided to commit suicide. Since he blamed the Taliban for his troubles, when he saw a Taliban truck come, he threw himself in front of it but lived. Now it was up to her to support the family, and she had opened this little bakery, thinking that at worst there would always be some bread for her children to eat.

"I think there are big differences between men and women. Women are more responsible and more faithful. If I had lost my father instead of my mother, she never would have left her children in order to go off and marry someone else."

Sabera

Sabera joined the resistance spontaneously. She had actually planned to complete a nursing class run by RAWA, but when they called for volunteers to work inside Afghanistan and Iran, she signed on.

Her path is a remarkable one, illustrating the potential that can lurk beneath the seemingly placid surface of women's lives. From a shy village girl who spent years in domestic confinement before obediently allowing herself to be married off to a stranger, she transformed herself into a determined, educated woman and a resistance fighter. And the man who encouraged her political awakening no longer works for his own political party; he has become an active supporter of hers.

One other thing is noteworthy in Sabera's story. Many political movements make grandiose speeches about the "wretched of the earth," the desperate and downtrodden masses they are hoping to liberate. But how many of them focus their energies on a depressed and reclusive middle-aged widow? Other groups might make her the passive beneficiary of their charity, but to see her as a valid person with a contribution to make, as a potentially effective political actor—there are not many movements this would occur to.

This approach allows RAWA to tap into an entirely new reservoir of political energy. As it turns out, that widow is not necessarily as passive or as insignificant as others might suppose. At first, the extent of her contribution might simply lie in not reporting on the forbidden literacy class next door. Soon she might be recommending the course to others. Next she offers shelter to the roving underground teachers who conduct the classes. And finally she decides to become a full-fledged member of RAWA. The passively grieving widow becomes an active fighter in the struggle to overthrow those who killed her family.

"I was fifteen when the Russians, using their agents, carried out the coup in Afghanistan," says Sabera. "We were living in the western part of the country at that time, and the head of our family was my brother, who was twenty-two. I had lost my father when I was four, to cancer. After the coup we decided to flee, so we became refugees in Zahedan, in Iran. My brother, like thousands of other Afghan refugees, started to do physical labor—that was the only thing a refugee was allowed to do. It was harsh work, for which he got paid very little. And my mother used to work in the kitchen of an Iranian household at night to earn additional money.

"In Iran, there were no schools for refugee children at that time, and they didn't accept us in their own schools. I was in third grade when we fled. With my two young brothers, I went to the nearest Iranian school and applied for a place. The principal told us that under no circumstances would he admit Afghans to his school. He further explained that Afghans are thieves and dirty, and he didn't want any students from among them in his school, as they create nothing but headaches.

"However, we had some nice Iranian neighbors, and the woman of the house was a kind person who had formed a friendship with my mother. She enrolled us in the school her own children went to. The principal of that school agreed, but she put forth a lot of conditions that we had to accept. One was that we had to try to speak with an Iranian accent. We had to cover our heads in the manner of Iranian girls. And, though we were Sunni Muslims, we had to change our style of praying to conform to the Shi'a way. It seemed strange to me at the time, but now I realize that she was doing something kind and forbidden by accepting us, and perhaps could have gotten in trouble herself, and just wanted to make sure that we would not stand out too much or be conspicuous. At any rate, we agreed, and we were at that school for a year and a half. Then my uncle came to visit. He lived in a city called Zabul, and when he came to see about us, he told my mother that she shouldn't let me go to school anymore, because I didn't have a father and people would be particularly observant of my behavior and would disapprove of a young girl going to school like that. And besides, he said, we were living among strangers in a foreign land, and who knew if it was safe for me to be outside of the house.

"His visit resulted in my becoming homebound. I used to spend all my time cleaning the house, cooking and washing clothes. Then, when I was eighteen, my uncle came again—with his wife this time, in all formality—and asked for my hand to marry his son. In Afghanistan this is customary. If there are two brothers and one has a boy and the other has a girl, then the children are encouraged to marry each other. Since I didn't have a father and my uncle considered himself to have authority over us, there wasn't really any choice, and I got engaged to his son.

"My uncle's son was eight years older than I was. I didn't know him at all. He was involved in the war against the Soviets, so after our marriage, I moved in with his family in Zabul. Living under the control of his father, I was just as locked up as before. My husband did not agree with this, so after a few months, he took me away to live in Quetta. RAWA had a workshop there, and from his own political organization my husband knew some RAWA members. So he asked me if I wanted to go and work there and live with the other women from the factory while he was away in the war, and when I said yes, he was happy, saying that he was struggling against the Soviets and I, by working with RAWA, was also contributing to the same aim.

"I was nineteen when I started working in that factory. I was a country girl and very shy. I spoke very little, but the other women were very interesting to me, and I observed them and studied them. They used to work with so much enthusiasm, and they were very nice. They all wanted to be closer to me and to help me. Over time I could feel that my personality was changing—I became more outgoing, and my confidence that I could do this work was increasing. I noticed in particular how others, with warmth and kindness, wanted to help me better appreciate the political situation of my country. Before that, no one had ever thought that it was worth the trouble of explaining such things to me. Due to this, my interest in RAWA greatly increased. In fact, I began to like many of my coworkers better than members of my own family, and I trusted them more.

"There were forty women in the factory. Some sewed; others did the buying of cloth and yarn; some went to the refugee camps, where we had small workshops, to distribute materials for sewing and to collect the finished items. Another woman and I had the job of washing the clothes that were brought from the camp and ironing them to prepare them for sale. Once or twice a month they would collect the things and take them to be sold.

"For everyone who worked in the factory, there was a literacy class, which met for two hours a day. My level of literacy was already good, so that enabled me to attend a political class which met three times a week. In this political course we analyzed the current situation; read documentaries and stories about life and resistance, especially women's role in resistance movements around the world; learned Afghan history and world history; and did some general studies about culture and literature. I thought of taking a nursing class, and even started it, but then they needed people to work in the underground resistance, working inside Afghanistan and Iran, and right away I decided to do that instead.

"My husband was the first person who opened the door for me, and I consider him my partner in all aspects. Now we live in Herat. My husband has a shop. He earns his living that way, and besides that, his shop is the regional contact point for RAWA. A shop is suitable for this, because it is not suspicious when many people come in and out of the door.

"My husband's brothers are in other cities and don't know the details of what we do. I suspect that if they found out, they would not accept it. They are very backward when it comes to the issue of women, and they would like their wives and daughters to stay inside the house sitting in some corner. I have tried to work on their wives and daughters so that they acquire consciousness and struggle against the backwardness and become more enlightened. However, the distance between my house and each of their towns is great, so I haven't been able to accomplish as much with them as I would like to.

"In Herat, I supervise six courses on literacy and three home schools. Each course has five to seven people. Now that the Taliban are gone, I hope we can combine the six courses into two. That will enable us to accomplish a lot more, and to use our mobile teachers more effectively.

"In one of the neighborhoods where we ran a school, neighbors told us about a woman who was very depressed and sad because her brother had been killed by the *jihadis* and her son and her husband by the Taliban. Her house was located next to the house where we held our classes. When I heard this, I felt concern for her, and along with one of the teachers, I went to her house. She told us that she doesn't have any more tears to shed, that she is staying alive instead of killing herself only in order to provide care for her daughter and her young daughter-in-law; otherwise she would have preferred to burn herself. She said she didn't know what to do, because no one heard her voice.

"Women's conditions such as this one make a big impact on me, and I especially want to help them. I used to go each week to the house of this woman. I wanted to rescue her from being lonely and hopeless and to share with her the good and beautiful aspects of life. I told her about myself and what my work meant to me. After a while she wanted to send her daughter and daughter-in-law to our literacy classes. Later, she invited the teachers to spend the nights at her house. Last year, when we had our tenth of December demonstration, she said she wanted to participate. She traveled to Pakistan and after the demonstrations she pulled me into her arms and said, 'My daughter, now instead of my tears for the death of my son and brother and husband, I will work with you. If I die, I will not be concerned because I will know that you, my daughters, will continue the struggle for the destruction of those who killed my loved ones.' Her words made us all very happy. My effort is to establish relations with such women and to create in them, by working with RAWA, a sense of life and direction."

What these women are engaging in is, of course, politics—politics of the highest order. In our luxurious contemporary version of politics, you can feel a sense of civic accomplishment just by going to your local elementary school or other polling place and casting your ballot—and if that ballot was confusing, you can spend the next two months complaining about the trauma it caused you and the vast sense of disenfranchisement you are now suffering from. In situations of violent political turmoil or radical oppression, to be political means a lot more than that and is quite risky. For many Afghan women, becoming politically involved meant regaining their sense of life and direction. One senses that Meena was speaking only half in jest when she told a young girl that she defined politics as a "wild animal." In situations where you might pay for political engagement with your life, it can indeed be that. Knowingly or unknowingly, her joke went deeper than that. Classical theory defines man as a *zoon politicon,* a political animal. Considering how these women, without prior education or guidance, take to politics as a means for shaping their lives, giving them purpose, and acting instead of permitting themselves to be brutally acted upon, it seems that woman is a political animal, too.

Mahboba

Mahboba required only a poem with three mobilizing lines to sense the promise that political action held. She might be bombed, pounded, driven into exile, but she did not have to remain completely helpless. Change meant people acting—people like her, one at a time. This insight can, as she describes, be accompanied by some elation, a feeling of empowerment. But Mahboba is not naive, an idealist caught in some revolutionary fantasy. Her explanation of how she resolved the issue of risk in her own mind and her poignant concluding description of the varying state of her emotions reveal an absolutely clearheaded choice.

The political situation she refers to at the start of her statement is the period when the so-called *jihadis* or freedom fighters ruled. After defeating the Soviets, they turned against each other in their struggle for power. In a thoroughly unsavory group, the worst of them all was Gulbuddin Hekmatyar, a fundamentalist of particular fanaticism. He was the one who in his youth, at the university, threw acid on female students. He is responsible for most of the destruction of Kabul; when the civil war broke out, he simply set up his armaments around the city and indiscriminately shelled his own capital and its civilians. For weeks, the population lived in terror, and many were killed.

"I cannot find the words to describe the political situation in Kabul, in 1992. When I remember those days, I want to cry for hours," says Mahboba. "The people in Kabul were inflicted with such a great sorrow and fear that their situation would correctly define the word *misery*. My best friend and longtime neighbor decided to leave Kabul for Pakistan. She entrusted me with her books and magazines. Two days after she left, I went through her things and came across an article about women's resistance against terror and tyranny. I showed the magazine to my father, and he advised me to be cautious. I still remember a poem from that issue:

> If I rise up
> If you rise up
> Everyone will rise up.

"Poetry was not my thing, but this particular passage spoke to me somehow. Soon thereafter, my family, too, was forced to flee Afghanistan. We went to Iran. I had memorized RAWA's post office box number, and once I was in Iran, I wrote to them. It took two and half months for the letter to go and the reply to arrive, and some of my questions remained unanswered. So the correspondence continued, and I received more literature, becoming more and more interested all the time.

"One day a woman showed up at my door and inquired about me. My intuition was that she must be the RAWA contact, and I was highly excited. My mother concluded that I must have met a boy somewhere and fallen in love, and that this woman must be his mother, come to ask for my hand on behalf of her son. It was the only thing she could think of to explain the happy grin on my face.

"After the woman had left, my mother asked me about her. I told her that she was a friend from Afghanistan whom I had met by accident in the market and given my address to. Well, this was the beginning of RAWA and me.

"After living in Iran for two years, I returned to Afghanistan having close ties with RAWA. I was engaged in political work as well as teaching literacy classes and holding meetings with women from different regions and provinces. Many of these women had lost a member of their family, as well as losing their houses and their belongings due to the war or because they belonged to minority groups the Taliban hated and were trying to kill. We found accommodations for these women, securing the welfare of their children and relocating their families to safer regions in Pakistan or Iran.

"In my opinion, the accomplishment of this task is neither frightening nor overwhelming. I think once you live under Taliban rule, you lose your sense of things being dangerous, and you can do my kind of work easily. Their way of dealing with women is barbaric and savage; it is really not possible to live under their rule. We, the women in RAWA, can therefore oppose them effortlessly.

"Sometimes when I have finished a mission, I feel content and satisfied; but sometimes I get really tired and then it seems to me that my contribution is only a drop in a bucket."

Sanobar

For RAWA's women, the decision to put their lives on the line is a political step with a deeply personal, emotional component. *Vengeance* is not the right word to describe what drives Sanobar. A better term would be *resolve,* a cold resolve born when, too young for such bitter insight, she first met the enemy.

"I was born thirty years ago in Kunduz. My grandfather was an important man in that province, a landowner; he had three hundred hectares of ground. Some of my family was traditional, like my uncle. He had four wives, who all lived in one household together with their children. My grandfather, however, was quite progressive in his thinking about women—for instance, he wanted schools for girls. When they started to discuss opening such a school in our area, he gave permission for it to be built on his property.

"I still remember my first day of school. I sat next to my cousin, and we fought over who would get the seat closest to the window. And I remember that there was a little brook in front of the school. Those lovely days lasted only a short time. Looking back, it feels like I only dreamed it.

"Pretty soon we heard the grown-ups talking about the coming of the Russians, and that they were *kaffir,* heathens. That they would be very different from us, that they would speak a different language and have a different kind of face.

"Soon thereafter, the bombs started falling. We had to flee. I remember it was morning. We hastily packed a few of our things and started to move in the direction of Pakistan. We were on the road for days and nights, all on foot. We walked, we marched until we could barely stand up anymore. Hundreds of other families were fleeing, just like us. Finally we reached a refugee camp. Every family got a tent. There were five thousand such tents in our camp.

"There were small hills around our camp; the other children and I used to play there. We would look down at the sea of tents and try to find which one was ours. From above, they looked like eggs, and I remember saying, 'Look, our chicken has laid a lot of eggs.'

"We were there for a year and my father was unhappy because there was no school for us to go to. Finally he heard about a school for Afghan children—it was called the Watan School—but it was too far away. It was not possible to move the whole family there. Where would we have lived, how to support ourselves? Our only home was the camp. So my father traveled to that school to discuss it with them, and they were very kind. They offered to let us live in their children's home, although it was normally an orphanage. That's how it happened that my father sent us there, me and two other girls.

"For all of us it was the first time that we had been separated from our parents, and that was very hard. During the first days we were very homesick. When no one could see us, we cried. The teachers tried hard to help us get adjusted.

"A week later, a lady came to visit us. It was strange because all of us children had the immediate feeling that we already knew her from somewhere, that she might be a relative. She hugged and kissed us and asked us lots of questions about ourselves, and then she talked at length about us to our teachers. From then on she came to see us every week. Our teachers were very nice and sweet to us, but the behavior of this woman was different—she acted just like a mother.

"This woman was Meena.

"In this school, I saw for the first time a map of Afghanistan. We worked on it with our teacher for a week and learned about the different cities and regions. Then when she showed us for the first time a map of the world, we were thrilled! We just couldn't believe it. So big! When we were still living at home in our little village, we thought that was the world. When we came to Pakistan, my horizon got much bigger.

"But now I know: The world, after all, is not as big as I thought.

"One day, after we had been in the children's home for about three months, Meena came and she had a big smile on her face. She said she had a surprise for us. She said: 'We have a new house, which is much bigger, and we have more money and more children can come to stay with us.'

"In the new home we were only three children to a room, plus a teacher. And each child had a special task. My job was to dispense medication if someone became sick. I had to write down what the sick child should get and at what time. And then I was allowed to hand it out.

"We had a storage room where the medication was kept, and none of the little girls was allowed to go in there except for me. That made me very proud and gave me a great sense of importance. I thought, 'If they have such a high opinion of me and if they trust me so much, then probably one day I will hold a big position.' I have to laugh now when I remember how important I felt.

"Meena liked poetry and songs. She often sang to us and read us poems. Later, the teachers practiced with us until we, too, could sing songs for her. Meena had tears in her eyes whenever she listened to us. The hours with her just flew by, we loved her so much. We waited impatiently for her if she was late.

"After about two years, my father asked the school principal if I and the two girls from our village could have a month's vacation because our mothers were missing us so much. She agreed, but for us girls the situation was strange. Of course we wanted to see our mothers again, but two years are a long time for a child and the school had become our home.

"Meena came to the train station for the farewell. She bought us some things for the trip and consoled us that we would be coming back soon enough. Her words, these feelings, the last farewell—I will not forget them until the end of my life. She forced herself to be cheerful, but there was great sadness in her eyes. I was only a child, but I could sense her unhappiness. I found out years later that she had just learned from some of her husband's friends that he had been killed. Yet still she came to the train station with us, and loved us, and put on a brave face and hugged and kissed us many times.

"When the month was over, my father didn't want us to go back. But we put pressure on him, and so after another month he told us to pack our clothes, and took us to Quetta again.

"Back in the home, we waited to see Meena. Four days passed, five days—she didn't come. We asked our teachers, and they said: 'She had some things to do, she is in a different city.' When we asked a second time, we got no answer at all. Then they called us together in the assembly room. They said they had to talk to us on a very important subject. We had no idea what was going on, but we could tell that something very serious must have happened. We sat there and waited for our teachers to say something, but it seemed none of them wanted to speak. They had trouble finding the words to begin. Finally one of them said: 'Today we want to give you the saddest news of your life. Tomorrow we must hold a large demonstration for Meena. She has been murdered.'

"I was overcome by pain. I could not see through my eyes. All the girls became very quiet. That night I could not sleep. I kept seeing Meena, her laugh, her warmth, her poetry. I fought hard not to cry, in order not to frighten the little girls even more.

"The next day we had a big demonstration. The women carried a large banner with a picture of Meena. Almost everyone was crying.

"My feelings for Meena had long been like those of a daughter for her mother, but now they changed and became even deeper. After all, RAWA raised me; they were my family. From each RAWA woman I learned something important for my life, and none of them had any other wish except to help me.

"I already knew that I wanted to work for justice and for other women. But on this day I felt a new hardness in myself. And I thought, 'I can do more than that. I can be a sword—a sword to drive into the hearts of those who murdered Meena and who are the enemies of all women.'

"Today I live with my husband in Mazar-i-Sharif. We both belong to RAWA, the clandestine part of the organization. We are the central contact point for the underground. We collect the reports and photos of Taliban executions and we deliver them to Pakistan. Sometimes we shelter people who have to hide. It is very risky, but I can handle it; already as a child I became acquainted with danger.

"Of course, we try hard not to be discovered. We asked my mother-in-law to move in with us. This makes us less conspicuous, to have an old lady in our household. But sometimes it is unavoidable to do some work at night—for example, we may have to write something to pass along with a person. Even this is dangerous, because if a light is on for a long time at night, the Taliban get suspicious and might come and check.

"Once, another woman and I had gone out to take photographs in the part of the city that we were assigned to cover. We were on our way home again when we noticed that we were being followed by a Taliban car. We realized that we had no *mahram* with us, which was strictly forbidden. The car with the Taliban tried to pass us, whereupon our driver stepped on the gas. The Taliban chased us and rammed into our car. There was a loud bang and we stopped moving. One Talib jumped out—he was furious. He rushed right up to us and put the barrel of his rifle directly against our driver's forehead. I thought that he was going to shoot him right on the spot, and I just lost control of myself. I screamed and swore at the Talib. He shouted to his companion to arrest me, to arrest this godless woman. As they pulled on my arm to get me out of the car, my friend was holding on to my other arm, pulling me back toward her. It was the most terrible moment of my life. All I could think about was what would happen when they found our camera and the film. I was desperately trying to think of an excuse, some explanation, but there couldn't be one. My heart was racing—I could hear it beating so loudly.

"They started to randomly search some of the men who were standing around. Then they remembered me again and wanted me out of the car, to arrest me. The men bystanders all spoke for us and asked the Taliban to let us go, to just let the women go. My companion wanted to appease them and calm them down. She started to cry and beg. She kept saying, 'Please, let us go, we haven't done anything.' And finally they did, they allowed us to go home.

"When I tell you this story now, my heart feels like it is burning. It makes me angry to think how we had to cry and beg in front of them. It would have been better to let them kill us, even slowly with a bow and arrow. It was terrible to experience so much fear and even worse to feel so degraded. But I tell myself that I had to do this. If they had arrested us, how many people would have died! Even if we had been strong enough not to answer their questions, still our house would have been searched and so many names discovered. It wasn't only about us—many other lives were at stake, too.

"Before I got married, my father was the only one who agreed with my work; the rest of my family was against it. Once in Pakistan there was a demonstration and my photo appeared in the paper. The family was very upset and told my father to forbid me to have any further contact with the group. That was one reason why I wanted to get married—to free myself from the control of my family. When a woman marries in Afghanistan, she does not belong to her family anymore, she belongs to her husband, and they can't interfere. My husband knew my ideals and plans and he agreed with them. He supports RAWA. Everything I do, he shares it with me. Day by day, even his three brothers respect me more and are becoming interested in my cause. My mother-in-law loves me and is proud of me. She is old and ailing but she helps us. She takes care of my little daughter so that I can continue my work.

"American sisters, where I am there is nothing but war

and guns, and from such a place I write to you. I am surrounded by many women who have lost hope. If you want freedom to be returned to Afghanistan and women not to be tormented and their lives destroyed anymore, then you should raise the voices of the women in the world and try to help RAWA."

CHAPTER 5

Shahla in November

I t's November 2001, and her name is Shahla. In October, it was Mariam. On her passport, it's something different still. Shahla seems unfazed by this—her head turns instantly when you call her by her new name. Life has obliged her to get used to changes.

Shahla has been a refugee for most of her twenty-seven years, and for much of that time RAWA has been her home and her family. RAWA plucked her out of a grim refugee slum, moved her into a house filled with other children and gave her an education and the love of caring teachers, job training and a mission.

They even vetted her future husband—my favorite mental image from this interview. I would give anything to have been there when her suitor presented himself to the stern scrutiny of a RAWA committee.

Shahla works in public affairs and in the schools. Now that she has learned English, she is sometimes sent on foreign assignments, lecture tours and public appearances. She has become one of the public faces of RAWA. With her determined ability to stay on message, her gift for turning a phrase and her regal air—when she spoke at the International School in Vienna, the children thought she "looked like a princess"—Shahla is good at this assignment.

Unlike Taliban delegations to the West, who became famous for their expressed desire to be taken to malls whenever they were abroad, or the September 11 terrorists, whose reconstructed days revealed a fondness for going to Gold's Gym and hanging out in pornographic video shops, it is difficult to get RAWA members to engage in casual leisure activities. They have a tendency to be very earnest and to want to work all the time. When Shahla arrived in Vienna, the organizers of the event sent a limousine and scheduled a city tour for her, but she politely declined. Time was short, she explained, and there was a lot of work to do. Besides, she said, glancing out of the window as the car passed the palatial buildings of Ringstrasse, she had been in Spain once and in Italy, and from the looks of it, Vienna was basically more of the same.

It was a good thing that Shahla was so unflappable, or perhaps just accustomed to the odder side of intercultural life. The event she had been invited to was a flashy awards ceremony; the honorees included Luciano Pavarotti, Mikhail Gorbachev, Ted Turner and Hans-Dietrich Genscher. Shahla had set up an information table showing facts about the situation in Afghanistan and the work of RAWA. The French film star Alain Delon approached, dramatically flung open his blazer and said that he would love to donate, but he had no money with him, not a single franc—in fact, he was not even carrying a wallet, see? But he did have something else to offer her that was more precious than money. So saying, he pulled out a huge silver crucifix with a miniature Jesus on it and held it toward Shahla, announcing, "He always helps!" As he strode away, one of the security guards came over, a woman. "I saw that," she said. "I'm sorry." Then she took out her wallet and emptied it on the table. It contained 700 Austrian schillings and a subway ticket, which she plucked up. "I need that to get home," she said. "But please take the money for the Afghan women."

The thing that struck me most, in Shahla's interview, is her concluding thought: "If people can help you, they usually will." To remember the spontaneous generosity of a random security guard and forget the self-righteousness of the famous Alain Delon, to focus on the huge wave of international sympathy and downplay the twists and turns of official foreign policy, to be capable of the kind of psychological arithmetic that will let you add up thirty years of war and destruction and come up with such an optimistic sum, is nothing short of wonderful.

"I was born in Kabul in 1974," says Shahla. "My mother was uneducated. She worked as a seamstress, and my father was in the army. I'm the youngest daughter; I have four sisters.

"Unfortunately I lost my father during the first years the Russians occupied Afghanistan. I don't remember much about Afghanistan, because I was too young when we came to the refugee camp in Pakistan—I was eight years old. Of course I was going to school when I was in Kabul, along with my sisters. The school was very close to our house, I remember that. But I finished only the first and second grades there.

"It was just a very horrible time for the whole family—not only my own family, but all families, especially those who were living in the cities, and especially those who were living in the city of Kabul. Because of the puppet regime of Russia, in my own family alone, just in the space of a few months, within two or three months, all the male members of our family were either arrested or killed. My two aunts lost their husbands; both were arrested. The youngest person of my family who disappeared was my cousin; when they took him he was twenty-five. I remember him—he was a very creative person, energetic and funny and very kind to all family members. Because of that, everyone loved him very much.

"He was a student. And one day he went to the university, as usual, and his mother was just waiting in the house for his return, but unfortunately he didn't come back. However, my aunt, his mother, is still waiting. She says, 'If I saw his body, it would be possible for me to accept that my son has died, but otherwise I will be hopeful always.'

"And her husband also disappeared, but at a different time. My other aunt, who has two daughters around my age, also lost her husband, but at least in one way she was more fortunate, because she could find the name of her husband on a list of the people who were killed, so at least she knew. This list was the list from a very famous prison, Charcheley, the biggest prison in the region.

"My family were just normal, average people. Of course, my father was anti-Russian and therefore against the pro-Soviet regime—most people were—but he was not politically active. He was very interested in the political situation, but he was not directly involved in any organization or any group. My oldest sister already had contacts with RAWA at this time.

"Then my family, what was left of my family, decided to leave Kabul and go to Pakistan, to the refugee camps. My grandmother also was living with us, and so we all—five daughters plus my mother and grandmother, just females—decided to leave. And the usual way to do that in those times was to contact some special people who had the job of taking families across the border. They asked for a lot of money, so whatever we owned, my mother sold all of it and collected the money, and in this way we lost everything we had.

"I remember the night we left. I was not informed that we were leaving for Pakistan; they hadn't discussed this decision with me, because I was the youngest. So I had nothing in my mind about Pakistan or another country or leaving my own city. I had no idea at all until my mother woke me at midnight, not in the morning as usual, and told me that we were leaving now, and to get up. Of course, I was very scared. I didn't know what was happening. My sister talked with me and explained that it was better to leave, and that we had to go now.

"We were supposed to arrive in Kandahar at night—that's the border city. But the road was closed between Kabul and Kandahar, because there was fighting between Russian troops and the mujahideen. The Russians were on the side of Kabul city and the mujahideen were on the side of Kandahar city. And we were in the middle. I remember that we spent that night in the bus, and we could hear the fighting and the loud voices. My grandmother was old, and she got out of the bus with some of the other adults, and my mother as well. They wanted to sleep in a corner of a nearby abandoned building. And in that way, we children could sleep on the seats of the bus. But suddenly a bomb hit that building. And very, very close to my mother and grandmother dropped this bomb, and my grandmother became injured a little bit, not too seriously. Still, it was a problem because she was old, but fortunately my mother had prepared for such a thing and had medicine and bandages, because she had thought that something might happen on the way. There was also a small child whose whole body was burned, and she cried all night, and of course no one could sleep anymore.

"In the morning, the fighting stopped and we could continue on the way to Kandahar. We were supposed to leave that city right away and cross the border, but unfortunately we couldn't. The Pakistanis had closed the border, and it was not easy to cross. You had to bribe people, and even that was not easy—you had to get the money for one person to another and another, and then you needed to arrange a special car, and of course it was dangerous, and you had to wait for a suitable moment. So without knowing anybody in this city, and having no contacts, we had to give more money to the same man who had brought us this far, and ask him to let us spend a few nights with his family. We went to that house and spent twenty-one days exactly.

"And in Kandahar city, I remember, every night we couldn't sleep. Especially for me and the next youngest sister, it was very difficult every night to hear the voices of the soldiers shouting, and to watch the scenes of fighting. We were small, but we could understand that this side is Kabul and this side is mujahideen. Then in the daytime we made a kind of game out of it, all of us children. Every morning all of us would get up and collect the small pieces of bullets and shrapnel, because there was a lot of firing and everywhere we could find these things. It was like a game, whoever can collect the most, and in the evening we counted how much we collected today, and also we counted the number of explosions and shots that we could hear during the night, things like that. But at the same time we were also very afraid, and that is why we tried to make a game out of it, I suppose.

"And there was no light. It was winter, I remember, and just after five or six o'clock it would get dark, and we would be inside the home from then until early the next morning. Even in the daytime, my mother tried to keep us inside the house as much as she could, because she was worried that something would happen to us.

"I remember the family of that man. He had three wives and a lot of children, and they were all working very hard, doing all the domestic work of the house, and fighting with each other every day over everything. And one wife was very old, and another one was very young and more power-ful among the others, and it was a backward family with backward traditions.

"When we were able to cross the border, it was a big relief. Living with this family was perhaps not so much of a shock for my mother, because within her extended family there were some who lived such a life, with three wives. And for me it was not so bad, either, because I was not of an age to understand all these things. But for my eldest sisters it was very upsetting, because they were educated—they were university students, both of them—and both of course were fighting for women's rights. They were in contact with organizations like RAWA. I cannot understand exactly what their feelings must have been, but I can understand that it was something very shocking. I think, in one way, it was a good experience for them, because you know, living in a city as we had been, being not very rich but certainly a middle-class family, and then coming to live in a village and being among these people and observing their lives, their traditions, and the situation of the women . . . besides being very sad and confusing, perhaps it was a useful experience also, that helped them with their future, because they learned to understand what life was like for rural women.

"During the time of the mujahideen, all of the schools were open, and girls were allowed to go. But unfortunately women could not really be outside their houses, because of the many rapes. This was the most powerful weapon in their hand, and so the mujahideen didn't even have to bother forbidding women to go out. And so basically we can say that school for girls was closed. Maybe the door was open, but in fact no girl could go there.

"Then when the Taliban came, the first day and the first house that they entered in Afghanistan, they said that all the schools will be closed after tomorrow, and women are not allowed to come out of their house, and they should not be in their jobs. They banned TV absolutely on the first days. They continued radio, but without music, without any programs for entertainment, just religious subjects, and there were some religious songs without instruments.

"When we first arrived at the refugee camp, we stayed the first few months under a tent. This was the second important experience for my family, to learn what it means to be a refugee. But it was not good for the health problems that my grandmother had.

"Soon we became able to leave the camp, but we did not go far. Very near, very close to this camp, we could rent a small house. It was not so much better than the camp. It was also without water, and it was the job of my sisters to bring water from outside. And two years after that, RAWA established the school in Quetta, their first school, and I was one of their first students in this school, which was a boarding school. At the beginning we were just twenty children. And I think these were the best days of my life, being together with my classmates. We were from very different ethnic groups, with different languages, but that also was good, because I could teach them Persian—I am Tajik—and they could teach me Pashtu.

"I had all the science subjects—mathematics, geography, biology, chemistry. Besides this I had Persian and Pashtu, which are the main two languages, and English only once a week, because we had difficulty finding an English teacher. One of our teachers was educated in German, and the other one in French, not English. Then, after the ending of the classes, we went to another room and changed clothes. We wore the uniforms in the morning, and then in the afternoon we wore our ordinary clothes, so that even though we remained in the same rooms, we could have the feeling that school was over, and this was our free time. It was good for us. After a short break, we did our homework, and our teachers were there to help us if someone had difficulties. During that time it was not so big a school, so there were classes with, for example, grade three and grade four together. This meant that many students in grade three had difficulties keeping up, and the teachers had to help them, and that's why we finished school so soon, because they worked a lot with us.

"Then in the evening, after five or six, we had entertainment, mostly sports—for example, jump rope and running, we had a big place for running—and after that we would drink tea. In the evening sometimes, perhaps two or three times a week, they brought us a TV set to watch. RAWA had just one or two TV sets, and we moved it to different places, sometimes for families, sometimes for school. Then at night we would have something to eat, and then go to sleep.

"In Quetta the refugee camp is very far from the city, but the school was midway between the two. Today that place is also a part of the city, because Quetta has grown so much, but at that time it was out in the middle of nowhere.

"We had very good teachers, very good. Unfortunately, we had a shortage of books and stories for children. We only had one little booklet translated by an Iranian, and some books that someone had translated from Russian. I didn't mind too much; I preferred painting to reading, anyway. I spent most of my time painting. Now I absolutely cannot paint anything—it was just my interest as a teenager. And also I was interested in music, and I was a member of the students' singing group.

"I went to this school for six years, and then, at sixteen, I became a member of RAWA. We had four teachers who were RAWA members in this school, and all of them were wonderful in my eyes. So I wanted to be like them in the future.

"One teacher was closer to the students. If one of us was sick, in the middle of the night she would come and ask if we needed something. And she spent most of her free time among the students, telling us stories. And another teacher, she was a bit more serious, the opposite of her, so of course some of my classmates said, 'No, I love the serious one,' but others said, 'No, I love the other one.' There were only five or six girls in my age group, but we were a bit educated already, a little bit, because we had been to school for two years in Afghanistan, so we started faster and finished faster. And one of our teachers worked with us so that we could finish on time, making up for the time we had lost as refugees.

"Usually during the summer or winter holidays we went to our families, but I remember that for two years the teachers decided not to give us the holidays, but urged us instead to finish our material. It was not hard for us, because we were happier in the school anyway. There we were many young people, and we had opportunities to play, to have games, to have TV. Because my mother was near, not so far, I could see her once a week.

"At first, being a RAWA member was not different from my regular life, because I was not old enough to do anything independently. It was more something symbolic for me to be a member of RAWA. I continued my studies, and I did some little things to help. In that year RAWA was going to publish its own schoolbooks, so I went to make photocopies, and this was my biggest job. I worked most of the time in the cultural committee of RAWA. Later we had computers, but during the first years we were mostly printing books for RAWA schools.

"Then RAWA decided to send me for more education, to an English-language course. And this was not within our own school system, but in a Pakistani language school, and RAWA paid for my tuition. I wasn't alone; they sent us in a small group, we were five. That was six years ago, when I was twenty. And my future husband was taking the same course.

"Our families were not known to each other, so ordinarily it would have been very difficult for us to get permission to marry. Mostly RAWA helped me, so that I could marry him. My comrades in RAWA were the first people whom I told that I had met a man and that I liked him. And they said, 'Fine, let's have a look at him.' Of course the other RAWA girls who were taking the class with me, they knew him already, and he had made a pretty good impression on them. Then a group of RAWA women spoke to him, and they found him to be good and suitable for me.

"So several of them went to see my mother, to ask her permission for an engagement. And he came to our house, and she met him. But still it took almost two years for everyone's objections to be overcome. My mother was the biggest obstacle. She was concerned about what people would say, knowing that I had found my husband on my own, from a family not known to ours. As a widow, she was always extra strict with us. She used to say, 'If I give you too much freedom and let you do as you like, then people will say these girls are running wild because they have no father.' And also she was worried for me. Since she did not know the family, she knew nothing about the boy, either, or what kind of a person he is.

"Yes, my husband is modern and supportive, but this is not so unusual as people in the West often think. I don't think his attitudes are so exceptional or so special; I think it is normal that he should be like this. Especially in my eyes, because we came from Kabul, and the men of Kabul were already much more advanced than the men in other parts of the country. Maybe the one special thing about him is that he is not so old. It is common with us for the husband to be much older than the wife—a difference of ten years is considered normal. For example, the husband of one of my sisters is twelve years older than she is, the other ten, the other six. But my husband is only three years older than I am, and many people believed that this difference was too small. But I like it this way, because I think it makes it easier for us to be close and to be friendly with each other.

"Once we were at my older sister's house, and I got into a heated debate with my husband, and my sister pulled me aside and said, 'Be careful, you shouldn't have this kind of a disagreement with your husband.' Her marriage is much more formal and stiff, because her husband is twelve years older. And personally I like my way much better, because the way we interact is much more relaxed.

"My husband knew from the beginning what he was getting into concerning my work. We regularly sent members to this English course, and the teacher knew all about us and therefore the other students also knew that we were a RAWA group. So my husband was forewarned. Even so, I had to do a little further work on him," she says with a laugh.

"If it had been up to me, I would not have wanted to have a baby so quickly, but his mother was putting a lot of pressure on us. She was concerned from the beginning that a political woman like me would not be a good mother for the children of her son, and now she is happy. The baby slowed me down, of course, at least in the beginning. But my sisters help me, and RAWA helps me a lot. My comrades are very happy about my son, and they always urge me to give him enough of my time. My husband is a businessman—he trades goods between Pakistan and Afghanistan, so he travels inside the country a lot, which is dangerous. When he is here he helps with our son.

"There is an inner circle of RAWA members who make the decisions, eleven women. I am not with these eleven.

There is a second circle, and I'm a member of this second circle. Each of the eleven is the head of a particular group—for example, RAWA's educational works, health care, financial committee, foreign committee, publication committee, cultural committee, relationship committee, organizing committee. . . . And I work in the cultural committee, and I have been on the publication committee also.

"At the beginning with our website, of course, some local people had to help us, but you know, even in Pakistan it was something very, very new, websites and the Internet, and nobody really knew a lot. So we needed to learn how to do this for ourselves, and some of our supporters from the United States helped us, they sent some CDs and other things that we needed to guide us. Our first website was quite simple, but I remember there were a few parts that were very nice. One of our supporters in Australia had done that work for us and sent it, because as he said, 'I don't have money to send you, but I can design this page for you.' And also from the beginning we always asked for the opinion of our visitors, and that improved our work very much.

"Of the eleven people who are the inner circle, most of them are inside Afghanistan, because that is the most important work, but at least two or three of them try to be in Pakistan, arranging the activities there. And from day to day they usually leave us alone to make the decisions ourselves. Of course we check with them, and they say yes or no, and explain why or why not. I think this is something very special about RAWA, that they are providing many opportunities for us, for the young members, to do independent work. Because as they say, 'I will not always be there for you, so you must learn to continue without me.'

"But in other ways I'm not so fortunate. When my older colleagues tell their stories, how they used to work, then I realize that things used to be very different, because mostly they were able to work among the students of the universities and schools. They had a much bigger forum and were able to live more openly, not like today. We are always hiding, always moving.

"Of course, we have contact with many women who were raped, and young girls come to us who lost their families and who were in danger of being raped but escaped, fortunately. And we have many stories, many reports, many contacts still inside Afghanistan that tell us of similar cases. The special difficulty of Afghanistan is that women who have been raped don't want to say it, even to their very close friends. And that's why it becomes difficult to help these women. But it is a very big number who are affected, especially during the time of the Northern Alliance, after 1992— there were a lot of cases, it was very common.

"But we need to do more work to help the women not to be shy and to be ready to tell what happened, or even to learn not to be an easy victim in the less serious cases. You know, sometimes it happens, especially for the young girls, that when you are walking in the street, a man comes and just touches you. Perhaps if this happens in the Western countries, it's nothing, absolutely nothing. But in Afghanistan it is something, even just a touch. And many girls feel ashamed to react, or they just want to keep it secret, not to be known by others. Of course they feel bad, they feel angry, they want to cry, to raise their voice, but they don't do it. And we are working very hard, especially among our young students, not to be so helpless—their life teaches them a little bit not to be quiet, but it needs still more teaching.

"It happened to some women who were raped that they got pregnant, and some of them don't want to give birth, they commit suicide. If they give birth, of course secretly, they don't want to tell their friends, their relatives or anybody, and they usually escape from one area to another, and they give their children away. Many people contact us wondering if we can get them a child from Afghanistan, because they have heard that many women who were raped give birth to children and don't want them. Also they contact the hospitals. In at least two cases with people that I personally know, women went to the hospitals and the doctors knew that in the next two months or three months this woman would be coming back for delivery, and they promised to get her child to give to someone. Mostly these children stay in Afghanistan, with women who can't have children, and so they adopt these children. But even then, usually they adopt boys, not girls.

"The support from the women of the Western countries is very important for us. RAWA would not be where it is today if we did not have these contacts and all these relationships with women, especially through our e-mail and website. Truly the establishing of our website was a revolution in our history.

"Of course the help is important, but one other thing is that our supporters make us hopeful, and they make us confident. We get a lot of strength from them.

"When we criticize the West or something that the West is doing, then it means the policy makers, the decision makers and the governments, not the people, never. We always had wonderful supporters, mostly among the U.S. people. We always criticize their government, their policies, their leaders, but never their people. And the same happens with the European countries, because we have many, many supporters. When we were in different meetings in different parts of Europe, we were so welcome, they were so warm, and they were so glad to meet with us, and they were ready to provide any kind of help for us.

"Of those people that I have met, my experience has been that those who have a better life, a better situation and the possibility to help someone else usually will help you. And because of our specific situation in Afghanistan, anyone can see that our case is very different from other countries. You could not find such a bad situation in any other part of the world, especially the crimes against women and the low level of education. It was this situation of Afghanistan that made people very interested to help us, and now, especially after the eleventh of September, even more people in the West became informed about the women, and when I am traveling this time I can see that people have more awareness and are even more supportive, not just of RAWA but of women."

CHAPTER 6

Books and Flowers

A fghanistan has the lowest rate of female literacy in the entire world. Only an estimated 7 percent of its women can read and write. The level of male literacy, while not very impressive, either, is nonetheless substantially higher. It is estimated at 35 percent. Unlike a difference in the educational level, literacy has a kind of absolute quality: You are either literate or you are not.

In a culture already marked by so many massive disparities in the resources and rights of the sexes, literacy provides one more reason for women to feel like the lesser group. It is quite usual to encounter Afghan families in which every man can read and no woman can. Nor is it exceptional for a family to send its sons to university while not providing its daughters with even an elementary school education. And male high school graduates are routinely paired up with illiterate brides.

When the Soviets invaded Afghanistan, the education gap between the genders was in the process of being significantly reduced, but the effort had just begun. Regional disparities and the rural-urban divide were slowly becoming more important than gender for predicting educational differences. In the cities, most families sent all their children to school, although the more traditional families and those of a lower social class would allow their sons more years of education than their daughters.

When the so-called freedom fighters or mujahideen (more correctly referred to in Afghan parlance as the *jihadis*) held sway over the Afghan refugees and later over the entire country, education generally took a steep nosedive. The fundamentalist ideal was the warlike male and the domestic female, and you didn't need much of an education for either of those roles. Their schools taught boys the Quran, political propaganda and physical education. The curriculum for girls consisted of the Quran and comportment, teaching proper dress and proper subservience.

Then came the Taliban. Fundamentalism is premised on the clear supremacy of male over female, and education is one of the means for achieving and demonstrating that superiority. In some Taliban areas, girls under the age of twelve were allowed to take part in some limited Quranic instruction, but real schooling was forbidden them. Confined to her house, a woman did not need to read anything. Not even allowed to shop for the family's basic necessities, she didn't need daily numeracy, either—she did not need to know how to count, add or subtract.

Afghan women, even those from very simple backgrounds, were embarrassed by their ignorance. Since this ignorance was statistically "normal," a fate shared by almost all women and proclaimed to be a proper part of their place in this world, we might expect them to have been accepting of it, but such was not the case. Most women regarded their inability to read, and their general lack of knowledge and education, as a painful deficit. That's interesting and noteworthy. It shows that even lifelong acculturation did not succeed in entirely stifling women's sense of themselves or their personal aspirations. Individually and collectively, women felt ashamed that they had not been schooled. They viewed it as an injustice that education had been withheld from them. As little girls, they had been told that their brothers were more valuable and more intelligent, that men were their intellectual and mental superiors. By the time they were grown, most women had studied the men around them carefully enough to know that this was not entirely the truth, that the story of men's universal brilliance and women's mental incapacity would not hold water in real life.

Still, socialization is a powerful tool, and Afghan women don't emerge from theirs unscathed. What if everything men say is true, and they just aren't smart enough to learn how to read and write? Maybe it really would just have been a waste of time and money to send them to school, given the limited academic capacity of their woman's brain. And even if it wasn't true then, when they were young, what made them think their minds could still absorb knowledge now, in middle age?

The decision to take part in a literacy course was, for most of the Afghan women we interviewed, not lightly taken. For most of them, learning to read and write was a lifelong dream, but one that they had nearly given up on. Then someone told them about a literacy class being offered in their camp or neighborhood, conducted by a women's organization just for women, and free of charge. Still, they hesitated.

They sought out women who had taken such a class, and studied them carefully. Well, those women were middle-aged also. They were refugees, mothers—ordinary women just like them. If they had succeeded, maybe it was worth giving it a try.

They tried the idea out on their husbands, who had no objection.

They signed up for the class and attended the first session with great trepidation, but they quickly made friends with their fellow pupils, all of whom were in exactly the same frame of mind and the same situation as they were. The teacher seemed confident that everyone could do this. They started to relax.

Soon they found themselves looking forward to the next hour. In the endless tedium of life in a refugee camp, the course offered a wonderful diversion. It wasn't just about reading and writing; you learned math, too, and discussed health and hygiene and better ways to raise your children.

The teacher, this educated, poised, self-confident and yet warm and encouraging person, was an education in and of herself. The women admired her, studied her, imitated her. They copied her speech patterns, her mannerisms, her confident posture. Her exciting stories about life in other countries inspired the imagination and raised many questions. In response to all the demeaning, insulting things they had grown up hearing about women and about themselves, this woman had uplifting and encouraging messages about the unlimited potential of women, their value and the many things they could contribute to the world.

Many of the husbands of the women in RAWA's literacy classes had themselves completed at least a few years of schooling. "He's an educated man" was how their wives would put it, which in Afghan common speech means that someone has, at some point, been to school. In the opinion of these wives, this explained why their husbands had given their approval for the literacy class. "As an educated person, he knows the value of learning. That's why he had no objection when I told him that I, too, wanted to learn how to read and write."

RAWA's literacy classes have five levels. In Pakistan, the average class size is fifteen. In Afghanistan, the groups had to be much smaller, in order not to attract notice. If more than three or four women had been seen regularly arriving at a house, this would have been suspicious—and teaching women to read was, under the Taliban, a very serious offense.

That's not to say that it was safe or easy in Pakistan, either. The border area was almost an annex of Afghanistan, with fundamentalists and their supporters in near total control. They didn't take kindly to the idea of female education. Just a year ago, one of RAWA's schools was raided by the police. Fundamentalists had reported that a brothel was being operated in that location—either because they really thought so, upon seeing large numbers of women go in and out of the building, or because they wanted to make trouble. As one can imagine, to be accused of prostitution in a strict Islamic environment is a highly traumatic experience. As soon as they learned that their students and the teacher had been arrested, RAWA dispatched a delegation to the police. Ultimately, everyone was released, but the police took their time about it, and the damage was done. After the scandal, the school had to be relocated.

A teacher explains, "The police of Peshawar took several of our students with them. When we went there to defend ourselves, to show that it wasn't what they were thinking, they wouldn't listen. After they finally accepted our explanation, we still had to abandon that location. Three of our students were so upset by the incident that they could not rejoin our class. Since then, when a new class begins, we discuss with all the students ahead of time what kinds of problems might occur. Then they will not be caught by surprise if something like this happens again, but will be prepared for it."

There are also other, broader psychological factors to be taken into account. Learning, the teachers have found, can't be separated from the context of these women's lives, past and present. The teacher continues, "Of course our goal is literacy, but we've discovered that we can't just plunge right in and start teaching. First we have to give the women a chance to talk about their personal situation and the problems of their families. Some are recent refugees. Within Afghanistan, the number of people lost to disease and war is tremendous—it affects our students a lot. Our teachers noticed that it is necessary to talk about these things first. You can't just push it away. At least the discussions can then be channeled in a way that is beneficial for everyone, and where the information that is spread will be true and safe and will have positive results."

Without a background in counseling or psychology, these teachers have intuitively hit upon the correct way to address trauma: by verbalizing it in the structured and safe setting of the group.

In this chapter, we will meet some of the women who attend these literacy classes. Their statements are fascinating, because they are the authentic voice of the Afghan population—not the modernized city folk, not the educated classes who have been exposed to global life, but the absolutely ordinary Afghan from a town or rural area, given her first glimpse of freedom and equality, allowed to think an independent thought for the first time in her life and grappling with the meaning and the possibility of change.

RAHIMA

"Just before we fled to Pakistan, one of my friends in Kabul told me consolingly that at least there might be a chance for me to go to a school once I got to Pakistan, because they had such things there for grown women. That is how I first found out about this course.

"I have always very much wanted to learn how to read and how to write, but unfortunately I was never able to realize this dream. Even when I needed to read something very simple and trivial, I always had to go to someone else and ask them to read it for me. That made me feel ashamed and it hurt me. There are two people among my relatives who have been to school, and maybe if things had been calmer and more normal they would have taught me, but all of our days were so filled with trouble that it was not possible.

"Now I have received this opportunity, and I am very determined always to go to my class and to learn as much as I can. So far I am very pleased, and I am hopeful that soon I will truly be able to read and write. Perhaps one day I might even get a job and work in an office. I would love to earn some income. And I want to read newspapers and books; I've always wanted that so badly.

"My husband is not against my coming to this course. I always do what is needed at home, in order not to give him any reason to be upset at my absence. My mother and my friends—almost everyone, really—are excited and happy for me to pursue this path. A few people in my family are against it, and they are men, distant relatives. Their reason is that if their Taliban friends find out that some men in their family are allowing their wives to go to school, then the word might get back to Afghanistan and it will embarrass them.

"Reading and writing—that in itself is not difficult for me. It is all the other problems that make it hard for me to focus. My mind is affected by many worries, and I feel that I am not concentrating in the way I could if I had a free mind. Reading is easier than writing, because there are words that have the same sound, but when you write them down, they are totally different. But such minor difficulties will not stop me.

"This is my third course. By attending these classes, I have come to know a lot of other women. All of them have been very nice and very interested to learn, just like me. This has increased my self-confidence, and I have become hopeful that as women, we are capable of learning. I feel confident and very lucky to have this opportunity. Learning to read will give me a better understanding of everything. It will open my eyes and ears [a Persian expression], and then it will be my turn to try to educate other women so that they, too, can become aware of what they are capable of. Our teacher says that if we women learn and educate ourselves, that will unite us and then we will have power and a voice.

"I want to improve my life, and I want my children to reach a higher level of education than me. My dream for the future is to start a course of my own, where I can teach other women. Then in the future, when we face men, we will be able to openly express our thoughts and ideas. I do not want to feel inferior to them from any perspective.

"My wishes and dreams are that one day I would like to have a safe life in Afghanistan. I wish that this condition of being without any rights will not exist anymore. And I also hope that the Taliban should no longer exist.

"I think that women and men, there is no difference between them in any way. And I have heard that in the advanced countries, there is indeed very little difference between men and women. But unfortunately in Afghanistan, the difference is immense. My teacher believes this also; she thinks that besides the physical one, there is absolutely no other kind of difference between men and women.

"All those abuses that women are facing in my country are due to the Taliban. They have no respect for human rights, and they are taking advantage of cultural beliefs that are empty of truth. As we can see, in more advanced countries such beliefs do not exist, and men and women, they work together and their rights are the same.

"But here, the differences that exist between men and women are so enormous. We are the prisoners of men. Against their abuses, we cannot even say a word.

"I can remember when the Taliban first came. I thought they would behave according to the Quran and Islam and would guide us on a better path. But soon we understood that what they were doing did not exist in any religion or any book. And now since I have begun to educate myself, I can see that the Taliban are only abusing women and making them inferior because they want to scare people, so that they will not stand up and defend themselves against them. As soon as anyone speaks up against them, they are quickly punished. And thus the Taliban have succeeded in making the people quiet and afraid. That number is half of the population. So half the population is in jail, the women, and the other half is really scared, the men. That's why they can control us very easily.

"Most of the men I know don't like these restrictions and are not happy about them. But there are also men who say that if these restrictions did not exist, women would become lost, and therefore women should obey men.

"And there are some men who are extremely happy with the way things are under the Taliban. They can marry any girl they want, one-fourth their age, and they can get her by force or by paying money. And therefore I believe that perverted men side with the Taliban."

NOORIA

Nooria is forty-eight years old. She is a resident of the Nasir Bagh refugee camp, where the literacy class is located. Nasir Bagh means "Nasir's garden," but if there ever was a garden in this spot, it must have been long ago. There's nothing here now but dust, scrawny shrubs on the order of tumbleweed and mud shanties belonging to the refugees.

Nooria is a lively, bright woman with a cheerful disposition, but her physical appearance betrays years of malnutrition and worry. She is scrawny, and her color is not good. During the course of our conversation, she shows us her fingers, cracked and bleeding from the cold. There's no fuel, she tells us, no wood, no gas, no propane. Sometimes the children are able to collect enough scrap paper to make a fire, enough to warm a meal on.

Nooria has eight children, three boys and five girls. Her family was forced to flee Kunduz two years ago, and from there they made their way to Nasir Bagh, where they were assigned a space and built themselves a little two-room hut. Two rooms for ten people—that's pretty tight. Holes covered with plastic sheeting form a kind of window, letting in some light. There's no bathroom; the camp has latrines that everyone shares.

At home, Nooria's husband was an office worker. Now he and his two oldest sons struggle to support the family by selling secondhand clothing.

"My husband is an educated man, who used to work in an office in Afghanistan. When we first got married, he asked me if I didn't perhaps want to go to a literacy class. I was very interested, but soon the war started and my hopes were cut short. After I got to this camp, a neighbor told me about RAWA's classes, and with my husband's encouragement, I signed up.

"I've been attending class for eight months now, and two months ago I was able to write my first letter, to my sister, who is a refugee in Iran. My husband and my children all support my effort to become educated. When it's time for me to go to class, my oldest son comes home to look after his little brother and his sisters.

"We've had our share of trouble with our class. Some men posted a flyer on the wall of the mosque saying that the purpose of the classes was to convert people to Christianity and that they wanted to warn the community. But people knew better, so no one paid much attention to their propaganda, and they failed to stop us from going to school.

"I have to tell you honestly that learning does not come easily to me. I have to work hard at it. It was the math class that posed the greatest difficulties for me in the beginning, but now I think I've got the hang of it. My view of myself

has changed quite a bit since I started coming here; somehow I feel more like a real person. Also, I have more interest
in the news. When I try to read magazines, though, I usually still have to ask my teacher to help me. I can't decipher
the really complicated texts on my own yet.

"If men read and write, then I think women should do it,
too. I want to be able to read many different opinions about
something and then form my own view.

"Of course there is a natural difference between men and
women, but women can accomplish the same things that
men can.

"To women in another country who might read your
book, I want to say this: Whatever you have heard about
Afghanistan is only a fraction of what we go through. Each
one of our days is more bitter than you can even imagine.
Under the fundamentalists, a woman is less than a bird in a
cage. A bird at least is allowed to sing, but according to
them, it is a sin for anyone even to hear our voice."

GULGOTAI

Gulgotai lives in the Old Jalozai refugee camp. It only got
that name recently, to distinguish it from the dreaded New
Jalozai camp, a place familiar to most of us from news
reports. When drought and war forced a new wave of
refugees to flee Afghanistan in the early fall of 2001 and
Pakistan refused to allow them entry, they landed in a god-
forsaken strip of desert that became known to the world as
Jalozai. And there they waited, without blankets, without
tents, without water, while the international community
tried to persuade Pakistan to grant them refugee status, so
they could begin delivering services.

Compared to that, the inhabitants of Old Jalozai were indeed lucky—though that would not be the first word that comes to mind when you view their place of residence. The place Gulgotai calls home is a dismal settlement of tiny mud cottages with only a sporadic supply of water.

"Coming to this class and studying has been such a good thing for me. Even if I'm not young any longer, I don't think that matters; no matter when you start to learn, it can be useful. I am forty, and I have two children.

"When I first came to this camp, one of the things I immediately noticed was that there were quite a few women here who were reading and writing. That was something new! I saw women writing letters, women who knew what their medical prescriptions said, even women who knew how to read the newspaper. I also noticed that they spoke nicely and could express their thoughts well. I discovered that they had gone to classes in the camp, even though they were no younger than me. Therefore I decided that I should go to this course as well, and now I can already read a whole book.

"Reading is useful for me personally, but I think it can also be useful for society. At the very least I will be able to teach a few other women to read, too.

"None of my friends or relatives lives in this camp; I am just here with my husband and my children. Although my husband is presently working as a bricklayer, he is someone who has finished high school and used to have a good position. He doesn't object to my going to the course, but to tell you the truth, I doubt that he concerns himself much with my comings and goings, because from four o'clock in the morning until the evening he is at work, trying to provide food for us. I'm sure you know that laying bricks is hard work. Right now he has a pain in his back and other such physical problems.

"The one who really encourages me to go to the course is my daughter, who is in fourth grade. When she gets home from school, she practically pushes me out the door. She tells me to go on to my class, and she will finish the housework.

"I'm not going to say that learning is easy. Doing dictation in Dari is hard for me, and math is also difficult. We learn a lot in our class, though. For example, we talk about the importance of being clean and preparing food in a clean way, and how to raise children nicely and never let them grow up in ignorance. Besides that, we also learn about what's going on in Afghanistan. We had heard the names before, of course—Gulbuddin, Rabbani, Taliban—but now we know a lot about each of them. In the past, I used to think that Najib was a fine man, because I remembered that he used to hand out coupons for free goods. Now I realize that this is not enough. If you want to judge someone's politics, you need to inform yourself more carefully. The way I think now differs from how I thought in the past.

"Also, in the past I used to think that I had no other value except in looking after my family and bringing up my children, but now I've understood that it doesn't have to be that way. Women can do anything—why not? Why should we be less than men? One thing I've learned in this course is that men and women are equal. Our mothers and grandmothers used to believe that women were created by God to be less than men, but now I think this is not right. Women can think as well as men can, and can work like men and be brave like men, and when I think back on my life and the men and women I have known, then it seems to me that there isn't much difference between us.

"In the village where we used to live, my father was a guard, and he also used to work as a gardener. One day he had gone to buy firewood for the winter, and as he was returning home a car hit him and he lost both of his legs. The doctors said that his bones had become black and needed to be amputated. After that he could only stay in bed. My mother became the man of the house, so to speak. I had older brothers, but they weren't living with us anymore; they had gone to Iran. My mother took on my father's role. She did the farming behind our house, she worked as a gardener, she did the errands for our family, and at night she took a gun and stood guard in my father's old job. What can a man do that is more than this?

"I often feel homesick. I'm not really happy here in Pakistan. When I'm all by myself, sometimes I cry, which of course doesn't help. I know that I am very fortunate when I compare myself with the thousands of families who have come to the New Jalozai camp—they don't even have a tent. At least we have a place to sleep and a bathroom. It feels bad not to have anything green anywhere around, though. There is one tree, but I'm afraid it's probably dead by now, because people keep chopping off its branches for firewood.

"I want my country to become peaceful, and the brutal Talibs and *jihadis* should be eliminated. If there were freedom, women would reject the burqa, reject not being able to go to school, and all those other crazy ideas. What the Taliban brought to the people of Afghanistan, neither men nor women like it. Even men who are the most backward in terms of their attitude to women are against the Taliban. The men who live in this camp want their wives to know how to read, and to work if they want to, and to go shopping, and to be free. However, there are some brutal men, too, and their number is not small. And there are men who just don't want to provoke the fundamentalists. They say that since these people are so crazy, maybe it's wiser for the women to just stay inside the house. However, I pay no attention to what these men say."

ANISA

Anisa is a warm and lively woman of obvious intelligence, someone with a lot of energy. She, too, lived in the Old Jalozai refugee camp. Even under the difficult circumstances of refugee life, her cheerfulness and determination shine through. One cannot help but wonder what she might have made of herself, given half a chance.

And one wishes that she could have flowers—the flowers she speaks of with such longing—which will never grow in the dusty soil of Jalozai.

"I'm thirty-five years old. I'm originally from Laghman. After that I was in Herat for a while, and now I've been a refugee for a year and a half. My brother came to Old Jalozai before we did, then we followed. For the first two months we lived with my brother, but it was difficult. He has two rooms, and he has five children; we have a nine-year-old boy, plus four adults, and so it was hard in such a small space. But eventually they assigned us a piece of land in a different corner of the camp, and with all of us working together, we built a room and a kitchen and a bathroom, and we managed to finish just before the winter. Unfortunately, the plastic for the windows didn't come, so there were just these holes in the wall, and the wind was always blowing in. We hung blankets over them, of course, but still it was very cold, and we all got sick. From the coughing I developed asthma, and even now, sometimes I feel like I can't get any air.

"The house has a little yard. Last year I planted vegetables, but then unfortunately there was a water shortage in the camp, so I couldn't give water to the vegetables and they died. That was a pity, because we really could have used them. But what I really miss is my flowers. In Afghanistan I had a fine house, and the garden was full of flowers, of all different kinds.

"The special thing about this camp is that it has a school for boys and for girls—that isn't the case in other camps. So my son is able to go to school. And when I arrived here, my sister-in-law told me that she was going to school as well, to a literacy class. I signed up, too, and now we are both at the second level. I caught up with her, because she is very busy with her five children, while I have less of a burden with just one.

"My husband helps out as a gardener sometimes, but usually he can't find work. This makes him very depressed and unhappy, and he has developed psychological problems. My brother works at making bricks, and our son goes to a neighbor's house to help make carpets. Our house is not large enough for a carpet frame, otherwise I would like to have one, too.

"I've wanted to learn to read ever since I was a child. The fact that the Taliban have outlawed literacy for women is just one more reason for me to want it, so I can do something that's against them. But my main motivation for going to the course was my sister-in-law. I noticed that she was learning a lot of different things there and was solving her life's problems in better ways. Her house was cleaner, she was calmer, her children were behaving better—and the same thing was true of the other women in the course. So I thought, I am not less than the other women in this camp. If they can do it, probably I can learn these things, too.

"My husband did not interfere with my plan at all. He did express some doubts whether perhaps, for him as well as for me, the age of learning had not already passed. Fortunately, though, it turns out that I have a good memory. I always get the highest grade in the class, and my teacher praises me.

"Since going to the class, I see many changes in myself. Before, I didn't know anything about the world, about my own country's history. Certainly I didn't know about the value of being a woman. I was narrow-minded and didn't know what was good and what was bad.

"When I was growing up, my family lived in a village. They used to emphasize big differences between me and my brothers. They used to always tell me that I was a woman and less able mentally, that I shouldn't talk too much, should just eat a little bit and sit quietly in the corner of the house. My brothers all went to school and then to university. I used to always think then that there was something missing in me, and therefore I couldn't do what my brothers did. Now I know that I may even have been more talented than them, because they always used to complain a lot about their learning and really have a struggle with it.

"My husband is a poor man who didn't receive much love in his childhood. He lost his mother when he was only two, and his family lived in poverty. From the time I married him, he has always been nice to me. All Afghan men are not like him, however. Many believe that women should work like animals, and that's it.

"I have seen many bad things done by the Taliban. When we were living in Herat, a young man was our neighbor. They came and took him away—they made up a reason by saying that he had a weapon—and three days later they gave his dead body back to his mother. The way his mother wailed, it burned me all the way to my bones. And I also felt so sorry for his wife and his little daughter. Men and women and young and old, everyone suffered under the Taliban and the *jihadis,* and we all hate them. My only hope is for peace so that we can go back home—the sooner the better.

"To the women of America I would like to say that we don't want the *jihadis* or the Talibs. These are oppressive people. There is no crime they won't commit, and we are all against them. So you should talk to your government and tell them this, that instead we prefer to have Zahir Shah come back as soon as possible."

SHAKRIA

Thirty-seven-year-old Shakria is very serious and deliberate. The condition she describes, of being always distracted by her grief and worries, was evident during much of the interview.

"I live in Quetta now, with my husband and my four children. I'm from Bamiyan, though. I had a little farm there; the house was on one corner, and the rest was a garden. I grew vegetables, mostly. Three times a week my husband would take our harvest into town, to the market.

"The people in Bamiyan are all quite poor, and in the last twenty years, things have only gotten worse. In these des-

perate conditions, the oppressors in Hizbi Wahdat nevertheless used to come and demand lamb meat from us, and
bread.* They took our young men to the war, and we lost
them in that way, for nothing.

"Two years ago, there was heavy fighting between the
Taliban and the Wahdat. We all had to flee. Our entire area
was almost completely destroyed. So we left our house and
our life, and we came to Pakistan. Here we pay thirteen
hundred rupees for one room. Quetta gets very cold in the
winter. Our room gets no sun, and we have to leave the gas
heater on all day. The children are almost constantly sick
during the winter, and we spend a lot of money on doctors
and medicine. And the room is very small. The bathroom is
inside the room, and during the summer the smell is very
bad. We share a kitchen with four other families.

"My husband works in a factory that makes *chaplaq*,
slippers. He gets twenty-five hundred rupees a month,
which is hardly sufficient to make ends meet. I have gone to
many places to find work, but unsuccessfully.

"One time I went to an Afghan women's clinic, taking
my daughter there, and since the doctor seemed nice, I asked
if she needed a servant in her house. She said, 'No, but if you
can read and write, I can hire you to register the patients.'
Unfortunately, I barely knew the alphabet, which I had
learned as a child from a cleric. When the doctor saw the
poor condition of my daughter and myself, she felt sorry for
us and didn't charge us for the visit, and instead said that if
I could learn to read and write within the next few months,

* Hizbi Wahdat is a fundamentalist party that is part of the Northern
Alliance.

she would hire me. I became very happy and started to look for a literacy course.

"Someone gave my husband the address of a school and told him that a woman runs it and that it has literacy courses. That was how I found RAWA and started there. And I registered my children in their school, too, which not only charges no fee but provides the books and other supplies as well.

"About eighteen women and girls are studying in my course. Unfortunately, my house is two hours away from the course, and we walk this distance every day. We finally decided to get a room closer to the school, but we haven't found one with an appropriate price yet. Since we are refugees, not everyone will rent to us; this limits our chances.

"It was my economic situation that made me want to learn to read and write. I think if my husband and I had been to school, we could have gotten better jobs. I know a girl who not only knows how to read and write but also knows English. She gets well paid. I will try to make sure my children learn all of these things. Then they will have a good life.

"My own life has been spent with a thousand unfortunate things. I don't even know which misfortune to start with. In the massacre of Bamiyan a year ago, six of my relatives were killed. Among them were two brothers of my husband, one twenty-five, one only nineteen. This shook me, and made me impatient and damaged my nerves. Several times I've decided not to go to the course anymore, but then when I think about it, I realize that being in the class and talking to the teachers helps me. My teacher is like a sister and mother; I can talk about any problems with her.

"Once I had an argument with my husband because of all of our problems, and it escalated and he hit me. I didn't go to the course for a few days, and the teacher came to the house to see how I was doing. When she learned what the issue was, she waited until my husband came home from work, and she talked to him logically and convinced him not to do that again.

"My husband is not opposed to my studying, but he doesn't encourage me, either. My mother-in-law is opposed; when she comes to visit she gives me a hard time, saying, 'What do you need to study for? You should always stay at home. It's not good for a woman to go out every day. You will give our family a bad name.'

"Since she's old and her mind is upset, I don't listen to her that much. Even with all these problems, I'm still going to my school, and I'm satisfied with it. Learning a lot is hard for me; my memory is not good. The teacher repeats things for me, but I still forget them. Before the death of my relatives, my memory was better. I can't always concentrate. I see other women who are older than me, yet they are learning better. The teacher is very patient, and she repeats the lesson separately to each of us, as often as necessary. The class meets in her house, which is only one room, and during the class she gives her little child to a neighbor.

"I have particular problems with writing, especially dictation, but I like math and I'm good at it. I get good grades on my math tests. And since math is used in day-to-day life, I can practice it. Now when I think about the expenditures in our house or when I go to the market, I can do the addition and subtraction myself.

"The general information that the teacher gives in class is

very educational. I learn about the conditions of my country, the world and women, and about the value of knowledge. With learning, there could be a big change in my life. When I see how educated women can solve their own problems without relying on a man, I would like to be self-reliant also. I am thankful that I can read and write, and my struggle is to learn more.

"With all the problems that we have, still I think my children are lucky. Many other children have become beggars, and from hunger, or from being homeless, or from getting sick and having no medicine, they die. At least my children have bread to eat and they can go to school. I don't know what will happen in the future, but I know this: If fundamentalists remain in power, then Afghanistan will not be peaceful and our future generations will all be wasted. But if we get the right government, and schools and hospitals, then it is possible that Afghanistan can change and become a free and developing country.

"There is no difference between men and women. They are both human beings. They both have a brain and the capacity for work. If a woman wants to, she can do any job that a man can do. A woman can become a doctor, an engineer, a pilot, and she can work in offices. The only difference that there is between men and women is from a physical point of view—men are bigger and stronger physically and can do heavier labor. Some of the Afghan men, when they are angry, beat their wives. This is terrible. I am against it, and my hope is that slowly they will be reformed and they will learn that women are also human beings. The Taliban are wild and illiterate. They assign no value to women. They don't think that they were born from a woman or that their mother and sister are women. They look down on women. This is one of the primitive and backward characteristics that they have. And in some of our villages, there are men who are not Talib, yet they are backward and don't give rights to women.

"Our American sisters, my request is that some of you come and visit and see our lives from close range. In these days after the bombing from America, lots of people have become refugees in Quetta. I feel sorry for them. I can't do anything for them. They are in a camp in the desert and nobody is helping them. Nobody really likes us or worries about us; everyone just throws their rocks at us. We haven't yet forgotten the Russian bombardment, and the bombardment by the fundamentalists and the bombardment by the Talibs, and now it's America's turn."

After talking to these women, the Taliban's approach begins to make a lot more sense. Indeed, if their goal was to keep women down, then a total ban on educating them was definitely the way to go. Given even the tiniest little serving of education, just a few months in a literacy class and some friendly encouragement, these refugee women came leaping out of the starting gate like pent-up racehorses.

These are women who are dealing with multiple and massive burdens. They have lost everything they owned, including their home. Most are dealing with severe grief and the aftereffects of shock and terror. They have been in war zones, been shot at, been bombed, been terrorized by one oppressive local and national power holder after another. Now they are refugees, eking out a miserable existence in some desolate camp or slum, coughing, freezing, crowded, unwanted. But listen to the lightness of their words. Consider how quickly they have arrived at powerful, sophisticated insights, as reflected in the statement of this recently literate woman: "For most of my life, I only heard one opinion. Now I see that there can be many opinions, and if I can hear what they are, then I can consider them and ultimately form my own."

Perhaps most amazing, consider the ease with which these women have shaken off the effects of a lifetime of demeaning messages concerning their gender, to embrace a new and quite radical vision of themselves. Obviously such thoughts preceded the confident messages of their literacy teacher and have just been waiting to receive articulation and support. It took a massive and concerted effort to keep women like these "quiet in the corner of their house," a coordinated system of injustice and forbidden opportunities. If just a tiny crack in that system can elicit these kinds of reactions, imagine what a level playing field would do for them.

And the fundamentalists appear to be fully aware of that. After all, if a group is genuinely inferior and incapable, you don't need a lot of threats and restrictions to keep them in their place—they'll stay there quite naturally. A useful political rule of thumb is this: The more force that is required to maintain a certain order, the more unfair and unnatural that order is.

If I were a fundamentalist, I'd be scared of these women, too—of their intelligence, their energy and their impulse to stand by each other.

CHAPTER 7

RAWA and the Men's Question

It is International Women's Day 2001 in Peshawar, and RAWA has organized a host of cultural, political and educational events. A large number of women are in attendance—and a very large number of men.

There they are, some in turbans and baggy trousers, others more urbane in raw-silk Nehru jackets and natty caps, perusing RAWA's incendiary pamphlets with admirable sangfroid, studying their posters, leafing through their magazines with nods of solemn agreement.

A play is about to be performed. Just offstage, Nabil nervously fingers the big wooden stick that will serve as his accessory in the role he has agreed to play. He will be portraying the evil Talib, and his college friends Samir and Assad will be the brave villagers who chase him away. The audience is already seated and waiting: elderly ladies with gauzy scarves pulled over their graying topknots, excited schoolgirls who have just finished their own song performance and are now ready to be entertained in turn, their proud teachers, a cluster of women who have been specially bused in from Afghanistan for the occasion . . . and hundreds of men, many in colorful ethnic dress, all of them come to hear RAWA's speeches, applaud RAWA's programs and help them observe this special day.

It probably should not have surprised me that large numbers of Afghan men were ready to take a stand for women and against the Taliban's oppressiveness. Time and time again, Afghan men have managed to exceed my (apparently too low) expectations.

I wasn't the only one who responded in that way. Anne Brodsky, an American academic who visited Peshawar in the summer of 2001 and toured RAWA's projects, relates her sense of alarm when a group of refugee men suddenly marched into the tent where RAWA was holding a convocation. In their turbans and *shalwar kameez* (traditional-style pantsuit), they looked like—well, frankly, they looked like trouble. Fundamentalists, Dr. Brodsky knew, often sought occasions to confront and attack RAWA. Throughout the presentation and ensuing discussion, she kept a watchful eye on the men. At first they just sat there, following the debate with grim expressions. Then one of them stood up. He had something to say, he announced. In his camp, RAWA was the only group that actually kept its promises. The others talked a lot, but RAWA was the only organization that was actually providing services. Then he sat down again, and the men around him nodded darkly.

"And I realized that I had to revise my stereotypes," said Brodsky, with a laugh.*

"People in the West have gotten the impression that every Afghan man is a fundamentalist," Shahla observed to me.

It wasn't so much that I thought they were fundamentalists; my problem was distrust. Part of me suspected men of

* See also her editorial on this subject, "The Taliban's Victims," *Washington Post,* Sept. 24, 2001.

deriving a measure of perverse satisfaction from the superi-
or status the Taliban had elevated them to.

"It's not really like that," Shahla insisted. "It's true that
our tradition contains some very negative values. That's not
surprising—it's the tradition of a very backward country.
But in practice, if an Afghan man is open-minded, then he
will support women and believe in human rights. I would
estimate that the majority of Afghan men by now are
against fundamentalism, because everyone suffered under
the *jihadis* and the Taliban, and we've all learned a lot from
that experience."

RAWA's work has always been inclusive of men. Their
high school for boys is a particularly brilliant undertaking.
While other young men were being raised as fanatics and
suicidal terrorists in the madrassas, RAWA was exposing
boys to the concept of equality and human rights. The
alumni of this school form a solid base of support for
RAWA's activities. To offer secular, democratic education to
both sexes was RAWA's concept from the start. Literacy
classes for men, by contrast, came about accidentally.
RAWA would set up a course for women, and soon the first
delegation of men would arrive at their doorstep. They
couldn't read either, they would say. They wanted to learn,
too. "Then how can you refuse?" Tameena asks rhetori-
cally. So RAWA somehow would find the funding and
organize a class for the men. When the situation is reversed,
others have no trouble refusing women—but it's entirely to
RAWA's credit that they take a different and more generous
approach.

Thus it is only fitting that the male supporter (to use
RAWA's phrase) plays such a useful and important role in

the work of their organization. The nature of this male support spans the entire range: vague sympathy for the goal of
equality, the occasional friendly attendance at a RAWA
event, help in distributing their magazine and publications,
selling the products of their workshops in their stores, even
direct participation in RAWA's underground work. In
Afghanistan, men served as couriers for RAWA and as an
"escort service," impersonating the male relative *(mahram)*
without whose presence RAWA women could not move
about in Taliban-controlled areas. If discovered in either one
of these functions, the men would have been killed.

The situation in Pakistan was not quite as perilous, but it
was extremely dangerous nonetheless. Many politically
active Afghans have been killed by fundamentalists in this
border region of Pakistan; it was here that the father of
Hamid Karzai, the current acting head of the Afghan interim
government, was murdered, as we've noted. Political activities that are completely harmless in the United States, such as
distributing leaflets, holding meetings, selling magazines and
holding a demonstration, are dangerous in Pakistan, especially in the border area, where the fundamentalists hold
sway. The country is a military dictatorship with a high
degree of instability. The government does not fully control
all of its institutions. ISI, for example, the Pakistani equivalent of the CIA, has a high degree of autonomy and is in
some ways an independent power center whose politics do
not necessarily always conform to those of the government.
There is no freedom of the press, and journalists take the risk
of being arrested if their writing is too critical. Some areas of
the country are only partially controlled by the government;
feudal structures, powerful landowning families, religious

leaders and tribes challenge the authority of the central government in regions such as the Northwest Frontier Province. There is a problem with police and bureaucratic corruption, which means that the laws may or may not be enforced. This causes an atmosphere of fear and distrust, as one RAWA member explains: "Everyone is jumpy. You can never be entirely sure where someone stands. Even friends and relatives can't automatically be trusted, because you can't know what ties they might have to a fundamentalist group."

RAWA's demonstrations are always in jeopardy of being attacked—and these attacks are not verbal but brutally physical. To see a peaceful crowd of women, including girls and elderly ladies, come under sudden assault by a furious mob of fundamentalist men, swinging sticks and throwing rocks and screaming threats, is frightening enough even on video—you may remember seeing one such scene in the CNN documentary *Behind the Veil*. Even in the case of legal, official, approved rallies, the Pakistani police cannot be relied on to provide protection. Many of them are pro-fundamentalist and turn a blind eye to violent actions.

Men who sympathize with RAWA therefore volunteer to serve as guards, to deter and deflect attacks like these. "Our demonstrations wouldn't be possible without our male supporters," RAWA members willingly acknowledge. "They form a circle around us, to protect us, not just during demonstrations but also for press conferences and other public appearances. They accompany us when we have things to do in hostile neighborhoods. Whenever I have an assignment in a neighborhood controlled by the fundamentalists, a volunteer bodyguard goes with me. Sometimes he is also my driver or my translator."

Some of these men come to RAWA through its publications or public events. Some are brothers or sons of RAWA activists. But many have an even more personal history with the organization, as Mariam explains. "If you've seen our male translators, you might notice that all of them are about the same age, twenty-one or twenty-two. That's because they're the first generation of graduates from our boys' schools. They learned their English or another foreign language in a RAWA school, and that's why they're ready to help us now by translating for us. And for the same reason they feel connected to RAWA, and they defend us. We were their teachers.

"Other men who often help us are the sons of our older RAWA members. The mentality of these men is not like the traditional one, because their mothers provided a different role model, and their home life was not traditional, either.

"And another group of men who support us a lot are the ones who come out of our orphanages. The first generation of orphans are young adults now. The men among them, they were raised in our homes and educated in our schools. They speak very good English. And now they stand ready to help their sisters."

Men who share RAWA's political vision. Men who don't like life under the fundamentalists. Men who were educated by RAWA teachers and absorbed modern, democratic ideas. Abandoned male children who were taken in and mothered by RAWA. That's the pool of recruits for the RAWA men's auxiliary.

From my own personal observations, I'd like to add one more source of supporters: young men who obviously find RAWA's resolute girls fascinating and brave and are eager to hang about on the periphery of the organization, making themselves useful in hopes of catching the eye of the one they like the best.

"A lot of young men are impressed by our girls," Tameena admits with a smile. "They'll say, 'We had totally another understanding of women. We thought they couldn't do the same things that men can. We feel embarrassed for the way we thought before.'"

RAWA WOMEN'S PERSONAL RELATIONS WITH MEN

In their personal lives and their relationships with men, the choices RAWA women make are affected by the constraints of their culture. Most RAWA women enjoy the active or at least tacit backing of their immediate families, in particular of the fathers, brothers and husbands who could otherwise cause them a lot of difficulties.

Given the importance of family, a young RAWA woman's situation becomes untenable if her relatives oppose her political involvement. Some RAWA women break with their families over this issue. The most common method of escape is to get married, taking care to choose a husband who is sympathetic to RAWA and who promises not to stand in the way of his wife's plans and activities. This is the easiest solution, because the woman can continue to have a good relationship with her family, who accepts her independence once she is married.

The other alternative, chosen by some but not many RAWA women, is to break with their family. These young women, along with other unmarried RAWA activists who are alone or are separated from their relatives for geographic reasons, are sometimes placed with families that support RAWA or in which the wife is a RAWA activist. Some single RAWA women share housing, living and working communally.

Men are the primary agents of social control in traditional Afghan society. Therefore, daughters of widowed mothers generally have more freedom. Sometimes their mothers encourage their political activism. If not, it is usually enough for them to mention vaguely that they are "going to school" or "going to their job" and then proceed with their plans unhindered.

Many of the newer members are widows, who learned about RAWA by attending one of their literacy classes or by getting involved in an income-generating project, and then decided to join. But the majority of RAWA members are married. As Shahla explains in the story of her own marriage later in this chapter, RAWA's reputation precedes it, and any man who marries a RAWA girl knows what he's getting into. This is actually a very interesting and revealing point. If there's a man on this planet with all of his marital options open—including legal polygamy—the Afghan man is it. If he should decide that he wants an illiterate, timid, subservient wife, he can find any number of candidates. A child bride? No problem.

Therefore, the fact that RAWA women—known for their independence, their pronounced feminism and the fact that an entire militant organization stands behind them—have no trouble whatsoever finding husbands, speaks for itself. And not just any husbands. They find husbands who aid and abet their clandestine feminist activities, who take over the housework and the child care while they are busy evacuating female refugees, who make up stories and provide cover to make sure no one will suspect that their wives are engaged in seditious independent political activities. "He is my beautiful companion," RAWA women say when talking about these husbands.

Asifa, whom we've met already in the chapter about Meena, is a member of RAWA's top leadership and has belonged to the organization almost from the beginning. She has one such "beautiful companion." Her husband used to be an engineer. Like most other men in Afghan cities, the war and the breakdown of the economy have forced him to try to make a living with petty trade, as well as being the backbone of the family and the primary parent to their three children, twelve, eleven, and five years old.

"My great joy is that I have a good husband, who from the day of our marriage until now has tolerated many difficulties for my sake. Because of my political activities, I have not always been a good mother to my children, but he has worked hard to make things up to them. And there aren't too many men who can do that.

"My absence from my home brings a lot of questions, especially from the neighbors. My husband makes up creative excuses. He is a beautiful companion to me. When the times are busy, especially during times when we have to send many new women refugees from Afghanistan to Pakistan, he takes over the housework. When I come home at night, my husband is waiting for me away from the house with his bicycle so that we come home at the same time so that the neighbors think we were together, that I was with him.

"The other difficulty is that for reasons of safety and secrecy, I have to move to a different house frequently. This is something that from time to time I feel embarrassed to inflict on my husband. He has sacrificed so much. If my husband didn't sacrifice all of this, there would be no way for me to do my work. I would have to either separate from him or give up my activities. And certainly my husband's and children's lives are also in danger because of my activities.

"The Taliban government has taken away everything—teaching, school, vacation, music, television. My oldest daughter loves music, but now it has become something that she can never have. We were obliged to burn all the cassettes, so that hearing some music doesn't give the Taliban an excuse to search the house and in the process find RAWA documents. In spite of these deprivations, their father is involved with their studies, so they don't fall behind."

MALE SUPPORTERS

The three male supporters of RAWA profiled here are average young men. Their families are traditional, with perhaps a slight inclination toward a more liberal view. The circumstances of their lives are typical for the refugee community. What made them so receptive to the ideas of feminism?

The first factor is probably age. Traditional Afghan society is hard on women, but it's very restrictive for young people, too. In families and in the larger society, young people of both genders are assigned a subordinate position and are expected to show deference and obedience to their elders and to let them make all the decisions concerning the young people's lives.

When young men criticize the traditional family, they usually mention three things that bother them about it. First, the women have no rights and no say, not even about the things that most intimately concern their own life, and that's not fair. Second, they'd like to have a different kind of marriage from the ones their parents had. Instead of the stiff, formal relationship common in traditional families, they want a marriage where their wife is a friend and a partner. And third, they want more freedom and independence for themselves—patriarchy, which we can view in its authentic and fully functional version in traditional Afghan families, doesn't just mean the domination of men over women; it means the rule of older men over everyone else.

As Fareidun, a RAWA sympathizer, explains, "I hope that my wife will be educated and, based on her desire and skills, will work outside the house. Before marriage I would like to get to know the girl I like and to discuss our joint life with her. The opinion of my family is important, but it shouldn't be determinative. It's good if the parents, in a democratic environment, talk about the marriage of their daughter or son and offer advice and share their experiences. They should act as a good adviser instead of the ruler. Unfortunately, in most households, young men and women are deprived of the right to choose their partner. Instead it is the fathers who determine the fate of their children, all by themselves."

And Babak, a twenty-six-year-old carpet dealer from Loghar, adds, "It would be good if democratic approaches could replace the current cold practices in the family. Often the head of the family just enforces his will by violence. My own family has some new influences but some older ones, too. Especially when it comes to my sister, my parents' views are old and out of date.

"In my view, whether in big entities or in small ones such as the family, exchanging views and expressing oneself is the best way to make decisions. A democratic environment increases the chance that one will not make mistakes. In my family, the absence of a democratic environment is a weakness. But to get the older men to listen to the logic of younger people and of women—that is very difficult."

In the classic days of traditional society, a younger man would either not question the system of patriarchal rule at all, because it would not occur to him that there might be an alternative, or he would patiently tolerate his own years of dutiful obedience in the knowledge that his day was coming, that he in later years would enjoy the powers of a patriarch. The current generation of young Afghan men no longer holds such an attitude. Most young men no longer want the dubious privileges tradition offers them. They don't want a distant, respectful, intimidated wife, and they don't want to rule over their children through tyranny and physical force. Mostly they don't want their future family members to view them with the same kind of resentment and resignation that, as they well know, their own mother feels toward her husband and that they and their siblings feel toward their father.

The men we interviewed were not Westernized in the least. They grew up in refugee camps, attended refugee schools, and now live either in Afghanistan or in the border area. None of them has been to another country. It's important to keep that in mind as we read their answers, which offer a true glimpse into the thinking of the average young Afghan man's views and attitudes.

Sheraz

Sheraz is twenty-one years old. Like most Afghans under the current conditions, he's hard to categorize in the usual demographic terms. Not merely literate but a high school graduate, he belongs to his country's small, educated elite. However, the economic contingencies of his destroyed country oblige him to eke out a modest subsistence as a grocer.

Sheraz is a very courageous young man. The work he did for RAWA under Taliban rule could easily have gotten him killed. Posing as the close relative, the *mahram,* of a woman when he in fact did not stand in any such relation to her would at the very least have sufficed as grounds for a flogging on adultery charges. If, after the arrest, his and the woman's connection to RAWA had become known, they could both have been executed for spying or treason. His other contribution, acting as courier to transport RAWA's films, was the most dangerous of all.

The interview took place in Kabul shortly after that city's liberation in the fall of 2001.

"I first got to know RAWA in 1987, shortly after Meena was killed. I was only eight years old, and my parents enrolled me in one of RAWA's schools. Their slogan, 'Freedom, democracy and social justice,' attracted me even as a young boy, and I felt that when I grew up, I should defend them. I agree with all of their policies, except for some points so small that I don't even want to mention them.

"I think the Taliban are the most regressive element that history has ever produced. Their harsh interpretation of Islam deprived women of any ability to play a role in society. They couldn't work, get an education or even leave their houses.

"The reaction of the Afghan men to such ideas is clear. After the defeat of the Taliban here in Kabul, you could see how everyone felt about them and their Arab masters. Everyone rejoiced that they were gone. And one of the biggest reasons why people hated the Taliban was their treatment of women. There isn't any advantage for men under a Taliban system. On the contrary, both men and women can benefit from RAWA's goal of freedom.

"I'm not extremely religious, but I do always pray. I try to have a modern way of looking at things. I completely want our women to be like Western women. Maybe that culture has some problems, too, but at least there women are treated like human beings. There are some negative aspects to Western culture—for example, I am told that they are not very warm or kind, but treat people as if they were machines. That can't be a good thing. However, from looking at their countries, you can clearly see that they obviously must work hard and have good plans and programs. I admire that about them.

"Why shouldn't women go to male doctors? In the past, Afghan women used to do that without any problems. It's only the Taliban who outlawed it. As to teachers, in the cities generally we used to have more women than men in that job. I think it's good that women should teach boys, since the way a woman describes things is likely to have more feeling and emotion in it, and that's a more effective way to teach. Women appear to me generally to be more patient, and this is also a good feature for teachers.

"When I marry, I want my wife not to be a kitchen woman.* She should work outside instead. When I choose my wife, the opinion of my family will be important; it will have weight. However, I want the selection to be mine, and my family can express their views. I think there should be

---

* Afghan expression for housewife.

democracy in the family, and even the youngest member should be able to express his or her view.

"I am from Kunar, but I live in Kabul. I have a small vegetable stand—that's how I make my living. There are only two remaining professions in Kabul: Either you're a shopkeeper or you're a beggar. However, the problem with being a shopkeeper is that not many people have the ability to buy anything.

"Once in a while I do some things for RAWA. I act as a brother or son, to accompany them on their missions. I have helped with taking photos and with spreading publications. A few times, with a lot of difficulty, I have managed to take some of their films and reports from Afghanistan across to Pakistan. I'm very proud of that. It was only RAWA that was telling the truth about what was happening in our country, and they took enormous risks in making the photos. They performed a great service to the people, and I felt good that I was able to help them."

Mohammad

Mohammad comes from a very different background. His family was among the one and a half million refugees who fled to Iran, not Pakistan. Iran was even less hospitable to its Afghan refugees, conducting forced repatriations. That is how Mohammad returned, somewhat prematurely, to his troubled homeland.

As in most of the other interviews, Mohammad's statements show that the values of civil society—equality, participation, critical thinking—are very attractive not just to an educated, Westernized class but to average young people from traditional settings. These values can definitely compete with the attractions of fundamentalism—provided that young people are exposed to them and are not left to the solitary care of fundamentalists.

In Mohammad's case, his encounter with a new and different world order came about through total coincidence, and during a time when he himself was living in an environment hostile to those values and attending a fundamentalist school. Still, in spite of his youth, he was able to compare the two mind-sets and make his choice. The passage in which he describes his first contentious contact with RAWA is not just amusing but also very revealing. It is regrettable that huge portions of this planet's youth are being exposed to the uncontested influence of fundamentalists. Given any sort of choice, many would come to the same conclusions as Mohammad—and the *jihadis* would soon run out of human raw material.

The interview with Mohammad took place at the start of November 2001, at a particularly perilous time. The U.S. bombing was in full swing, but the Taliban had not yet been routed, and the outcome of the war was as yet unclear. His concerns for the safety of RAWA members are to be seen in that light.

"The first time I became aware of RAWA's existence was thirteen years ago. I was living in Iran, studying in one of the refugee schools. Another boy had somehow gotten hold of a copy of *Payam-e-Zan*, and I was glancing through it. I read that there had been an Afghan women's demonstration in Pakistan. This was something completely new for me. The camp I was growing up in was run by the *jihadis,* and they were opposed to women. Women weren't able to do much of anything there, certainly not anything political. It hadn't occurred to me that there might be places in the world where that was different. So I was curious. I wanted to discover as much as I possibly could about this, so I wrote to their address.

"I had many questions, and to be honest, some of them were pretty obnoxious. But the RAWA women didn't seem to get angry about that. They answered all of my questions completely and patiently, and this fact alone already brought me closer to them. Their attitude was quite a contrast to the *jihadis* I was accustomed to—if you asked any questions of them, you were immediately accused of being an unbeliever. If we ever questioned anything, our teachers would get very angry and say that we were just trying to cause trouble and obstruct their work. But here was RAWA, and not only did they not become angry, but they encouraged me to ask more questions if I had any.

"Since then I have always found RAWA to be well organized, fearless and at the same time kind and patient. It is an organization that has a widespread presence and works hard night and day and with conviction, not just for their half of society but, since they are trying to bring democracy, for everybody.

"Peshawar, you know, had become the international capital of the fundamentalists. And the men didn't have the guts to stand up to these people, but the women from RAWA were carrying out demonstrations condemning them. And there were even violent physical encounters, but still RAWA did not become afraid. That was pretty impressive. How could I, if I loved my country and suffered its pain, not join an organization like that? They want to have a country where religion is separate from politics. I hope that the UN and others who want to play a role in forming the new government embrace this idea. We really don't need the mullahs and Talibs and fundamentalists, with their worry beads in their hands and with their long beards and their hats, sitting in the seats of the ministers again. Congratulations to RAWA for putting things clearly on this issue.

"My only difference with RAWA is, I think, that they are sometimes too bold, not giving enough value to their members' lives and taking too many risks. Even now, they are working so recklessly right in the middle of war conditions that they make me worried. Although I have become used to a lot of losses in my life—and I don't tell them this directly because they might think I'm a coward—nevertheless I worry about them a lot.

"As I told you, I went to a *jihadi* school, not a RAWA school. But I've met lots of people who attend such schools. You can tell the difference this school makes, especially with girls from rural areas. Such girls tend to be very timid, very shy and withdrawn, but after they've gone to these schools for a while, they really blossom. Their whole family blossoms.

"I don't think there's ever been anything as brutal or as stupid as the Taliban, not in the entire history of the world. Educated women were locked up at home. On the streets they had to stay completely covered under the *burqa*, even in 110-degree weather. And if a Talib had even the slightest objection to their appearance, he could simply beat them. We men were very displeased with this, and it was one reason why we hated the Taliban. I know men whose wives were sick, and they had to watch the women die just because the only doctor in their town was a man and he wasn't allowed to treat them. Don't you think that such men

Meena, the martyred founder of RAWA,
in an early, undated photo.

A RAWA schoolgirl protest rally held in the early nineties in Islamabad, Pakistan. The effigies of Rabbani, Gulbuddi and Dostum are hanging from a post.

The Pakistani police crackdown on RAWA's schoolgirl demonstrators, also in Islamabad.

Police beating back RAWA participants in a procession protesting the bloodshed in Afghanistan. Because of the restrictive policies of the Taliban, many of RAWA's public protests and activities were held in neighboring Pakistan.

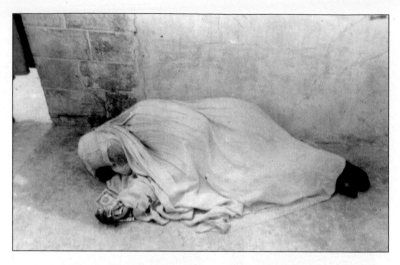

A widow sleeping on the street, clutching alms.
Under the Taliban, women were not allowed to work, leaving
widows without a livelihood. Many were
forced to beg to survive.

Secret video stills taken by RAWA on August 26, 2001, show
two Taliban of the Department of Amro bil Mahroof (the
Promotion of Virtue and Prevention
of Vice) beating a woman in public.

A Taliban fighter dangling the recently severed right hand and left foot of an accused thief. Upon achieving power, the Taliban imposed Islamic Sharia law, which they said would prevent criminal activity.

A RAWA teacher leads an underground literacy class.

RAWA distributes quilts in Jalozai camp for Afghan refugees on the Pakistan border.

"Where are the women?" read the cover of the Nation, *next to this photo of the participants in the Bonn meetings, convened to negotiate the peace in Afghanistan in December 2001. A RAWA member joined the proceedings on the third day.*

Cheryl Benard standing among the men in the Haripur Afghan refugee camp on her first visit to the Afghanistan border in 1982.

The boys of the Nasir Bagh camp enjoying "exercise" in the form of military drills. It was in the camps that the fundamentalist mullahs of Pakistan recruited and trained the boys who would go on to become the Taliban.

would greatly hate the Taliban? I personally know of several such cases.

"My family is religious, though not excessively so. They do not in any way oppose female education, and as to the burqa, they hate it. The men among us do not like having to wear a beard. And my family finds it ridiculous and insulting that when we travel by bus we can't sit together, because our men and our women have to be in separate sections. Also, we'd like to watch TV and use the Internet. That doesn't mean we aren't moral people and good Muslims.

"I live in a small town that you have surely never heard of, in the province of Farra, near the Iranian border. I've trained as a teacher, for Dari and for math. I've never been to Europe or any other Western place, and without seeing it for myself, I wouldn't like to form any opinions about it. But I have read books about other countries, and I've seen movies. I know that women there can get any sort of an education, that they are not forced into any marriages but can decide for themselves whom they want to marry, that they have jobs and that they are allowed to travel alone. In my view, these are all good things. I have further heard that some Western women are only interested in their own amusements and have no sense of responsibility. This part I do not like. They should know that in the world there are lots of women who have serious troubles, such as the women in Afghanistan. Instead of wasting their time, they should maybe think about what they can do to help these other women.

"I am married. Both I and my family had a role in the selection of my wife, but ultimately I decided. I think it's wrong for the choice to be made by the family alone. This kind of marriage, which has been common in Afghanistan, has had bad results. It leads to marriages that are very unhappy. I believe that everyone in the house should have the right to speak, and that things should be democratic."

Javed

Javed is thirty years old. His family is quite traditional, and most of them never left Afghanistan. Javed himself "commutes" between Peshawar and Afghanistan, bringing goods for the little business he runs with his brothers. His frequent travels across the border and the fact that he is known to be a trader on official family business provide him with a good cover, enabling him to be very helpful to RAWA.

"About ten years ago I saw a copy of the magazine *Payam-e-Zan*. I became interested and wrote them a letter, and got an answer and some further publications. Their beliefs appealed to me, and as I studied their activities more carefully, I got the feeling that I should help these brave women with all my power.

"Besides the fact that I shared their political goals of freedom, democracy and women's rights, I was also intrigued by the bravery and boldness of their members. They were the first Afghan organization that demonstrated against the coming to power of fundamentalist terrorists. They opposed them from the very beginning, which is something no one else can claim. In those dark years, RAWA gave voice to the thoughts not only of women but of ordinary Afghan men as well. I have been pleased to see that, over the past few years, their message has been increasingly spread worldwide by radio and television and important global information agencies. Just a few days ago I saw a report that in the first month after September eleventh, its members had been interviewed by more than three hundred news agencies.

"Because of my job, I travel back and forth between Afghanistan and Pakistan, and I can attest to the fact that RAWA's magazine is read in various Afghan provinces. This in itself is unprecedented in the history of Afghan political movements. And have you heard the music cassettes of RAWA? They are popular with many people.

"A few things worry me about RAWA. In *Payam-e-Zan* I have seen a defense of those who like same-sex relationships. In my opinion this is going too far for such a backward country, as the population at large will not understand this view.

"Also, in a situation where the fundamentalists are in charge, and RAWA members are killed if they are caught, I don't see how they can continue to advocate nonviolent resistance. That does not seem logical to me.

"I am very familiar with RAWA schools, and they are exemplary, really a model for schools in a free Afghanistan. The statement of purpose of these schools is a very good one, to make children familiar with human rights and democratic values, as well as with the usual school subjects. Nothing like this exists in other schools in Pakistan or Afghanistan.

"When I see pictures of girls' schools run by the Northern Alliance, I notice two things about them. First, the girls they show are always very young, little girls. And even they are covered with the *hijab*.* I ask myself why, from the very

---

* *Hijab* is the generic term for all variants of Islamic veiling or concealment of women. In areas controlled by the Northern Alliance, the burqa or *chaddri* was not universal. Many women wore a regionally specific version of the veil, more similar to the Iranian style—a kind of huge scarf that covered not just the head but the entire body, leaving the face free. For girls, this style is especially inconvenient, since it needs to be held shut constantly with the hands and any sort of playing is impossible.

beginning of their lives, they have to be taught about religion in a way that insults them and limits their freedom.

"When I see pictures of RAWA's girls' schools, the girls can be of all different ages, and they don't tie anything on their heads. The girls seem happy, and I feel in myself the wish that all over Afghanistan women and girls should one day be able to go to educational institutions without being insulted or restricted. It would be good if the future schools of the country were run by RAWA; then people like me would not worry about the education of our children but would think that they are in good hands.

"I, as a person who supports democracy and equal rights for men and women, am full of hatred toward the Taliban's view of women. I don't see anything in their system that would be attractive to any man who has even the slightest sense of honor.

"I am a Pashtun from Kunduz. None of my family supports the Taliban, but most of them are nonetheless quite traditional.

"When I am with my Pakistani friends and there is a picture of Afghan women from previous years in a magazine, showing them without a burqa and in normal clothes, then I feel a little bit proud. I feel glad that the Pakistanis should know that Afghanistan was not always what it is today, men wearing beards and women covered from head to toe, that Afghans have not always been strangers to civilization and freedom. I want Afghan women to be free to wear whatever they want and to be more like the women of the developed world. I personally do not care for outfits that are very extravagant and immodest; nevertheless, I don't support taking away the right of women and girls to wear whatever they want.

"In my view it is completely ordinary and natural for women to visit male doctors. Even fifty years ago in Afghanistan there were male doctors of gynecology and women routinely went to them. At the same time, men should be proud to be taught by women professors. In the past we had this already, and women taught at our universities. Especially in a place like Afghanistan, it is good and necessary that women should be professors, so that men can realize that women are not less than they, and this itself over time leads to a recognition of equality. Knowledge does not distinguish between a man or a woman.

"If in the future my wife, in selecting her profession or continuing her education, were to encounter any sort of opposition from me, then this should be a cause of embarrassment to me, as it would indicate that I wasn't really serious about the equality of men and women, but have only been lying to myself.

"I have convinced several Afghan and Pakistani friends to be supporters of RAWA. Through my travel I can help them, and I support them financially as well. Also, after my marriage I intend to introduce my wife to RAWA and hope that she will become a supporter and a real help to them."

We have explored why younger men might feel sympathetic to RAWA and its exciting new ideas. But when we try to analyze the structure of who supports RAWA and who criticizes it, the picture becomes surprising. We would expect traditional Afghans, older men, very religious people and rural people to be leery of RAWA's newfangled values and disapproving of such bold and outspoken women. But that is not the case. Traditional Afghans tend to see RAWA members as "good girls," self-sacrificing, earnest and patriotic. Because most of their work centers on providing social services, on distributing food and blankets to new refugees, running schools and orphanages and helping widows, it is honored and appreciated by conservative, traditional and older Afghans.

This leads to a recurring, somewhat ironic interaction between older Afghan men and RAWA's activists, as Tameena relates. "Whenever we're in some public place like the market, distributing our leaflets, older men almost always come up to us and express their respect. They say that we put men to shame, that we are the only ones with the courage to speak out, that we are braver than the men, who are afraid to stand up to the fundamentalists. Often they conclude their speech by taking off their turban and politely offering to trade it for our scarf. They are trying to say by this that they have failed in their duty as men, while we have had to step in and do their job, and therefore they should trade places with us."

It's meant as a compliment, but the irony is not lost on RAWA. The underlying premise—that women are supposed to be the timid ones while men are brave, that it's the men's job to change society, that it's an honor to wear a turban and a sign of humility to exchange it for a scarf—those messages are not very flattering. Nonetheless, RAWA accepts such compliments in good grace and hopes that their elderly admirers will grow accustomed to seeing women as full-fledged partners and participants instead of admiring just a few of them as amazing spectacles of supernatural female achievement.

As surprising as this unexpected source of praise may be, RAWA also attracts at least one surprising criticism, pertaining to their policy of nonviolence: They take risks but refrain from properly defending themselves. Javed is not the only one who finds this stance incomprehensible—there are many, including some European supporters, to whom this does not make sense.

RAWA AND MEN

RAWA is a feminist organization. Their publications cite "overcoming the dominance of men" as one of their fundamental goals.

In an Afghan context, you don't have to look very hard or very far to see what is meant by "the dominance of men." It is a social order that deeply, profoundly and overwhelmingly favors men, granting them special privileges, more rights and greater power in all aspects of life, at all ages, in all situations. As it happens, many Afghan men don't want those privileges, those rights and that power—at least not that much of it, so crassly displayed.

As we have already seen, many younger men prefer a more egalitarian, democratic and friendly world populated by free women—and quite a number of them are prepared to risk a lot, including their lives, to get rid of fundamentalist patriarchy and help bring about such a world.

A group from which we might expect greater opposition are the middle-aged refugee men. After all, they're just about old enough to start regarding themselves as the local alpha males, and they've spent their entire lives immersed in tradition. RAWA comes into frequent contact with these men when, for example, their wives want to attend a literacy class. By and large, they can be quite receptive to new ideas. Many support their wives' desire to get a belated education; in fact, they are often the ones who, knowing of their wives' long-standing wish to learn how to read, locate the class for them.

One tends to think of a backlash as being a reactionary phenomenon, but the Afghan case shows that it can just as easily go in the opposite direction, toward progress. If they seize the moment and use the impetus provided by the widespread, gender-spanning, Taliban-provoked liberal backlash, Afghan women may be able to move their society historically forward a very considerable distance in a short amount of time. This will require work on the part of women, and RAWA is fully aware of that—equality has to be claimed, taken possession of and then defended.

Those necessities, however—claiming, taking and defending—do not come easily to Afghan women. They require a degree of assertiveness and independence that life in the traditional extended family does not typically encourage. In those families, you are cared and provided for, but you are also assigned a very definite place in a complex hierarchy determined by status, age and gender.

The "democratic" family that so many young men rave about will require profound changes in the habits and the mind-set of all concerned. RAWA's teachers are aware of this. Mariam, a member of the education committee, reflects: "Of course it's important to work with the boys, and we want to do more of that, but in the end, since our resources are limited, I suppose it will depend even more on the girls, and we have to focus most of our efforts on them. Because if we want women to achieve their rights, and if we want to make them more active, then the first thing they will have to learn is how to assert themselves within their family. The first battle of Afghan and Pakistani women will have to be conducted in their own houses, where they will have to assert themselves against their brothers, their fathers and so on.

"Of course it is also important to change the thinking of the boys and the men, so that they will give way and let the girls have more opportunities.

"Whenever we start to work in a new location, the first thing we have to do is talk to the families. We have to discuss their attitudes with them and change their minds. We have to persuade them that girls are capable of learning, too, not just boys.

"And we work on the boys in our schools, too. 'Your sister is the same as you'—that's our fundamental message. That's what we need to get across to them, that they are no different from their sisters."

Whenever people live together, conflicts of interest occur and have to be resolved—that's just a fact of life. Women have to learn how to articulate their wishes, negotiate compromises, resist encroachments, find solutions and sometimes simply stand firm.

And then there are conflicts and threats that no individual woman can handle on her own: organized abductions, mass rapes or the coming to power of a regime that oppresses them. Against enemies like that, collective action is essential.

During the last decades, women have found new and highly effective ways of acting, not only for themselves but for each other. Bosnian women had no chance against rapes by armed Serb soldiers, but women in the outside world were in a position to turn this into a major issue. Throughout history, such assaults had been tacitly tolerated as the "inevitable" consequence of war. Those days are now over. The new climate of awareness made it possible for the individual victims in Bosnia to come forward, which in turn allowed for accountability; those responsible were brought before the war crimes tribunal. This required a lot of courage and strength on the part of the victims, but the effects were powerful. From being the secret shame of the victim, these rapes became a public shame for the perpetrators and their state. International awareness that rape was a war crime was achieved, serving as a deterrent to soldiers in future wars.

When women's groups worldwide became engaged in this effort, they could not have guessed that this deterrent would soon make itself felt in distant Afghanistan.

In the early 1990s, Northern Alliance troops exercised no self-restraint whatsoever as they rampaged through Afghanistan. Besides large numbers of killings and other abuses, they freely engaged in rape. Other than a few human rights organizations that published reports about it, the world paid little attention.

In 2001, when the Northern Alliance was again on the march, the issue of rape was raised with their leaders, and they were warned that the situation was very different now compared to their last military onslaught. This time, the international press was watching, and world public opinion would turn against them if incidents of rape were reported. Western diplomats issued specific warnings to them in this regard. It has become politically risky to allow soldiers carte blanche against women, and that is a big step forward.

What Afghan women experienced under the Taliban, though, was not just one kind of assault. Several of the Afghans interviewed for this book remarked that the Taliban's treatment of women was so extreme as to be unique in human history, and one can probably make that case. Western journalists often used terms such as *medieval* or even *stone-age* to describe Taliban attitudes, but even those terms were probably too mild. In the face of such an extraordinary exercise of total power by men over women, you might expect the women to become disillusioned and distrustful toward the nature of males in general.

On the whole, though, RAWA refrains from such generalizations, and with good reason. Many men support and help them, and many others turned against the Taliban precisely because of their treatment of women.

At RAWA's meetings, men are welcome to attend. It's a women's organization, so only women can be members, but men can offer suggestions, propose changes or activities and exercise criticism.

Still, in a society that, even in the best of times, practiced an extensive degree of sexual separation, and where disparities were so marked, we wondered what women really thought of men. One of the questions in our interviews addressed this issue.

The answers differed, but one word recurred in almost every statement: *chashang*. It occurred with such regularity that even I, with only the most rudimentary sense of Persian, began to notice it through sheer repetition. The translators had to struggle a little to find the exact English equivalent. It is a nuanced term, apparently meaning something along the lines of "mean" or "harsh," but with an undertone of deliberate malice. Here was what they finally came up with: *Chashang* is when you have the inclination to treat your fellow human beings with deliberate and indifferent harshness.

Chashang was the word almost all of our women interviewees selected to describe the nature of men, even when they otherwise had many good and friendly things to say about them.

"Men have a free hand when it comes to abusing women in the family," observed Mahboba, a twenty-seven-year-old underground fighter.

"From puberty on," another woman pointed out, "our girls are forced to stay in or very near the house, while boys have every freedom in the world. That's got to have an impact on the later mentality of the sexes."

"Many Afghan men, if they're angry or nervous about something or if they're under stress, then they beat their wife," observed Shakria, a refugee. "That's not good and I don't like it, and I hope they will change their thinking soon and realize that women are human beings, too."

"The fundamentalists assign women no value at all," her friend noted. "I don't know what they think, who brings them their life in the first place. They look down on women and don't ever seem to think that they have mothers and sisters."

The statement of Nooria, a forty-eight-year-old refugee woman who lives in the Nasir Bagh camp, was representative of the general view. Nooria believes that men and women are essentially the same, capable of the same achievements and driven by the same desires. In her opinion, fundamentalism and its accompanying hostility to women are fringe views, repugnant to the vast majority of Afghan men. While her basic attitude toward men is positive, she doesn't completely trust them—too many observations and experiences stand in the way, and the enduring power imbalance obstructs genuine friendship.

"Of course there is a natural difference between a man and a woman, but women, like men, can work and participate in society equally," she says. "Those Taliban, they grew up in mosques and madrassas, and that's all they know of the world. They have no other idea except to enslave women and keep them at home. Not all Afghan men are like Talibs. My husband, my brothers and the husbands of the women who attend the literacy class with me do not believe as the Talibs do.

"However, I believe that men are generally inclined to be harsh and mean. Although my husband is a good man, his temper easily flares and then he takes his anger out on us, and we can't defend ourselves. Based on this experience, I have formed the opinion that men have a brutal nature."

Husai is twenty-eight years old, the mother of three and a RAWA member of long standing. Currently she serves as the principal for three of RAWA's schools in Pakistan. As it happened, this question about the nature of women and men was something Husai has spent a lot of time thinking about.

"Although I have read that there are no fundamental differences between men and women, I have felt for years that there are some such differences. For example, it is obvious in the history of humanity that most of the wars and mass killings and quite a number of other crimes and aggressions against the rights of others, have taken place on the orders of men, and been carried out by men. It's true that the number of women leaders compared to the number of men leaders is very small, but still, from these few women you don't ever have the likes of Genghis Khan, or Hitler, or Suharto or Khomeini.

"When I look at Afghanistan, I see that it has been in a condition of war for twenty years, and those who are responsible for this tragedy have been, without exception, men. Both among the nonreligious tyrants of our country—Taraki, Amin, Babrak, Najib—and then with the religious tyrants, the Talibs and the Northern Alliance, Osama Bin Laden and al-Qaeda, the same is true. No doubt there are a few female fundamentalists, too, but they aren't running any criminal regimes.

"I would like to study and read more about the causes of this, to see if there is a scientific explanation. Just based on my own observations, though, I believe that men are *chashang*.

"I am also doubtful about the claim that they are braver than women. If being kind-hearted and being warm and loving, and worrying about the fate of others—if you think those indicate a lack of strength, then yes, women suffer from that. But I don't think this has any bearing on a person's courage.

"Another point is this. In the history of humanity, it has been men who have beaten women and have oppressed them and never the other way around. Isn't this an indication that there is a difference between men and women?

"In short, my answer to this question is that if there is a difference between men and women, then the difference is that men are less kind, not that they are braver. And this isn't something they need to be proud of."

CHAPTER 8

Boxing with Hashemi

I n the spring of the year 2000, when the Taliban were still firmly in charge of Afghanistan and the rest of the world was still unsure what to make of them, they sent a representative, one Mr. Hashemi, to the United States on a lecture and PR tour. He crisscrossed the country, giving interviews, holding speeches, appearing on talk shows, reading statements.

At one point he was asked about the purpose of his visit, and he summarized it in one surprising sentence. He was there, he replied, to "do battle with feminists."

I'll always remember that reply, if only because it provoked such an absurd response in me. I, a suburban liberal pacifist vegetarian, the kind of person who worries about her karma before smacking a mosquito, felt an alien wave of archaic barroom bravado wash over me, on the level of "Oh yeah, buddy? Bring it on." Moments later I regained my composure. But there was no denying it: The sentence had gotten to me, had struck a nerve.

It wasn't too difficult to figure out why. Hashemi's words gave the lie to the Taliban's claims that their draconian restrictions against women were only intended to protect them, to show respect for the honor of Muslim women and to keep them safe in troubled times.

It exposed as naive the belief, still widespread at that time, that the Taliban weren't really cruel and malicious, just ignorant, misguided and unfamiliar even with the true precepts of their own religion.

His sentence made it clear that the Taliban knew precisely what they were doing, that they felt contempt and hostility toward women and were determined to push them down and keep them there forever.

And if somehow they could, they'd love to do the same to me.

In that light, his resentment of "feminists"—a category that presumably included any woman not wearing a burqa, able to read and write, and unaccountably permitted by the lax men of her culture to roam the streets unsupervised—was quite understandable. First, the very existence of this sort of woman belied the Taliban's existential premise that societies would collapse if women had such freedom. And second, they were a painful reminder of one of the Taliban's more serious political miscalculations.

The Taliban had thought to eliminate women as any sort of humanly significant factor in their society, to make them invisible and irrelevant. But instead women had become a huge global thorn in their side.

In fact, the Taliban's plight was reminiscent of those comedies that revolve around clumsy murderers trying unsuccessfully to rid themselves of their victim's body.

The more the Taliban tried to push Afghan women into invisibility, the more they got noticed by the rest of the world. The more they tried to nudge them into the background, the more everybody else became interested in even the most minuscule details of Afghan women's lives. In trying to erase Afghan women from public view in their own country, the Taliban only succeeded in turning them into a global diplomatic issue. Major aid projects got canceled or suspended because the Taliban would not allow women to share in the benefits. International bodies refused to admit the Taliban because of their stance on women.* I think it is safe to say that the Taliban found this baffling in the extreme. They had not expected any opposition to their plans for women.

Taliban foreign minister Wakil Ahmed Muttawakil, groping for an explanation, concluded bitterly that "Jewish women" must be running the United Nations.† He knew

---

* Though only one in very many, the World Food Program's standoff with the Taliban was probably the most dramatic because it affected the largest number of people. This program, which was feeding an estimated 40 percent of the population of Kabul, needed to conduct a survey in order to ensure that rations were reaching the intended recipients, to include the neediest families. Those in greatest need were the households headed by women, in particular widows. Since women were not allowed to work, these families were in literal peril of starvation. Acceding to Taliban sensibilities, the WFP very accommodatingly proposed to use only female surveyors to visit the households of women. The Taliban refused to lift its total ban on female employment; the WFP announced that though they were willing to conduct the survey in a way the Taliban found culturally acceptable, if they could not conduct it at all and thus had to conclude that they were failing to deliver aid to the neediest women, they were shutting down the program. For an extensive overview of the Taliban's conflicts with international organizations, see Ahmad Rashid, *Taliban* (New Haven: Yale University Press, 2001). Another major showdown involved the powerful international agency CARE. That organization had, through laborious negotiations with the Taliban, gained permission to hire female health care workers, only to have these women dragged from the organization's vehicle and beaten by other Talibs. This incident is described in the organization's own report (Jonathan Bartsch, "CARE Afghanistan Case Study: Violent Conflict and Human Rights," CARE Afghanistan, Peshawar, 1998).
† This is in the context of the WFP standoff described above. The specific Jewish designation probably occurred to him because of the simultaneous scandal over the Taliban order that Afghan Hindus were to mark themselves by wearing a yellow badge, criticized as resembling the Jewish star of Nazi days.

184 ~ *Cheryl Benard*

better, of course. Along with the rest of the Taliban's leadership, he was at that time receiving delegation after delegation of foreign men, all trying to get the Taliban to at least modify, if not abandon, their stance on women in regard to education, access to health care, and the right to be employed. Male journalists, development experts, aid workers and diplomats were appalled by what came to be called gender apartheid, and its terrible consequences for the quality of Afghan women's lives.*

However, it is true that women tended to rank the issue higher on the scale of political significance. Repeatedly, for example, the U.S. government seemed inclined to let the woman question slide into gentle oblivion, if only the Taliban would accommodate them on the issues of terrorism and drug traffic. Only the women's lobby—often led by the Feminist Majority—stood in the way of this sell out. Their pressure on Congress would result in a hearing, and eventually the State Department would be ordered to get back on message: terrorism, drugs *and* human rights for women. Afghanistan is a case study of an extremely successful lobbying effort, perhaps the first such one, by women on behalf of women's fundamental rights.

The level of engagement and determination was impressive and at first glance surprising. Apparently, I wasn't the only woman willing to duke it out with Hashemi in the parking lot—but why? The abuse of Afghan women was far away, remote from our lives, impacting us not at all—but that wasn't how it felt. It felt personal. They were being per-

* For example, see the article by Howard Kleinberg, "Afghan Women, Not Statues, Need to Be Rescued," *Baltimore Sun,* March 8, 2001.

secuted and insulted because they were women, and other women minded that.

In recent history, there have been two instances where American and European women were noticeably more hawkish than men. The first was Bosnia, where by a clear statistical margin, women favored an intervention sooner and more decisively than men did. The second was Afghanistan, where you could find many male but few female experts proposing that Western governments should "try harder to engage the Taliban" or—this after September 11—"try to work with moderates inside the Taliban." The Serbs, and the Taliban, had declared war on women, and as it turns out, doing so may be unwise—not necessarily because women are so immensely powerful or are "running things," but because, in labile diplomatic situations, they may tip the balance.

Tactical advice for ethnic cleansers and terrorists: You may wish to refrain from mass rape and systematic abuse of your country's women. In the case of Afghanistan at the turn of the twenty-first century, women noticed, women cared and women were in a position to do something about it.

One outstanding feature of RAWA has been their willingness to capitalize on that. Many Third World and Muslim women's groups could be similar beneficiaries of worldwide female solidarity but are sidelined by nationalist concerns, unwilling to accept criticism of their own culture's men and feeling it's disloyal to be helped by another culture's women. RAWA avoided these errors from the outset.

"Welcome to the website of the world's most oppressed women." That's calling it like it is, and that's how www.rawa.org serves it up. The situation of Afghan women under fundamentalism is terrible, bad enough to be in a league all of its own, and RAWA isn't planning to justify or excuse or rationalize it. They're not planning to give you any lectures about tradition or religion, or to instruct you to mind your own decadent Western imperialist business. No, you are very welcome here, and your help is needed.

That approach works; women the world over (and men, too) have responded fabulously. A brief RAWA appearance on *Oprah* led three hundred thousand American women to the website in one evening. When the site broke down under this onslaught, American Web advisers quickly helped install mirror sites. The website mentioned that if only RAWA had digital cameras, they could better and more safely document Taliban atrocities—and two weeks later, RAWA was up to its ears in state-of-the-art photo equipment. By the end of the month, they could have opened up branches of Circuit City in Quetta and Kandahar with the surplus.

Islamic women's groups have by and large disdained to use the international women's response as a resource—or have simply not known how to harness it. RAWA was smart enough to recognize what a powerful tool the Taliban handed them when it made Western women angry; the group was creative enough to realize that cosmopolitan Western feminists could be the natural allies of women who were forcibly being kept at the opposite end of history's spectrum. Soon they had a highly educated, skilled, multilingual, affluent cadre of foreign sympathizers at their disposal—translating their texts into Portuguese and German, writing protest letters, opening bank accounts in California and poster depots in Washington, D.C., functioning as their chauffeurs and press agents during lecture tours and composing reams of poems about the veil and oppression and solidarity. These appeared promptly on RAWA's website and in their brochures. In fact, you could almost get the impression that of all the gifts and services they receive, RAWA likes the poems best. It's in their history. RAWA started out as a troop of schoolgirls holding street demonstrations that at times turned deadly, confonting armed troops with nothing but their chanted poems to protect them.

Foreign sympathizers do, in addition to money and technical support and labor, at times offer advice. Some of it is accepted, and some of it is not. Perhaps the most contentious issue has been RAWA's name: Revolutionary Association of the Women of Afghanistan. Repeatedly the word *revolutionary* has been an obstacle. This is not so much the case for the supporters and sympathizers, although many of them are middle-class, middle-of-the-road, even right-of-center people who do not feel entirely comfortable with that appellation. Still, they will generally tend to make an informed decision about the group's ideology and affiliations, then attribute the name to an entirely different setting and cultural framework and not mind it. The real problem arises when these supporters try to garner third-party help and support. Embassies, government agencies, even international organizations balk at the word *revolutionary*. It can be frustrating to come close to landing a support deal for RAWA, based on the substance of their work and a project that clearly deserves it, only to have the whole thing fall apart because one word in the organization's name is unacceptable to the sponsor. With regularity, foreign supporters urge RAWA to rename itself, citing pragmatic considerations as well as linguistic ones: *Revolutionary* sounds dated, and the world of social change has long moved on to other

188 ~ Cheryl Benard

catchphrases. Can't they call themselves something with *civil society* in it, for example? *Empowerment* would be okay, too. How about *participation?*

RAWA accepts such suggestions graciously. "Million heartfelt thanks for sisterly advice," the answering e-mail will say. Then they'll just go ahead and keep on calling themselves RAWA. Their reasons make sense. In the course of recent Afghan history, they'll tell you, so many sleazy people have changed sides so often, so many groups have shamelessly reinvented themselves, from Communists into fundamentalists, from agents of the KHAD secret police into "freedom fighters," that it disgusts them, and they don't want to be like that. RAWA is the name they started out with, and people know it and would only mock them as opportunists if it suddenly changed. Besides, they'll say, if Afghan women learned how to read and write and became part of society, that *would* be a revolution. Lastly, they'll remind you, they're a democratic organization. Something as fundamental as a change of name would require a lot of debating and a lot of thought, followed by a referendum, and there just isn't time for that right now, not when the situation is so dire. All of this makes good sense, and even if you don't agree, it doesn't matter, because it's their call.

Besides the name, RAWA's political style is also likely to strike you as slightly dated. Leafing through RAWA's publications is like entering a time warp. It's almost as if RAWA's linguistic clocks stopped when the Russian invasion forced them to leave the 1960s world of campus politics and sloganeering to join the diaspora. RAWA literature still describes its enemies as "stooges," "lackeys" and "thugs." Add in the translation factor, clearly at the hands of someone who is highly motivated but far from a native speaker of English, and the results can be nothing short of astounding.

Persian is a flowery, dramatic language, given to the lavish use of adjectives and metaphors. To produce an effective English text would require heavy editing, to lower the decibels in conformity with our more understated style.

It doesn't matter. RAWA is proof that political values can travel on lumbering wings, that thoughts can be conveyed even in the absence of skilled rhetoric and that like-minded people will understand each other despite such obstacles. Jaded Western urbanites are perfectly willing to suspend literary criticism in order to heed RAWA's call. The mission statement, as formulated in Peshawar on the occasion of International Women's Day 2000, is clear to all of us. We have to "make ourselves a sharp arrow in the eyes of the fundamentalists and blood-thirsty, dunder-headed anti-women elements in every nook and cranny of this restless world."

I couldn't have said it better myself—well, maybe I could have. But it doesn't matter. As it turns out, it's not the spin after all. You don't have to do a professional sales job. If your message is powerful, you don't need the hourly opinion polls or the wardrobe consultant or the PR agency. If your ideas resonate, then however you state them, they will travel gracefully to every nook and cranny of this restless world.

In the case of RAWA's ideas, this is certainly happening. One day, browsing some international press reports online, I happened across an article describing RAWA in the highbrow German-language daily *Der Standard*.

The newspaper has a readers' forum, allowing people to react to what they have just read, and there I found the following exchange:

MICHAEL
subject: idea

Various international bodies are struggling
to put together a suitable post-Taliban government plan for Afghanistan. So far they've
come up with the Northern Alliance and,
believe it or not, that ancient mummy, the
country's former king.

Why not RAWA?

What if the international community
gave governance to an activist women's
movement? That would be a truly interesting experiment.

But given the Stone Age patriarchal ambi-
ence that still dominates global politics, such
a solution is probably unthinkable.

BYRON
Re: your idea

Great suggestion! Your idea has my full sympathy and support.

ASTRID
Re: your idea
power to women

The suggestion to place the fortunes of that
state in the hands of its women is an excellent one. Now the question is: how can this

idea be publicized, and how can those powers who are deciding the destiny of Afghanistan be persuaded to support such a suggestion? One thing seems certain: women would definitely take a different problem-solving approach and would have a deeper commitment to social justice.

TOM
subject: heroes

I feel deep respect for these women who risked their lives to help their fellow human beings. That is true courage. They are the heroes, not the men with the machine guns or in the bomber jets.

HELMUT
Re: heroes

My ungrudging admiration for these brave women. But there's one thing I don't understand. How can one move effectively against a regime that rules through violence and brutality, without employing force oneself? How can you make someone who is ruling over you with a machine gun put his weapon down, except through force? To operate in hiding and basically just wait for them to catch you and kill you—that can't be the right approach.

All the really fundamental issues raised by RAWA's experience are contained in this short online exchange.

Why is world diplomacy, in the end, still so basic and so primitive, its intellectual and legal and ritualistic trappings just an elegant veneer to cover up the fact that in the end, the warlords of one kind or another have the greatest voice in determining the peace?

Isn't it time to try newer and more innovative approaches, including ones more inclusive and respectful of civilians and noncombatants, especially women?

Diplomacy is one of the least innovative sectors of our society—and we can't afford to have it stay that way. Consider the Middle East "peace process," which has been caught for decades now in the same deadly, monotonous circle. Conventional diplomacy reacts to this stalemate by persisting with methods that have produced nothing but failure—an antiempirical, dated, irrational approach. If it's manifestly not working, to try yet another summit and sign one more accord isn't even diplomacy anymore; it's ritual and form.

These ordinary Internet citizens, thoughtfully reflecting on the world around them, seemed far ahead of institutions and diplomacy in their political ideas and values. And I began to believe that we are in the midst of a very exciting global development, a new people's politics of which RAWA is just one small manifestation.

There are many examples of the lag between people's politics and institutional politics, but one clear illustration is offered by the case of Bosnia. In 1991, appalled by the slaughter and persecution of a minority there, world public opinion demanded an intervention, but governments were stalling and hedging, allowing the aggressor to violate one useless agreement after another. Instead, well in advance of their governments and their militaries, civilians acted. U.S. Jewish organizations, led by the American Jewish Congress, funded a powerful media campaign on behalf of the endangered Bosnian Muslims. The reports of "ethnic cleansing" and the images of desperate and miserable Bosnian refugees reminded them of their grandparents' persecution in Europe not so long ago. Nor did Western Europeans, who had the advantage of geographic access, wait for their governments to act. Church groups held donation drives, then loaded the supplies onto pickup trucks and headed for the Croatian border. Without permits, without papers, without even a clear sense of where they were going, these people negotiated with border guards, discovered the location of impromptu refugee settlements, argued their way across checkpoints and ultimately got their little shipments of medicine, food and clothes through. In the case of Bosnia, and again in Kosovo, the citizens of Western democracies held what amounted to a kind of spontaneous referendum. Their expression of will ended up driving the foreign policy of their reluctant leaders.

Now let's consider the unknown Michael's proposal, from the website, in that light. Give a women's group a shot at things, he says. His suggestion is a radical one—or is it? Let's look at the candidates whom international diplomats envisioned installing as the new government of Afghanistan in December 2001. First, the Northern Alliance. This is a loose association of warlords who governed the country once before, from 1992 to 1996. This period is remembered as a time of gross misrule. Extremely severe human rights violations on a scale that would justify a war crimes tribunal took place during that time, as is well documented by neutral outside agencies and disputed by no one. Consequently, the Northern Alliance is widely feared and disliked by the population of Afghanistan. Diplomats have found them extremely difficult to deal with, aggressive, rigid and prone to breaking their agreements. Its various factions are also at odds with each other. Some of them are fundamentalists. None of them is democratic.

Another contender for power was Zahir Shah, the former monarch, a man in his late eighties with benign social values, an engaging affection for feminists and some sentimental meaning as a national icon but no infrastructure, no military, no money, no cohesive following, no organization. Unlike some other deposed monarchs, he did not set up a government in exile and did not participate in either the military effort or the humanitarian programs in Afghanistan or for the refugees. His solitary virtue is that some people, especially the older ones who remember his family, are nostalgically fond of him as the symbol of better times.

These are the two parties that Western diplomacy could readily envision installing in the seat of power. The critical word here is *installing,* because in the case of post-Taliban Afghanistan, the international community will be deeply involved in choosing, creating and shoring up the next power holder.

Neither the Northern Alliance nor the former king has the slightest glimmer of a chance to attain such power on their own. The Northern Alliance fought against the Taliban for five years, losing city after city, province after province. By the fall of 2001, they had been driven back into the last little corner of the country, which they were clinging to in desperation.

The killing of their most effective commander, Ahmed Shah Masud, by al-Qaeda assassins was widely considered to have been the final blow—until September 11, that is, when the Northern Alliance became the foot soldiers of the U.S. military. The massive use of U.S. air power so completely intimidated the Taliban that they went down without a significant struggle, and it was left to the Northern Alliance to accept the surrender of one city after another while the Taliban fled in disarray. Given that level of U.S. air support, a middle-school soccer team could have taken Kabul.

Now let's consider RAWA. RAWA had established something very much like a government in exile. Without calling it by that name, they were actually exercising many of the classic functions of a state. While others were committing human rights violations, they were receiving human rights prizes, including the highly regarded human rights prize of the French government for the year 2000 and Japan's human rights prize for 2001. They had set up a functioning political party respected by men and women alike. They were running schools and health programs. They had a kind of foreign policy, with ties to other countries. They were running an effective underground, with a network across the entire country. They were multiethnic.

Why *not* RAWA? Here was a party led by women who had managed to pull an amazing set of civic services practically out of thin air, with a proven ability to provide leadership and organization and an impeccably democratic record. Why shouldn't they run the country, too? That was "unthinkable," to use Michael's term. Except that it wasn't unthinkable, apparently—he had thought about it, and he wasn't alone.

Even as the experts and academics are writing book after book about the "new world order," pondering what kinds of new political delineations, conflicts and behaviors it will bring, people are living that order and carving out a place for themselves in it. They are conducting their own highly personalized foreign relations, experiencing their own cultural exchange, carrying out their own development aid programs, forming their own alliances.

RAWA is both a benefactor of and a catalyst in this new global exchange. There is a vast network of international supporters, women and men who maintain economic, cultural and other relations with RAWA, exchanging goods, money, songs, poems and ideas, developing joint political platforms and doing many of the other things usually performed by embassies, ministries and envoys. How did these foreign supporters discover RAWA, and what did they hope to accomplish through their affiliation?

We posted these questions through RAWA's e-mail exchange and soon heard from a colorful, worldwide assortment of lay diplomats. There was a marine biologist and the head of a band called Star Vomit. Replies came from the Fiji Islands and from India. There were writers, engineers, artists, academics. German rock icon Nina Hagen responded; she may be a recent supporter, but she had already organized a benefit concert, and her answer contained the largest number of exclamation marks. The cultural program was a lively one. Besides the poems, people were also inspired by RAWA to write and perform plays, to compose and record songs. Some had a primarily emotional relationship with RAWA; others saw it in an intellectual or political light. The common threads were the shared values of equality, democracy and human rights. Their answers are a window into the new people's politics.*

ELEANOR, 27, ENGLAND, INTRANET WEBMASTER

"In late 1997, I received one of those e-mail petitions about Afghan women. Even then I was a pretty experienced Internet user, so it was obvious to me that the e-mail petititions were meaningless and weren't going anywhere. The account they had come from had probably been terminated long ago. In any event, I felt that in order to achieve anything, you probably had to do more than forward an e-mail.

"Still, I had been wondering what happened to Afghanistan after the USSR left, so I did an Internet search and discovered RAWA's website. I read it thoroughly and sent them a message of support and some money. They replied. Later they asked me to find them a few books and a part for a digital camera they could not get in Pakistan, and it went from there.

"I agree with their principles. RAWA proves that you don't have to be 'woolly' to be a liberal, and you don't have to be unprincipled to be practical. And then again, how could I refuse to help a person who does such acts of amazing courage, braver than you see in any war film, and then signs her e-mail 'love and hugs'? The courage of women is never recognized, because the women themselves take it for granted and don't muddle it up with maleness, or with recklessness, or with aggression.

"I've set up a deal with a TV company for them, given presentations about RAWA to university groups and acted

*Some of the statements were abbreviated for this text.

as a trustee for donations. I'm familiar with the cultural interventionism debate, but in my opinion, it doesn't hold up to scrutiny. Every person has the right to help another person who asks for help, and RAWA has a right to ask. The Taliban represented no one but themselves. Yet 'respect our culture' is what the Taliban say in support of their evil practices. What a surprise—it would suit them very well if 'their' women were just their beasts of burden and didn't have any friends or rights."

MARIA CELINA, 30, MEXICAN-INDIAN-AMERICAN, LAW CLERK

"I am a Muslim. I am tired of factions of all races and religions condoning heinous acts just because they are of a like agenda or religion. Muslims do this also. This is akin to being a party to the crime. The oppression of women in a Muslim country is particularly moving to me. The negative and false stereotypes of Muslims in America are fueled by fundamentalists. Most importantly I cannot permit my beloved Prophet and sacred Quran to be blasphemed anymore. Mohammad wanted a safe and loving environment for women. The Taliban made a nightmare of Islam, and made life on earth a living hell for women, men and children.

"I like RAWA because these women have what is so rare in humans. These women live by their beliefs. They literally risk their lives for what is right."

MARGARET, 69, ENGLAND, HUMAN RIGHTS LAWYER

"I met RAWA at a UN meeting. I like their clarity of vision, their sense of purpose in realizing the need to overthrow all forces of fundamentalism, their intelligence and their brilliant communication skills. The role of outside supporters is to channel their voices, to use our influence with our own governments and with the UN, network from the grassroots up to national governments and the international community."

LORRIE, 41, AMERICAN, WRITER AND MUSICIAN

"I read several stories in the newspaper about the plight of Afghan women, got very upset and went online trying to find a group I could work with. I found RAWA. I got in touch with them and started writing songs. I wrote the song about Meena that is on the RAWA website—I'm Dr. Lorrie, and Star Vomit was the name of my band, but now I'm called Sugar Rat. Currently I'm making a CD of songs about Afghanistan. I've also organized speaking events, and we've set up a local support group.

"Over the years, everything I've seen or heard about RAWA has made me like them more. I really do believe that they are the one totally sane group involved in Afghanistan. I appreciate their website—every time I visit it, it's a very draining experience, but I feel more and more admiration for everyone in RAWA.

"Under the Taliban, women and girls were targets of unprecedented oppression. When half the population is being systematically killed off (emotionally and physically), I believe the world community should intervene. The world community intervened and took the Serbians to trial at The Hague. Why did the international community wait so long to notice the Taliban? Women in my country take their rights for granted and completely dissociate themselves from the women's rights movement and feminism. But I think anything's possible. If I don't help the women in Afghanistan, they won't be around one day to help me.

"RAWA rocks!"

MARIANNE, 35, DENMARK, PUBLIC RELATIONS MANAGER

"I support what was said by one of Denmark's most famous writers, Suzanne Brogger, who stated, 'Once in a while you can have your doubts about whether you are a feminist or not. But you cannot, even for a second, doubt that you are an Afghan feminist.'

"I consider nonviolent fighting for human rights, including women's rights and democracy, to be beyond cultural differences. These are global rights for global citizens. For a long time, a lot of Danes have been suffering from mysophobia when it came to interfering with other cultures. We have been too lazy and too afraid of being disrespectful.

"RAWA and the women in my country are kindred spirits even though our history and situation differ significantly. I consider Afghan women as being, overall, strong and independent women who see education, careers, womanhood and motherhood as compatible. The generation before me fought for women's rights here in Denmark. Now it's our turn and the scene is set outside Denmark, that's all."

SHABNAM, 44, INDIA, ACTIVIST

"I think one of the most important things for any fighter to know is that he or she is not alone. That there are other people who support their cause. Therefore I feel it is very important to provide moral support to RAWA, as well as of course monetary and material help. I remember distinctly even now, after thirteen years, that after my brother was attacked and killed while performing near Delhi, we received thousands of letters from all over India from the artistic community, from intellectuals and from ordinary citizens. That gave us enormous strength.

"What the Taliban did to Afghanistan and especially to women has no parallel. However, I would like to add that the right-wing forces in India have a similar ideology and there have been many attempts by them to impose similar restrictions on women. The Muslim fundamentalists in Kashmir and extremist groups in Punjab have also tried that. The position of the majority of women is quite pathetic in India, but at the same time there is a strong women's movement that can openly fight for their rights."

ALEX, 23, UK, EDUCATOR

"I learned about RAWA from a friend in the United States who heard one of their activists speak at a university. I particularly admire their bravery in risking their lives to collect evidence, so that there cannot be any convincing 'historical revisionism' about the behavior of the *jihadis*.

"Oh, it's interventionism to demand human rights? Isn't the introduction of Kalashnikovs and U.S.-made shoulder-fired weapons intervention in and alteration of the traditional culture, too? Tell them to go back and read the Quran and see if there is any incitement to do what they are doing to women, men, children, and to thought and civilization.

"I wrote a play, using research provided by a RAWA member. It was produced by the Stockyards Theatre Company in Chicago in May 2001."

VIJAYASHREE, 28, INDIA, SOFTWARE TECHNICAL MANAGER

"I learned about RAWA through an e-mail sent by one of the members in a technical group mailing list. What I like is that they aren't just complaining about their situation but trying to fight it and doing a very good job with their limited resources. I was impressed by their website. I wouldn't have expected it to be so sophisticated. They put forward their story with good visual impact. My first impression was that I ought to help them.

"It's interesting that countries don't think they are interfering in other cultures when they engage in trade, or push their products and hence their lifestyle. They only start worrying about culture when it comes to treatment of women. The world is becoming more and more interdependent, and basic human rights should be implemented in the whole world.

"As I come from India, and we do have a lot of problems there in the treatment of women, RAWA is an example of how a women's rights organization can use modern technology to spread their cause and reach out to a larger audience. I feel they should be more aggressive, though, in demanding a say in the future dispensation in Afghanistan after the Taliban. I hope and pray that these women will achieve what they are striving for. Let me correct myself—I am sure they will, only I hope it is without any harm done to any of them."

LEE, 40, AMERICAN, COLLEGE ENGLISH TEACHER

"In America, we also have fundamentalists who lust for power and who would reorganize America according to their narrow views if given the chance. Just listen to some of them and you will hear faint echoes of the Taliban and their absolutist mentality."

PARVIN, 60, IRANIAN-AMERICAN, ELECTRONICS ENGINEER*

"I learned about RAWA in 1994 after my sister, Dr. Homa Darabi, self-immolated in Iran protesting the oppressive treatment of women by the Islamic Republic of Iran. I received a note of condolence from RAWA. Now I support them, because women living under Islamic laws must become united in order to defeat a code of law that considers women less than a human being.

"Interventionism? If there happened to be a cannibalistic society on earth and they started eating their neighbors, would we say it's just their culture and it's okay? The Taliban were devouring Afghan women. It would be cruel and unjust for anyone to stay silent about an oppressive culture.

"In Iran, my country of birth, we are fighting the same evil of Islamic laws regarding women, and we must work together to achieve our goal, the establishment of secular democracies."

NINA, 46, GERMANY, SINGER-SONGWRITER

"I saw a documentary about RAWA just a few weeks ago! They are fighting for their human rights! I am supporting them with all my heart, especially the hospital project!

"I believe that human rights should be available to all

---

* Parvin Darabi is the author of *Rage Against the Veil* (Amherst: Prometheus Books, 1999).

women in this world, no matter which culture or religion they may come from! When women cry out for help, because they have been robbed of all their human rights, then it is our human duty to try our best to be of help for them! I have only love and respect for RAWA! And I hope that more and more women in the whole world will help RAWA more and more!"

GRACE, 22, ENGLAND, AID WORKER

"RAWA doesn't pander to the status quo. They are not passive but outspoken, even when the cost to them is possible death. They put to shame the condescending Western liberal elite that could speak freely, without danger to itself, yet doesn't.

"I believe those of us in the richer and more powerful nations have a duty to impact the political decisions made in our respective countries that will have an effect on Afghanistan. Collaborations provide a creative opportunity for shared learning, friendship and solidarity. Western policy muddles into other nations' business, then abandons them."

SALLY, 25, AUSTRALIA, ACTIVIST

"When I first visited the RAWA website I was pretty much uninformed, so everything I read there surprised me. I felt that just signing their guest book was not all I could do. So I held a benefit night for RAWA. I have also done public speaking and written articles about these great women. Seeing women so powerful in the midst of so much sadness, I was drawn to them.

"Their work inspires me every day. They've shown me that no matter what you are facing, what is wrong is wrong, and anyone can work to change it."

RAWA's ability to attract supporters and unleash their creativity by tapping into an underlying stream of political values was revealed to me in a somewhat surprising way while I was working on this book. My research institute employs an intern, twenty-two-year-old Alfons, who works with us as a statistician. He was comfortable with feminism, otherwise he wouldn't have chosen this particular workplace, but he didn't appear to be overwhelmingly interested in politics. His after-hours career with a rock band was clearly of greater importance to him. Then came Shahla, from Islamabad to Vienna and straight into his life. Alfons disapproved of the things he heard concerning the Taliban. He was pleased to hear that RAWA wasn't taking this lying down. Next thing we knew, he was spending his nights in the studio, recording a fund-raising CD for RAWA and talking about how meeting this group had changed his life.

RAWA has a large music division. They produce cassettes of patriotic and political songs that are very popular among Afghan refugees. For Alfons, that was the most logical level of connection. His story helps illustrate how political affiliations develop in this postmodern world.

"I decided to become active on behalf of RAWA because they're obviously fighting against a massive injustice. The Taliban are using the most vicious means imaginable to dehumanize their society. They seem to hate and to want to persecute anything female. To oppress one gender by forbidding education, forcing them to conceal themselves to the point of having no human form, ordering them to walk soundlessly and enforcing similar rules amounts to a kind of torture. Those guys wanted women to be invisible, mute and, if possible, completely ignorant. That's a kind of slavery. And by withholding education, they wanted to make sure that women would never be able to break loose from that system. In my opinion it's just a fact that everybody has the right to equal treatment, regardless of their race, their class or their gender. I don't think one should differentiate people by those criteria to justify inequality. Those are archaic distinctions; they don't even make sense anymore. You'll never get a peaceful and tolerant world if you're going to focus on categories like that.

"I see that Afghan women have begun to defend themselves, because they've realized that they are being oppressed. As their weapons, they've chosen education, humanitarian aid, information and medical services, not bombs or missiles. That makes it my obligation to help them.

"The most realistic thing for me to contribute is to help them become better known here in my own surroundings, so that more people will want to support them. They need material and political help. I think it's in my own best interest to help bring about a more open and equitable society and to stand by those who are being treated inhumanely. If only in a minor way, I want to be part of the fight against injustice in our world. It doesn't take too much sensitivity or empathy or global thinking to see that this isn't just about some gray, anonymous mass in a faraway place. These are people like us, getting treated as though they weren't human beings. There's no cultural excuse for that, and any pseudo-tolerant rationalizations would be inappropriate. You have to take a stand. Otherwise you're just showing tolerance toward intolerance.

"I felt good when I made the decision to help RAWA. It

gave me a sense of purpose. A sort of relaxed feeling came over me, the feeling that I was doing the right thing, that I could maybe take the things I believe in and help move them forward a bit. The situation of women in Afghanistan is so impossible, yet they keep at it and are effective. They're extremely brave under very dangerous conditions. In my situation, then, I ought to be able to accomplish quite a bit, even if I just summon up a moderate amount of guts.

"Music is my thing, so that was the first level of involvement that occurred to me. I downloaded their songs from the Internet and immediately felt the strong emotion transported by their music. The hoarse voices of women and children in their songs, calling out for justice, the sense of desperation—it was some of the most powerful and intense music I've ever heard. It created a strong mood in me as I listened. Since then I've discussed it with a number of friends, and they all felt the same level of impact. We decided to create a remix in our own style, using European beats, sounds, harmonies and basses, leaving only the original voices of the women and children. I communicated with RAWA about it, and they said it's something they've been thinking about, too, and it would be great if I did it. I plan to put other information about RAWA and their projects on the CD, too, maybe even some video.

"We started last week—we, that's the Electronics Project Blockwerk. On the second remix we plan to incorporate rap elements, because that's another good way to include verbal messages. We get together at nine p.m. or so and usually work until about four in the morning.

"Ever since Shahla came, my life has basically been all about RAWA. During working hours we're doing projects and organizing information campaigns for them, and at night I'm remixing their music. For me, music is the best medium. It transmits moods, situations and feelings. It's more honest than spoken language, and it has no borders."

There's a cliché that every population has the government it deserves. I think this is patently untrue. The world is filled with people who are far more creative, more democratic and more culturally advanced than their governments, their foreign policies and their diplomats. When fed up with their country's foreign policy, they do more than complain. They get on the Internet, go to the recording studio or pull out the checkbook and make their own.

CHAPTER 9

RAWA and
Postmodern Politics

T he fighter is riding a donkey (antiquity). He is carrying a Kalashnikov rifle (last century). He is communicating with his superpower ally, who will be providing air cover, via a satellite phone (high technology) in his backpack. In the Afghan war of the winter of 2001, this was the image that fascinated so many commentators. We were in a new age, and this image captured it. The combination of ancient and cutting-edge was typical for the postmodern conduct of war and conflict.

An oppressive regime rules the population through fear, imposing rules intended to return the country to the Middle Ages. Women, completely subjugated by this regime, form an underground resistance movement. They move about on foot, using the burqa (antiquity) to conceal their movements and to transport contraband. They communicate with international helpers, who provide funding, technical support and political backing, via the Internet (high technology). Deprived of formal education, with no political venue whatsoever, they piece together and publicize a coherent ideology capable of motivating illiterate village women and highly educated foreign sympathizers equally. The combination of objective powerlessness and amazing efficacy is typical for the postmodern conduct of social change, and part of RAWA's significance is that it may well turn out to be the world's first postmodern resistance movement.

POLITICS AND CONFLICT
IN THE THIRD MILLENNIUM

September 11 was a painful turning point for most of us. We realized that we had a mortal enemy, one not to be taken lightly. But we didn't know who or where he was, what his goals were, where he would attempt to strike next. Suddenly we were on new and hostile terrain. Our prior certainties no longer held; where would the new ones come from? What kinds of wars did the third millennium hold in store? Where was the front line? Who was the opponent? What were we even fighting about? Were we dealing with a "war of civilizations"? Struggling against "evil ones," as President Bush indicated? Would things eventually, blessedly, go back to the way they had been before? Was this perhaps just a kind of "correction" on a global and political scale, a terrible but temporary setback—like a recession, only with human casualties? And if the new conflict scenarios no longer fit into the old scheme of conventional nations fighting familiar wars, how would we best deal with them? With propaganda? With bombs? With some combination of both? After the first moment of paralysis, a flurry of activity ensued. New agencies were created. Stringent security measures were introduced. Military courts were established. And endless numbers of experts spent endless numbers of CNN hours talking about the lethal complexities of al-Qaeda.

Yet from their "bases" in the border area of Afghanistan, untrained women civilians were operating covertly against the Taliban and, through them, also against al-Qaeda.

One likely reason why they had been able to take these

opponents on was that they knew them. The Taliban and al-Qaeda were unfamiliar to us because they were the product of new global configurations, a complicated mix of poverty, backwardness, frustration and imported foreign ideas randomly combined with aspects of tradition and high technology. Poverty, backwardness and frustration made them volatile, exotic ideological combinations made them unpredictable and access to modern technology made them effective.

RAWA, in a sense, had grown on the same soil. As the same garden can produce lethal digitalis and benign achillaea, RAWA was a kind of mirror movement to al-Qaeda. From the global ideology mix, they had picked democracy and equality; al-Qaeda had drawn anti-Westernism and authoritarianism. From their joint cultural background of gender segregation, RAWA had retained the inclination of women to comfort each other and used that to form operating units composed of small groups of women, but the organization was very inclusive of men. Al-Qaeda took the same background to extreme lengths, forming a pathologically anti-woman, ultramale cadre.

Both of them have a certain advantage over us: While we were comfortable and at home in modernity, they had never gained a foothold there. To have modernity shift into a new and as yet unfamiliar form is not as disconcerting for them as it is for us.

The current term to describe this newly emerging era of social and political reality is *postmodern*. If there is no real consensus yet on its defining features, then there are two good reasons for this. First, it is always more difficult to understand and analyze something when you are still in the throes of it; assessments are usually and more readily made at a historical distance, the way we now speak of the Dark Ages, whereas while they were being lived, they certainly did not have that appellation. Second, this new era is in its beginning, which obviously makes it harder to define than an age that has unfolded more of its character.

Contemporary theory is currently inclined to operate with three categories. There is the premodern age, roughly equivalent to the Middle Ages. Albert Borgmann defines its characteristic features as "local boundedness, cosmic centeredness and a belief in divine constitution."* In other words, that age—which lacked the facility for easy transportation—kept people geographically and mentally confined to their own local area, while their religious beliefs centered around a hierarchical, divinely sanctioned form of rule and a strong belief in the hereafter that gave purpose to earthly life and explained its tribulations. Individual freedom and independent judgment had no role in that society. Nature and society were ordained and structured by God, and human hierarchies reflected his authority.

The modern age represented a colossal and dramatic shift. Though it took time and many significant social upheavals, the order that eventually emerged gave central importance to the individual, believed in human domination of nature through science and technology and gave rational thought the primary position in explaining the universe and ordering the world.

Postmodernity reflects a departure that might turn out to be at least as radical as that between the Middle Ages and

---

* Albert Borgmann, *Crossing the Postmodern Divide* (Chicago: University of Chicago Press, 1998), p. 5.

the modern age. While its extent and nature can't yet be completely defined, some of the emerging qualities are a focus on communitarianism, extreme flexibility, "informed cooperation" as the basis of political legitimacy, a high degree of information processing and a great tolerance for particularism combined with a wholly new sense of global unity. What jumps out at us when we review the qualities ascribed to postmodernism is the word *contradiction*, even *paradox*. If the premise of postmodernity is borne out, then this is an order that rides roughshod over most of our existing boundaries and structures, unites and combines things that would earlier have been considered absolutely incompatible, finds commonalities where the naked eye sees mainly vast and unbridgeable differences, dissolves prior systems into irrelevance without even bothering to confront them—and does all of this with natural ease.

RAWA, sending out a call for help into the anonymity of the World Wide Web in clumsy English from a remote location, then receiving an outpouring of support and forging deep bonds with distant affluent people who had never heard of Quetta before and really had no logical reason whatsoever to concern themselves with this matter—that is postmodern politics in its pure and quintessential form. It is postmodern because it initially seems illogical or paradoxical. With a paradigm shift, it suddenly attains coherence—like those 3-D pictures that were popular a few years ago, which held an image visible with one particular focus but were just a scramble of elaborate patterns with any other.

If we look at the world through the focus of modernity, we see nation-states, powerful financial institutions, negotiated trade relationships sealed by treaties, ethnic groups, religious groups with their attendant leaderships and hierar-

214 ~ Cheryl Benard

chies and codes. But shift the paradigm and a whole alternative system that relies on totally different affiliations and allegiances can potentially reveal itself.

The existing order of modernity is understandably determined to continue, to defend its paradigm against the lure and the claims of this new rival. The institutions of modernity suddenly have a collective interest in their shared survival, even if they were formerly enemies. The tendency of fundamentalists from religions that in the past have bitterly opposed each other, to the point of crusades and wars of liquidation, to suddenly form bonds and cooperate is one powerful example of this process. The sudden friendship between the United States and Russia, two powers whose monumental struggle defined important stretches of the modern age, is another illustration. In the struggle for its survival and dominance, all institutions of the current paradigm become allies—even those who have in the past traditionally been enemies. This is logical, but it is also ironic, because the inevitable strategy of forming a natural but paradoxical alliance is a postmodern one—one that will contribute to the paradigm shift, even as it tries to block it.

One of the leading authors of postmodern theory, Walter Truett Anderson, refers to this struggle on the part of the old system to keep its structures in place as an "autonomy project." Ensuring that people's first and foremost loyalty is to their nation or to their ethnic group is an example of an autonomy project. But the postmodern world, with its increasing numbers of displaced persons and refugees and mixed marriages and emigrants and expatriates and multinationals and travelers, creates a growing body of people who no longer feel identified by just one racial membership, one nationality or one ethnic group. In his terminology, these people are "consciousness minorities." Presciently, in 1991, Anderson predicted that women would play a particularly central role in bringing about the new postmodern paradigm—logically, because the old paradigm didn't offer them a very satisfactory place. "Women are a very large consciousness minority, and I think they'll be doing the most to subvert the autonomy projects of any identifiable group," Anderson surmised.*

RAWA and its global supporters fulfill that prediction. They not only subverted the autonomy project of the Taliban, which was trying to restore premodernity, but are currently engaged in subverting the autonomy project of modern diplomacy, which wants to mold Afghanistan into a nice conventional male-preponderant nation-state according to the old criteria of ethnic composition, in a setting where ethnicity is not a relevant identity for most citizens anymore and where ethnicity has caused nothing but havoc and destruction in the past. And why does conventional diplomacy want this? Because the autonomy project—preserving the existing world order of modernity—is the overriding goal.

Look at RAWA's statements, and you will find that the organization moves easily and fluidly, unselfconsciously, in the dual universes of modernity and postmodernity. Consider, for example, Tameena's previously cited statement concerning their "foreign policy" toward the West: "When we criticize the West or something that the West is doing,

---

*"Postmodern Politics—An Interview with Walter Truett Anderson," *Reclaiming Politics,* fall/winter 1991, p. 32. See also Walter Truett Anderson, *Reality Isn't What It Used to Be* (New York: Harper and Row, 1990).

then it means the policy makers, the decision makers, and the governments, not the people, never. We always had wonderful supporters, mostly among the U.S. people. We always criticize their government, their policies, their leaders, but never their people. And the same happens with the European countries, because we have many, many supporters. When we were in different meetings in different parts of Europe, we were so welcome, they were so warm, and they were so glad to meet with us, and they were ready to provide any kind of help for us."

The nation and its population are no longer the same entity. There are significant areas where they need to be considered as actors independent of each other.

RAWA AS A POSTMODERN MOVEMENT

When you think about it, the sheer existence of RAWA is a political implausibility. How could the most backward country in the world have produced one of the most daring women's movements in the world?

There's a certain symmetry and justice to that, yes, but it's not usually how things work. It would be far more realistic to expect those poor women to huddle, cowed and demoralized, in their shacks. Even as a fictional movie plot, RAWA would be a tough sell.

A country in which 93 percent of the women can't read, a country run by a terrorist regime that doesn't even allow them to walk on the street without a male supervisor, with rules enforced by floggings and executions—and the most effective civil resistance comes from a women's group that operates in the underground? That sounds like some sort of oriental fairy tale. That's not Machiavelli. Maybe it's Scheherazade.

Yes, Scheherazade. The ruler of her kingdom hated and distrusted women and had embarked on a systematic killing spree to eliminate them. Scheherazade could have kept herself safe, but instead she deliberately put herself in the path of danger to stop him, volunteering to be his next sacrificial bride. Scheherazade was something of a pioneer in the realm of asymmetric conflict. Her opponent was the lord of the realm, with every conceivable power at his disposal. Scheherazade had nothing but her imagination and her intelligence, and with those she outwitted him.

Besides an equivalent skill at asymmetry, RAWA has a number of other features that mark it as a postmodern political movement.

- *RAWA's operations use a combination of simple, premodern and sophisticated, high-tech methods.*

If premodernity is local and parochial, while modernity represents the efforts of metropolitan centers to conquer and assimilate outlying zones, then postmodernity depends on technology to form new kinds of nongeographic communities and to affirm local identities without reducing their members to that affiliation alone.

The Internet is an essential tool for postmodern movements. It is absolutely necessary to the planning, funding and logistical support of their operations. The Internet and e-mail turn what under other circumstances would be just a small, localized group into a multinational movement, capable of sharing information and planning coordinated actions whose effects are immeasurably enhanced by the ability to act in concert.

This capability is a great equalizer. Powerful institutions have the capacity to act in locations of their choosing, because they have the mechanisms to put that into action. But with the Internet, opposition movements have speed and presence. Their members are already in place and, given information, are increasingly in a position to *re*act just as quickly as the institutions can act.

Going online was a qualitative turning point for RAWA. The day they decided to post a website was a fateful moment in their history. They didn't realize it at the time, but they certainly know it now, and refer to it often with a certain amount of awe. The Internet enhanced their safety and political effectiveness—thousands of people all over the world, many of them very vocal and with at least some measure of access to their governments, were keeping a watchful eye on their RAWA friends and making sure their activities stayed on the media's radar screen. Their donations made RAWA's ongoing work possible.

But RAWA's success hinged equally on an obsolete item of clothing that dated back centuries. The most dramatic and high-impact information that RAWA was able to distribute via the World Wide Web had been gathered with the help of a very different kind of web—the little strip of mesh sewn into the burqa at eye level. Afghan women were compelled by force to wear the burqa, but RAWA turned it into one of their secret weapons by hiding their cameras beneath it and shooting photographs that condemned the Taliban more surely than a thousand words could.

- *The organization is decentralized, with a high degree of autonomy for the individual committees or cells but simultaneously with a high degree of structure. The struc-*

ture consists of a series of concentric circles, of which the innermost circle is clandestine.

When the Taliban was in power, RAWA operated under extreme conditions, especially where its activities in Afghanistan were concerned. Obviously, it wasn't possible to clear every decision with "headquarters." A Taliban garrison was being moved into your neighborhood—should you move your school? An official from the religious police had been overheard muttering his suspicions about someone—should you warn that person? To wait for directives was impossible, much too risky. Local groups and individuals had to be relied on not only to come to independent judgments but to plan and initiate action entirely on their own. Certain basic principles were agreed upon, and if necessary, the individual or the cell had to take it from there. For example, all literacy classes followed the same program and structure. But if they had three members or twenty-five, if they continued to meet or were suspended indefinitely, was a local, ad hoc call.

That al-Qaeda is an exclusive men's movement while RAWA is a women's movement is obvious from their style. Al-Qaeda negates and seeks to suppress the emotions of its members. The manual found in the car of one of the hijackers after the World Trade Center attack gave detailed and explicit instructions on how to deaden one's emotions and suppress one's human feelings, including the fear of impending death. Terrorists were given a set of stock phrases and advised to repeat them mechanically in order to stifle their doubts about the mission.

After the attack, the FBI meticulously reconstructed the movements of the terrorists during their final days and hours, revealing a fascinating set of choices. They prayed together and read from the Quran. They visited Gold's Gym, enduring the manager's spiel on how an annual membership would be so much more cost-effective than the short-term membership they were insisting on. And they paid repeat visits to an adult-video store, where they attracted the notice of the owner because they browsed for hours without ever actually renting a movie. All of these activities fall into the category of sublimation and compensation.

Al-Qaeda schools train boys to be unfeeling. There are no women in these schools; there is no mothering, no tenderness. The only parental figure is the stern Quran teacher who stands at the front of the room reciting *surahs*. The effective operative is one who has killed all feeling in himself and feels no pity for innocent others.

RAWA operates at high risk and high levels of danger, but they don't deny emotion. To the contrary, they consider a very emotional style of interaction to be normal and good. They have also discovered that emotion is an effective conduit for political communication. People may be drawn to RAWA because its schools are free and because it offers certain services. But what wins their loyalty and gratitude is the feeling that someone cares about them. A free literacy class is good. But a teacher who takes real interest in your personal situation, tries to help you with your problems, struggles to find new ways to explain things to you when your many worries destroy your concentration—that can affect you deeply.

The scope of the Afghan tragedy far exceeded RAWA's abilities to help. On several occasions, for example, the Taliban engaged in massacres of ethnic minorities. To the extent of its abilities, RAWA tried to support the survivors materially, to help them flee the endangered area and to shelter them once they arrived at the border. But their first act was to attempt to dispatch someone to the area so that the affected people at least should not feel they had been forgotten and abandoned.

RAWA does not shy away from feelings. Sorrow, affection and concern are an everyday part of their political interaction. This is so much a part of their style that it even marks the etiquette of their communications. As one of their American supporters notes, you know that you are dealing with a new sort of underground resistance group when, even in the midst of turmoil and crisis, they sign their e-mail notes to you with "love and hugs."

The role of poetry in their movement is another outstanding feature. On the website you will find a catalogue of grim, almost unbearable photographic documents of poverty, degradation, violence and barbarism. And you will find a catalogue of poems, some by Meena, some by other RAWA members, as well as many sent in by foreign sympathizers. Those of us who have been bashed by other Muslim women, who can at times be roused to indignation even by a well-meant expression of support and solidarity ("You can't understand our culture; this is not for you to judge"), will perhaps flinch preemptively when reading some of these poems. Doesn't RAWA find it odd in the extreme, maybe even a little presumptuous, to have women from North Carolina or Montana compose and then mail off to Pakistan poems describing how it feels to wear the burqa, when they have never worn one and perhaps never even seen one except in a photograph? RAWA genuinely does not seem to look at it this way. They might perhaps post these poems on the website just to be polite, but they do much more than that. They print them in their brochures, refer to them, use quotes from them and give every sign of honestly appreciating them. They appear to consider that woman in Montana, whose real wardrobe ranges from Levi's to a strapless Anne Klein evening gown, perfectly capable of emotionally and psychologically placing herself in a burqa. And why not? In terms of postmodern political communication, the burqa is a shared and powerful image, a symbol representing a joint stance. It makes sense, yet is surprising nonetheless, that RAWA will accept input from outsiders, using an image "owned" by them, without blinking an eye.

Despite its emotion-based, interactive and open style, RAWA is quite highly structured—although this aspect contains yet another paradox. RAWA has a formal level of membership and leadership that is structured and organized, but it handles the informal, "shapeless" body of its international support system with equally impressive management. Every signal of interest, every piece of advice gets a response. American companies, ever striving to improve their level of "customer care," resort to recording random phone calls for supervisors to monitor "for training purposes." They can only dream of the level of "customer care" RAWA provides with apparent effortlessness. With the exception of the highest point of U.S. bombing, when you got an automatic response and had to wait for forty-eight to seventy-two hours for a personal answer, each and every e-mail receives a prompt, serious, thoughtful, individual reply, and if you write more than once, your earlier correspondence is remembered and factored in.

It is obvious on many levels that RAWA values good organization and has a talent for it. Where does this come from? We can suppose that it is a response to the high level of anarchy, chaos and instability that have marked the last decades of Afghanistan's history. Try to imagine the psychological costs of living in such an environment. Your home gone, relatives disappearing, governments changing at the drop of a hat, family members suddenly dead, local leaders changing sides—the feeling of disruption and disorientation must have been massive.

Shahla, who grew up in a RAWA dormitory after losing all the male relatives of her family and being forced to flee, remembers the comfort she found in her new school's thoughtfully and reliably structured day. There they were, in the middle of the desert outside Quetta, a few dozen girls and their teachers, with only a small school building to call home. The teachers decided to delineate the day by following a clear program, which was further marked by changes in dress—school clothes for the school hours, casual clothes for free time. Assigned jobs gave the girls a feeling of personal competency and control. Sanobar recalls how important she felt when she was made responsible for dispensing medicine to other students at her school. Logical, orderly systems and structures provide an antidote to the surrounding chaos and encourage rational thinking.

- *There is a charismatic but remote leader.*

Perhaps because individual identity is downplayed, a charismatic individual becomes a kind of joint figure of identification. This leader takes on a powerful symbolic

224 ~ Cheryl Benard

role. The guiding precepts of the group are authored by this
leader, but in an abstract way. Day-to-day decisions are
made by others; the leader provides the overarching guidance. In daily life, this leader tends to be remote and unap-
proachable.

In RAWA's case, Meena is a constant guiding presence,
although she has been dead for nearly fifteen years. Her
legacy is carefully guarded, and she is considered to be a
martyr.

Even before America's pursuit obliged him to go into
hiding, Mullah Omar was a withdrawn, remote figure.
Images and photographs showing his face were forbidden.
He did not appear in public. Bin Laden lived in the desert, in
the mountains and in caves. He allowed himself to be
filmed, but only in transient quarters, reclining outdoors on
a blanket drinking tea or leaning against a cliff. Iranian
political mythology centered around a "hidden imam," a
leader who had gone into mystical hiding but would reap-
pear at some apocalyptic moment.

Such legendary leaders have concrete life circumstances,
but only the vaguest outlines of them become known. There
are a number of photos of Meena, but I have not unearthed
one that showed her with her husband. You have to dig
deep to learn that she had three children.

Concerning Mullah Omar and bin Laden, it is known
that they married and had children, but there is little concrete information. They are said to be polygamous. Report-
edly they make a habit of marrying their children to the
offspring of other terrorist leaders in order to cement
alliances. Mullah Omar and bin Laden actively encouraged
the mythology surrounding themselves. As vicious terror-

ists, they strove for a lyrical aspect. Bin Laden spoke softly, even when the substance was threatening and deadly, and liked to look into a philosophical distance. Mullah Omar spoke not at all.

- *The ideology is hybrid, a mixture containing elements from many different philosophical and political systems.*

If their methods and instruments of action are a wild mix of old and new, indigenous and imported, so are their beliefs—and the combination will not always appear coherent to the outside observer. It is entirely possible for things a Westerner, mired in modernity, may regard as mutually exclusive to go unselfconsciously into the mix of a Third World postmodern movement. Fundamentalism, socialism, feminism, Islam, Communism, pacifism, secularism—please yourself, mix and match. Globalized antiglobalization? No problem.

Maybe we need to think of it in culinary terms; that may help us not merely come to terms with it but even enjoy it, which will certainly make life in the postmodern age more comfortable for us. After all, why do we enjoy Thai, Greek, Vietnamese, Turkish or Indian food? Because it surprises us with unfamiliar tastes, with combinations of spices we would never have thought of ourselves. At first, we may have found them odd. Sweet and sour? Spicy but with yogurt on it? Salt in your tea? Some will always revolt you. Some you'll try once and never again. Others you will find intriguing, growing to like and eventually even to crave them. In previous centuries, people mostly stuck to their own national cuisines, with a few exotic imports brought by explorers or invaders—coffee and croissants courtesy of the Turks to the Austrians, or noodles carried home from China in the luggage of Marco Polo. In the modern age, we dine from the global buffet. If it's true for food, maybe it's equally true for beliefs, values and codes of conduct.

RAWA describes itself as feminist and antifundamentalist, as democratic and secularist. Its members want equality, free elections, and a separation of church and state. Their vocabulary sounds leftist, even somewhat Marxist, but they are virulently anti-Communist and there's not the slightest little hint of class warfare anywhere on their horizon. I think it's that postmodern culinary thing again. Looking for formulations to express certain categories of injustice and resolve, these were the phrases they found. Unaware of the context and free of the mental and historical associations those terms might evoke in others, they borrowed them for their new political vocabulary.

There's an Austrian restaurant in Washington, D.C., where first you choose a main course from one portion of the menu and then you choose two side orders from a separate list. It is very interesting and entertaining to watch the faces of Austrian patrons when their American guests place this order. To an Austrian, the correct combinations are obvious and there is little room for innovation. An American, lacking this knowledge, is inspired to improvise—sometimes causing near-physical pain to his Austrian companion. As any Austrian knows, a schnitzel goes with potato salad, maybe cucumber salad, and that is it. A schnitzel and red cabbage? A schnitzel and a dumpling? Never!

RAWA and other Third World movements use phrases and terms that to them sound interesting and evocative, without understanding or perhaps caring what they mean to a Western ear, which combinations we consider appropriate and which subtexts we read into them. This causes confusion, because at first reading, RAWA's language can sound predominantly Marxist; people may quickly label them as Communists and then be surprised to encounter a virulently anti-Communist diatribe on the following page, because Communism, to RAWA, means the Soviet invasion of their country and its consequences, mass killings and the destruction of Afghanistan's political order.

Another strikingly postmodern feature is RAWA's attitude toward commerce. The website sells T-shirts, posters, coffee mugs with the image of "martyred Meena" and men's boxer shorts stamped with the RAWA symbol.

Not many prior political movements, feminist or otherwise, possessed the innovative flair to come up with a product like this last one, entertaining, commercially successful and, at the same time, subversive. On one hand, you had the Taliban trying to impose an ultra-Victorian puritanical order, and on the other, you had RAWA, outfitting men in underwear stamped with a socialist-realist image of five combative women raising a banner imprinted with the words "Freedom, democracy, women's rights." What would be the correct term for this? Irony? Feminist capitalism?

- *Members are recruited through schools or charitable services affiliated with the organization.*

The Taliban were the product of Pakistani madrassas or religious schools. Fanatical religious leaders went to the camps, rounded up the boys and enticed their parents into handing them over by promising a free education, room and board. Today, the appeal of these madrassas continues to hold, not only in Pakistan but throughout the Islamic world. For impoverished parents, the offer that someone else will feed, clothe and educate their sons is simply too good to refuse.

The curriculum of these schools is designed to condition and indoctrinate. Little boys spend hours doing nothing but chanting verses of the Quran in Arabic, which for them is a foreign language. Even in Arab countries, where the children theoretically understand the words, the text is much too complicated and archaic for them to make any sense of it. Their recitation is loud, fast and accompanied by a rapid rocking motion—almost a form of hypnosis. If other subjects are taught, it is done only in the form of indoctrination. History is a tirade of hate slogans against the West, against Jews and Christians. Physical education is a series of military drills. The heroes they are taught to admire are terrorists and "martyrs"—suicide bombers. A violent death is held out as the desirable goal of their lives.

But schools are not the only recruiting tools fundamentalism deploys. There are also soup kitchens, clinics, banks that give interest-free loans, counseling services, legal-aid facilities and a host of other social services that attract the needy masses, gain their trust and gratitude and spread the influence of fundamentalism. In postmodern politics, it isn't necessarily the state that provides social security—movements perform that task, thereby circumventing the state, rivaling it as a power center or even discrediting it altogether. Though the results are opportune, it would not be entirely fair to describe these undertakings as purely opportunist. In much of the Third World, the states are failing. They are unable or too corrupt to provide the functions and services expected of them. Through their provision of social services, these organizations and movements provide desperately needed help to their populations and advertise their leadership abilities.

RAWA conducts the traditional activities of a political movement: They organize demonstrations, set up information stands, print pamphlets, hold rallies. And, like other postmodern organizations, they provide social services. Their schools and literacy programs are an important source of new members.

"After graduation, some girls enter into marriages arranged by their families, but many decide to join RAWA," Tameena explains. She herself is one of them. These new members, and especially the women who come to RAWA through the literacy classes, have transformed the social makeup of the organization from an upper-middle-class movement to one with a high representation of rural, working-class and minority women.

- *The organization has an international network of supporters and sympathizers.*

The classic Third World movement of the last century condemned the prosperous West in the most vituperative terms.* The postmodern movement gets its financing from that West.

This happens to be a highly effective way to put the disparity in wealth to creative use. For the Third World movement, the support provided by the West amounts to a very

---

*It would be more accurate to use the term *North,* as in "North-South divide," but for reasons of coherence I will refer to the industrialized countries as the West.

significant amount of money. The Western supporter gets an unrivaled degree of buying power—to use common parlance, a "bang for the buck" that he or she would have to pay ten- or hundredfold for in his or her own political setting. A $20 donation is not very much for a Western organization or political party. In the Third World, that same amount can pay a professional's salary, cover the rent for a refugee family for a month and generally go a very long way.* Among Westerners, it is generally not the Bill Gateses, Ted Turners or Rockefeller heirs who support Third World movements, but factor in the exchange rates and the standard of living, and the donors might as well be as rich as those individuals. This difference in scale is one of postmodernism's secret weapons. Formal organizations are not able to take advantage of it—they have to pay Western overhead and Western salaries to their experts.

Besides money, supportive Westerners provide knowhow, contacts and other necessary contributions. Nonviolent organizations such as RAWA get gadgets, printers, school supplies and software. Less benign groups may acquire bombs, biological weapons and arms of all kinds.

- *Even if the organization is democratic, it has a strong collective element. The group has priority over the individual.*

Changing their names often is a security measure for RAWA members, but the ease with which they accomplish it

---

*In Afghanistan under the Taliban, a surgeon's salary was U.S. $5 per month.

reveals their deep connectedness to their organization and its purpose. This degree of flexibility is classically postmodern; it also expresses the degree of their commitment to a larger political purpose.

On one level, the lack of a real, constant personal name can be comforting, because it makes someone a more difficult target. On another, it may lend expression to a fundamental psychological insight: No matter how much a woman's circumstances change, turning her from a peaceful grade-school child in Kabul to an orphan on the run, from a sheltered Muslim housewife to a refugee, a widow and her family's breadwinner, her self can be stronger than those circumstances and can endure those changes. Whether she is called Khadija or Omeira, she can keep her sense of her self.

I think that RAWA's refusal to change the name of its organization, at considerable financial and political cost, is also related to this dynamic. The names of the individual members may change, but there are two lodestones, two unchangeable pillars of group identity: Meena and RAWA.

In the case of severely traumatized individuals, it seems clear that their membership in RAWA has a therapeutic side. In some of our interviews, women and girls described clear symptoms of post-traumatic stress disorder. They experienced memory loss and disorientation, recurring nightmares, severe depression, suicidal impulses, apathy, high nervousness, an inability to concentrate and other such symptoms.

The traditional Afghan way of dealing with tragedy— namely, to deny it, lie to the victims and hold out false hopes—often intensified these symptoms and the suffering. Children and youths who had lost their parents were told that their mother or father was fine and would be returning shortly. To lend credibility to the story, a specific date for their return might even be given; they would be back tomorrow, or next week or in ten days. This date would pass, and a new one would be mentioned. Eventually, the individual would become suspicious. This was intended to provide a kind of cushioning of the blow—by gradually coming to suspect the truth, the person was supposed to be prepared for it. Instead, what this method usually accomplished was to destroy any last remaining shreds of trust and security, as the individual realized that those closest to her had blatantly lied, and that even confident-sounding assurances could not be believed. By the time they encountered RAWA, many of these girls and women were in desperate emotional straits. They spent their days crying, listlessly dragging themselves through the tasks of their day or even contemplating suicide. RAWA managed to convert many of them back into a fully functional, even happy state.

Politics becomes therapy in a twofold way—by providing an explanation for events that seemed so terrible as to defy comprehension, and by offering a venue for action. What had been lost could not be brought back, but in the larger sense, justice could perhaps be restored. The grieving survivor, who had been immersed in her own personal tragedy, was encouraged to take a broader perspective: She was not alone, many were suffering—in fact, many were suffering more than she was and needed her help. She was not powerless, but could act.

RAWA members will occasionally say things like "I don't matter; my personal feelings don't matter." This sounds alien to our Western ears, because we have been raised to believe that problems have to be confronted, grief worked through. At the same time, we recognize that some kinds of grief that reach the level of trauma require medication, because they can't be "dealt with" anymore. In the context of the kinds of feelings these RAWA women are referring to, a way to escape unbearable feelings of grief can be welcome and healing. In this context, their comments are not a denigration of individual importance but a comforting mantra.

Nor is RAWA hostile to individualism on principle. On the contrary, the organization encourages individual initiative and autonomy. Their educational programs and their income-generating projects aim at making women independent, and the organization systematically grooms its newer members to take on responsibility. Shahla felt appreciative, though sometimes daunted, by her mentors' persistent efforts to push her out of the nest. Recall her words: "I think this is something very special about RAWA, that they are providing many opportunities for us, for the young members, to do independent work. Because as they say, 'I will not always be there for you, so you must learn to continue without me.'"

Al-Qaeda practices the elimination of individualism for the purposes of violence and destruction. It produces people so devoted to the group that they are literally prepared to erase themselves, commiting violent suicide. For RAWA, the group has the opposite purpose—it reintroduces desperate, even suicidal individuals to functionality by giving them the sense that their life has purpose, that it is worthwhile to continue living. Mohammad Atta encouraged himself and his co-terrorists to overcome their fear of the planned mission by hating this life and thinking only of the next. RAWA tries to give women a sense that they can accomplish things in this life. "I wanted to rescue her from being lonely and hopeless and to share with her the good and beautiful aspects of life," says one RAWA activist of her personal effort to reach out to a severely depressed widow.

Still, few things are more difficult than the attempt to get a RAWA activist to talk about herself. It's not that they are introverted, not at all—they are friendly, open, accommodating and sociable. It's more that the cult of the individual is something they don't subscribe to. In particular, those activists who are sent abroad on lecture tours don't like to answer personal questions; in their view, they've been sent to talk about their movement and their country, and anything else would be egotistical and frivolous. The American supporters who hosted Tameena on her visit to the United States during the fall of 2001 had their work cut out for them, preparing her for interactions with American journalists. She would be asked about herself, about her life, her background, her personal thoughts, her feelings; there was no escape, her hosts warned her. It took three interviews, three insistent American journalists pressing for some up-close-and-personal human-interest tidbits, before Tameena, bemused to discover that her advisers had not been exaggerating, bowed to her fate. That didn't make it any easier for her. An impromptu lecture on the problems of recent refugees? No problem. Her personal biography? Tameena really sweated over that assignment, scribbling down notes with an intent and unhappy frown.

- *Its behavior in a conflict is asymmetric.*

In the traditional warfare of yore, there was a battlefield, and there two hostile armies met. Similarly equipped and roughly equal in strength, they advanced toward each other, clashing until a victor emerged. This was classic symmetric warfare. But as time went by, this became rare.

In the Cold War, the main opponents never clashed directly at all. They kept each other at bay through a careful, enormously expensive "balance of terror," fighting occasional skirmishes and even full-fledged wars through the use of proxies. This was more complicated than the old style of warfare, but it still had symmetry: Two superpowers, who were or at least appeared to be roughly equal, kept each other in check.

And indeed, many potential conflicts were suppressed by the tacit agreement of the Soviet Union and the United States to avoid direct confrontation. But these conflicts erupted as soon as the Cold War ended—an obvious consequence, though in the general atmosphere of jubilation over the fall of the Soviet Union, it caught many of us by surprise. The wars over Bosnia and Kosovo are two examples.

With the end of the Cold War, the nature of conflict and warfare changed yet again. The former superpowers no longer seemed inclined to fight each other, but a large number of other global grievances remained. In many of these, a great power stood in the way of what a smaller power wanted. Historically, smaller powers do declare war on larger powers—and it is not that rare for them to win.* This kind of combat is known as asymmetric warfare, because the smaller power has to find ways to make up for its relative disadvantage. Symmetry would not work for such smaller

---

* For a number of very interesting historical case studies, see T. V. Paul, *Asymmetric Conflicts* (Cambridge: Cambridge University Press, 1994).

powers because it would likely lead to their crushing defeat. In symmetric warfare, the outcome is directly related to strength, and therefore, you maximize your chance of victory by matching as closely as possible or, preferably, exceeding the resources of your enemy. If he has four hundred tanks, then you will want to have at least that many tanks, and more if possible; ideally, they should be newer and better. In asymmetric warfare, you have a significant difference in strength and resources, but you still have a degree of symmetry—both sides are states, for example, or both sides are struggling for the same thing, namely, the right to be the government. Since one side is significantly weaker, however, it needs to bring its other resources to bear: stronger motivation, better knowledge of the terrain, greater desperation to win because more is at stake and so on. These give it an edge.

In asymmetric *conflict,* as opposed to asymmetric warfare, a mere edge is not enough. The disparity is so great that any kind of direct confrontation would be pointless. Also, other levels of symmetry are absent in this kind of conflict. Terrorists, for example, can be lacking in affiliation with any state at all; their purpose might be to help the cause of Palestine, of which they are not even potential citizens.

In an asymmetric conflict, logical ratios are not just inverted but completely set aside. As recent events demonstrated, the greater the disparity in objective power, the more insignificant that issue of power can be: Men with box cutters can inflict upon a nuclear superpower one of the worst blows in its entire military history. The asymmetry was enhanced by the lack of any kind of standard format—there was no declaration of war, there was no known enemy, no one identifiable country was involved, there was nothing resembling a classic hostile confrontation.

After September 11, strategists and military experts worldwide realized that they had not sufficiently anticipated this new shift in the logic of conflict. As they hastened to develop appropriate safeguards and responses, it was obvious that they were worried and uncomfortable. This was not their customary terrain—which of course is the whole point of this kind of conflict. You refuse to engage the opponent on the terrain where he has the advantage, and instead find other points of action.

For RAWA, which also faces a vastly superior opponent, asymmetric action comes naturally. Its postmodern quality is enhanced by the fact that here is an organization involved in an asymmetric conflict against a renegade state, one that "should," if things were proceeding normally, be the agent and not the target of asymmetric action.

For American strategists, asymmetric proceedings are disorienting. Not so for RAWA. Never in their lives or in their history as a group did they experience a level playing field, a political situation where they could act directly and stand a fair chance. Even when they were just organizing nonviolent demonstrations of schoolgirls, their opponent would assert his massive force, firing on them and killing the young demonstrators.

Even so, wherever the risk seems tolerable, RAWA engages in overt and direct political confrontations. In Pakistan, they continue to hold demonstrations and to operate in the manner of a political party. Harassment by fundamentalists (and occasionally by profundamentalist police), threats and acts of destruction and violence remain at a level that, in RAWA's judgment, falls within the range of what is bearable. The alternative would be to shut down all overt operations, which would too greatly limit the ability of the organization to be known and make itself heard.

In Afghanistan, however, to confront the Taliban directly would have been pointless and suicidal. An asymmetric approach provided the only possibility for action. Using the anonymity of the veil, RAWA took secret photographs and was able to move its operatives around the country undetected. RAWA turned a simple roll of film into a powerful weapon. The laughing face of a teenage Talib, dangling the chopped-off hands of his victims by a string—these and hundreds of other images were the equivalent of a massive military strike against the Taliban.

This should not be underestimated. At one or two critical moments, these images may well have played a defining role in shaping the policies of the outside world. The BBC/CNN documentary *Behind the Veil,* which featured extensive segments of RAWA footage, was broadcast again and again in the initial weeks after September 11. Following RAWA's incendiary footage of men hanged from the goalposts on a soccer field and a cowering woman shot dead at point-blank range by a Talib on the same field, filmmaker Saira Shah discussed these incidents with Taliban foreign minister Muttawakil. Smug and complacent in his garden, he first announced that executions of wrongdoers were occasions for joy and therefore a suitable leisure event in a public sports facility, then went on to say that if the world community did not like a UN-funded soccer stadium being used for this purpose, it could always fund a separate execution site. When this selfsame Muttawakil was briefly nominated as a "moderate element inside the Taliban" with whom the West might perhaps cooperate instead of over-throwing the entire regime, RAWA's graphic images and his own words condemned him, defeating what would have been a catastrophic idea.

CHAPTER 10

No Place at
the Men's Table

"There is no place for us at the men's table."
—The Portuguese Letters

T
he setting for the 2001 Afghan peace talks was
spectacular: a castle on the outskirts of Bonn,
perched on a hill above the river, imposing, Bis-
marckian, dramatically shrouded in the fog of a German
November. Here, the "parties to the conflict" were to gather in order to hammer out an accord for the future of their
country.

The event was embedded in the usual rituals of diplomatic formality—speeches, receptions, red carpets, crystal
chandeliers—creating a soothingly civilized atmosphere . . .
until you looked more closely at the participants.

Among them were men who had brought endless misery
upon their people, embroiling their country in death and
destruction for the sake of their own greed and ambition.
Some of them were directly implicated in betrayals, massacres and murder. And now they were "parties to the conflict," to be wined and dined and coddled. Meanwhile,
those who had lived as ordinary citizens, or risked their lives
with humanitarian efforts to ease the suffering of their fellow citizens, got no such celebrity treatment. They certainly
weren't invited to Bonn.

Four "parties to the conflict" had been invited.

The "Rome group" was composed mostly of modern, well-meaning individuals, expatriates who have built success-ful new lives but who still grieve for the many tragedies that befell their homeland since they left it twenty or more years ago. Some toy with the idea of going back—not right now, but maybe later, if things seem safe and stable. Not to live, but for the occasional visit, and to show their children where they came from. Some, members of the former elite or an impor-tant tribal family, have grander plans. They remember lives of luxury, houses full of servants, winter residences in Jalalabad, offices in Mazar-i-Sharif, summer homes in Herat.

The Northern Alliance, they were the warriors. As one of them explained quite bluntly in my hearing, "We are the ones who did the killing, so we deserve the most power." How crude. How medieval. The world doesn't work that way anymore. However, count how many seats the spon-soring UN diplomats assigned to each group, and you'll find that yes, apparently it does. Although they represented a small minority of the population, the warriors were given the most votes, by far. The dossiers of their human rights abuses could fill libraries, but by a "gentlemen's agree-ment," everyone had decided to politely overlook this.

The Cyprus Group and the Peshawar Group were com-posed of expatriate Afghans with ties to the governments of Iran and Pakistan, respectively. In return, their clients had made sure that they were at the table.

All of this was known to all involved. You have to be pragmatic, they said. Nobody in Afghanistan has clean hands. There aren't any nice guys.

I was having a hard time with this, frankly. This isn't how they teach it at the university, not how they describe it in textbooks on politics and international relations, not what they allege at the conferences on conflict resolution and diplomacy. I was having trouble with the disconnect between nice, modern, civilized theories and blunt reality. At Harvard's Kennedy School of Government, Swanee Hunt has started an initiative called "Women Waging Peace," and books with titles such as *Getting to Yes* explain how to obtain civilized compromises through rational discourse. In reality, the warriors and the agents and the carpetbaggers meet to carve up the spoils, hosted by the United Nations.

The table at which the participants were to gather was enormous, a huge square structure in a palatial room. It was a men's table, definitely.

The Bonn meeting had been in the works for several weeks, and the international women's lobby had been agitating from the start to have RAWA included. Petitions had been handed to the UN organizers, Francesc Vendrell and Lakhdar Brahimi. Telegrams had been sent. The Green Parties of various countries had tried to intervene. In Kabul, women had held demonstrations and tried to get letters to the UN. High-ranking women diplomats had weighed in. But all this was in vain—Brahimi had selected his "parties to the conflict" and said that they could include women if they wished.

The Northern Alliance had brought along one heavily draped woman who hid behind an enormous scarf, kept her eyes on the ground and never spoke. When journalists insisted on a statement, she mumbled that she was "honored to have been allowed to come."

The Rome Group had brought two women from the exile community, an American-Afghan and a German-Afghan, educated and well-spoken but with no recent first-hand knowledge of their former homeland's women, their wishes, their experiences and their problems. It was exasperating, unbearably unjust. Afghan women had done so many courageous things, had been so active, and now they were excluded—not one single independent Afghan woman was present at these talks. RAWA's international friends launched a last-ditch lobbying effort, unleashing such a barrage of pleading and persuading and calling in of favors that the Rome Group agreed to cede one of its as-yet-unassigned seats to a RAWA member.

This truly generous act redounded to the credit of the former king, who had always been a friend to women and to the issue of women's rights. In fact, even in his old age, he was capable of sudden bursts of feminist rhetoric. (In a statement for International Human Rights Day 2001, for example, he announced that any country that covered the eyes of its women made itself blind. The aging king's radicalism is regularly toned down by his entourage, who frequently deliberately mistranslate his bold statements. "I don't think you captured what I was trying to say," he will protest mildly. He doesn't seem to realize that he's being systematically censored.)

The promise to give up a seat to RAWA did not please everyone—actually, it would be more accurate to say that upon its becoming known, all hell broke loose. You would have thought one was proposing to make each delegate sit on a live hand grenade. Factions and counterfactions promptly formed to renege on the deal. (Sad footnote: The American-Afghan, Sima Wali, was particularly opposed, perhaps at the prospect of being upstaged by the real thing, an Afghan-Afghan activist.) The men lamented the loss of a seat upon which they could have placed one of their buddies. And a RAWA woman—that was an incalculable quantity. Those were not tractable, cooperative women. They were independent, fierce, reckless enough to take on even the Taliban. What might such a woman do? What would she say? Would anyone be able to control her?

Fahima is a member of RAWA's inner leadership. Throughout the period of Taliban rule, she lived in Afghanistan. When Rome agreed to include RAWA, she was the one chosen by her organization to represent them. Upon receiving this message, she departed Kabul and made her way to the border, a dangerous and arduous journey under the hail of American bombs, past the beleaguered city of Kandahar, where the Taliban were barricaded for what many thought might be their last stand.

Arriving in Islamabad, she hoped to join the UN flight that was transporting the other delegates to Bonn, but her name was not on the list. The plane left without her. The German embassy, with regrets, was unable to issue travel documents. The Italian embassy, familiar with RAWA's work and kindly disposed toward them, gave her a visa. Foreign supporters collected money for an airline ticket, and Fahima flew to Milan. There arrangements were finally made for German travel documents, and she proceeded by train to Bonn. A retired German ambassador and his feminist wife offered her the hospitality of their home until matters could be sorted out. Fahima's backers sat with her in the couple's living room, reviewing the steps that had been taken, trying to discover what they had overlooked. "What you've overlooked is, you don't have any Kalashnikovs and you haven't killed people," said the ambassador gently. Though he didn't like it, he had come to terms with the disconnect between theory and realpolitik long ago.

The major events of international diplomacy—the summits, the negotiations, the peace talks—are invariably conducted by a vast preponderance of men. There they are, lined up for the photograph, taking questions at the press conference: men. It's not really what the world looks like anymore, and it's not the case in other areas of public life. Where are the women? Why aren't more of them represented? If pressed for an answer, most of us would probably assume that this is because of one or more of several reasons:

- There weren't enough qualified women at that level.
- Women just weren't that interested in this aspect of politics.
- Women didn't feel self-confident enough to demand to take part.
- Women hadn't been involved in the preceding events (the war, the economic negotiations, etc.) and therefore didn't really have a role here.

Those same assumptions guide both public policy and feminist efforts. In the field of democratization, a significant number of institutes have been created to deal with these supposed obstacles to women's greater political participation—to school women, empower them, teach them the techniques of public speaking, and raise their self-esteem. The Kennedy School of Government's Women and Policy Program is one example. Women in Development, based in Washington, D.C., is another, and there are hundreds like it all over the world.

However, the above list of obstacles is not really what is preventing the greater presence of women. They aren't underrepresented because they haven't positioned themselves properly or tried hard enough or felt sufficient motivation or radiated enough self-confidence or wanted to be there badly enough. In Bonn, as in a laboratory, one could see what really kept the women out.

Fahima was definitely qualified—more qualified than many of the male participants. She had been at the scene of the action, actively engaged. She was extremely interested, highly motivated and confident that she could make a contribution. She had made her way to Bonn in the face of great obstacles. She was politically experienced, part of a democratic movement. Yet every conceivable discouragement and obstacle was thrown in her path. To witness this was enlightening, fascinating, sobering, radicalizing and enormously depressing.

In Afghanistan, women had met all of the qualifications demanded of them as conditions for acceptance into the "club." They had fought. They had risked their lives. They had persisted. They had educated themselves. They had worked for the common good. But the fact was that the club just didn't want them and had absolutely no intention of letting them in.

The story has a happy ending of sorts. Ultimately, on the third day of the conference, a renewed round of pleading, persuading and calling in favors finally took effect, and Fahima was in. An activist, feminist woman, representing an independent women's movement, actually sitting at the table of the official peace talks, if not from day one, then at least from day three—it was a historic moment for women, a triumph.

And yet how modest was this achievement—and how grueling the struggle had been to achieve even this much. Sixty percent of the Afghan population is female—but to get just one independent female delegate in required a monumental battle. The autonomy project, operating through conventional diplomacy, was waging a war of attrition, a war of exhaustion. They were going to make women fight for every millimeter of turf.

However, as Bonn also shows, there's no reason to be deterred. Victories might be small and difficult, but they are attainable. Women can take the castle. But that's just the first step. Then they have to defend it.

SIMA SAMAR

The Bonn conference appointed an interim Afghan government. Of the thirty members, two were women—thus granting the larger half of the population a representation of 6 percent. Whether that seems adequate and appropriate even for a traditional, backward society, I will leave to the readers and to history to judge. Some tried to put a positive spin on things. Two women, that wasn't a lot, but on the other hand these were cabinet-level positions. Suheila Siddiqui was put in charge of public health. An undeniably tough, resolute person, she had never manifested an interest in women's issues. As an army surgeon, she had spent most of her life in the company of men and was called "The General." Sima Samar, by contrast, minister of women's affairs, had headed an NGO and run health and education projects for women in Pakistan and, like RAWA, some secret schools inside Afghanistan.

When I met her in January 2002, the "autonomy project" was holding her in check. She was the only minister who, five weeks into the administration, had not been given an office, a staff or even a telephone line. Sympathetic for-

eign women had bought her a satellite phone, but at six dollars a minute, she was afraid to use it. She had no money;
who would pay the phone bill? Her colleagues missed no
opportunity to demonstrate their non-acceptance, starting
with the inevitable phrasing of each decision. "So, if all the
brothers are in agreement . . . ," Karzai would say, and she
would rap her knuckles on the table to signal that at least
one voting member was not a brother. This kind of persistence did not come easily for her, Sima confided. Sometimes,
the treatment was so insulting that she felt near tears.
Pressed for details, Sima hesistated, then shook her head.
"Let's just say this much," she summarized, "I am among
difficult people." To get through those moments, she would
remind herself that "I represent ten million women, all of
whom have suffered a lot. My colleagues don't want to hear
from me, they don't want me there, but I push and keep
pushing. I don't want to, but I have to, because it's not
about me alone."

THE FUTURE OF RAWA

The interim government is just one step on the road to a
lasting Afghan government. And RAWA, which has reinvented itself several times since its founding, will again have
to choose a course to match the changing circumstances.

In doing so, they face a dilemma that is certainly not new
in political activism: how to decide where pragmatism ends
and selling out begins. They have to avoid being co-opted,
but they equally have to avoid becoming irrelevant. Their
relationship to government and power is the issue they will
need to confront in the coming years. Several paths are open
to them.

• *They can become a political party.*

This would require refining their stance into a platform and running for office when elections resume in Afghanistan in (one hopes) the not-too-distant future. This would be an exciting choice, in keeping with their pioneer role. They could keep their principled stance, but they would have to come to terms with pluralism in a new way. In parliament and in government institutions, they would have to find a way to work with people and groups they despise, whom they currently condemn out of hand for their past human rights violations. This might be difficult for them.

However, RAWA will not be the only group facing this problem. After all the things that have happened, Afghanistan will need a national reconciliation program similar to that in South Africa, to help people overcome the past and move forward.

• *They could become a more classic women's movement.*

At times RAWA has expressed the hope that if things settled down in their country, they could abandon some of their more peripheral activities such as food distribution and focus more exclusively on women's rights.

• *They can become an NGO.*

This would mean focusing on their educational and health-related services. This is a feasible outcome and has some merits. RAWA's fund-raising over the last months has produced enough money to allow some initial, exciting projects in the area of schools and hospitals. However, depending on how the Afghan government develops, their work inside the country could be curtailed, and they might be limited to working with refugees in the Pakistani border area, who at some point will be repatriated. For example, if the Afghan education ministry centralizes the school system, then independent RAWA schools will not be possible.

- *They can remain an opposition group with the capacity to work underground.*

Given the many uncertainties of the current Afghan situation, this outcome has some merit also. It is not at all certain that the international community's plan for Afghanistan, which foresees a transitional period followed by elections, will materialize. Along the way, some group may attempt to unilaterally seize power, one of the temporary governments may decide to declare itself permanent, renewed civil war may break out or any number of other unfavorable developments may bring about a new crisis.

The first turning point in RAWA's history came with the establishment of the pro-Soviet regime, which consisted of two brutal and warring factions, and was followed by a Soviet invasion. This obliged RAWA to transform itself from a campus-based student movement to a political opposition group.

The breakdown of order in their country, followed by the forced flight of most members to the refugee camps of Pakistan, was the second. RAWA now developed its social programs and developed its base within the population.

Fundamentalist rule, first under the *jihadis* and then

under the Taliban, ushered in RAWA's third phase, marked by underground work.

Now RAWA needs to reflect on the overthrow of the Taliban, assess the international effort to establish a peaceful government and choose its place. If I were a voting member of RAWA, I would probably choose to become a political party, which keeps all participatory options open but doesn't necessarily close off the critical, oppositional role. Because in the end, the best way to deal with the men's table is to sit down, grab some silverware and help ourselves to a nice big slice of everything that looks good.

CHAPTER 11

Gender Apartheid and the Political Order

> *To prevent beard shaving and its cutting. If anyone is observed*
> *who has shaved and/or cut his beard, they should be*
> *arrested and imprisoned until their beard gets bushy.*
> *To prevent washing cloth by young ladies along the water*
> *streams in the city. Violator ladies should be picked up in*
> *a respectful Islamic manner, taken to their houses and*
> *their husbands severely punished.*
> *Women, you should not step outside your residence.*
> —*Taliban decrees issued after their conquest of Kabul, 1996*

W hen the Taliban began meticulously removing everything female from public view, and instituting a system for strictly separating the sexes, the outside world devised a technical term to describe this new order: "gender apartheid." This term was very apt, because it immediately made clear that this separation was occurring by force, that it was a political and not a cultural or natural separation and that it had negative and discriminatory consequences.

Unfortunately, as RAWA consistently points out, Afghanistan is not the only country where fanatics are trying to institute such a system—nor is the battle yet won in Afghanistan. The Northern Alliance includes any number of fundamentalists. Even after the defeat of the Taliban, Islamic fundamentalism continues its activities in many parts of the world, and gender apartheid is a basic element of their program in all of those locations. But why is this issue so important to them, and what role can it play in their political aims?

Much of the Islamic world is suffering from grave economic, political and social mismanagement. Besides the immediate problems of hunger, lack of shelter, poverty, high levels of crime, corruption and violence, what demoralizes people and makes them desperate is the thought that things will never change, will never get better. It's one thing to get through a few bad years, quite another to think that even one's children will still be living in similar misery. A lack of hope and progress understandably makes populations restive.

Movements and governments based on Islamic fundamentalism don't have a coherent plan for solving the many grave problems facing their societies. Instead, they base their strategy on a shrewd psychodemographic calculation. By and large, men are much more prone to violent expressions of discontent than women, and in traditional societies, they are more important and hold more power. By giving men the feeling that their situation is improving *relatively,* if not absolutely, fundamentalists can appease and win over that half of the population at the expense of women, who are the weaker and more peaceful segment of society anyway.

What those societies really need is an improvement in their standard of living and in their level of culture. But fundamentalism can't deliver that. It doesn't have the skills, the ideas or the mind-set to actually make people's lives better or to tackle the very real problems these countries face. But what it can do is to achieve a kind of optical illusion. By pushing women down even more, men receive the illusory sense that they are being lifted up. Fundamentalism degrades women, then invites men to compare themselves with women and to feel relatively much better off, more important and more free.

And there is another factor at play. For its various radical activities, fundamentalism requires a pool of fanaticized young men, who must be kept in a condition of overheated readiness to follow the commands of their leaders even unto death. One way to do this is to keep them in a persistent state of low-grade sexual frustration. Young fundamentalists live in a rigid, completely masculine world. But, like everyone else, they have hormones and impulses. When these are repressed, it creates a level of tension and anger that can be channeled into whatever direction their leaders choose.

Lastly, if you want to inculcate blind obedience, you have to discourage people's faculties of critical thinking and their propensity to ask questions. Instead, you want to encourage them to think in absolute terms, to dichotomize their mind, eliminating subtleties and gray zones and leaving behind only stark opposites: good and bad, black and white, right and wrong, friend and enemy. The absolute division of male and female helps to conceptualize and make graphic this dichotomized world.

The deep rifts and problems that underlie these developments will have to be addressed, soon and effectively—that is the one clear lesson of September 11. We failed to develop a successful approach for Afghanistan, and as a result, that country turned into a giant terrorist base harboring a network of our lethal enemies; the people of that country suffered years of terror and destruction; and in the end we had to go to war.

Unfortunately, this was an outcome to which we contributed, partly through mistakes we made and partly through lethal defaults. Looking forward, we need to explore the reasons as they pertain to our policy, our diplomacy and our values.

FAILURES OF POLICY

Before September 11, most people registered only the occasional shocking news item about Afghanistan—a remote and backward country with no real relevance for the United States.

In the community of policy makers and academics, however, Afghanistan was an ongoing topic, and the experts were involved in a deep and ongoing dispute over this issue of how to assess, understand and deal with the Taliban.

International aid organizations and human rights organizations were locked into painful soul-searching over ethics and tactics. The Taliban's stand on women and their brutal treatment of minorities offended the deepest tenets of international human rights and demanded action. But the only available response was to boycott them. Given how desperate their economic condition was, the threat of withdrawing aid that a shocking 50 percent of the urban population depended on for its daily survival might frighten them—or it might not. The Taliban were notoriously indifferent to the material well-being of their populace. Organizations that provide health care and schooling have it written into their statutes that they must not discriminate on the basis of gender. The Taliban, however, did not allow them to provide services to girls and women. Some organizations closed down their operations in protest. Others felt it was unfair to punish Afghan men and boys for the sins of a government they hadn't chosen, that it was better to help half the population than no one at all. Additionally, many international aid organizations had to deal with threats, intimidation and insults to their foreign and national staff, to the point where they could no longer guarantee their safety. Many of these employees were dedicated individuals who had come to feel a great sense of pity and empathy for Afghan civilians and preferred to tolerate personal danger and psychological abuse rather than abandon them.

At times, their different perspectives put honorable people at odds with each other. Human rights organizations tended to argue for withdrawal and boycott. In the long run, they believed, the only solution for Afghans was to get rid of the Taliban. Providing aid would only prolong the misery by extending the survival of an untenable government. Aid organizations agreed in principle but couldn't bring themselves to take that step. It sounded all right in the abstract: put pressure on the Taliban, isolate them, boycott them, impose sanctions. But in Kabul or Herat, where they worked, those phrases meant that innocent civilians would die by the thousands or even tens of thousands.*

With considerably less emotion, the theory and policy communities grappled with similar issues. They saw three basic choices on how to deal with the Taliban.

One could engage them, continuing to work with them

---

* The title of this NGO study reflects the moral dilemma that shaped the work of aid organizations in Afghanistan: "Violent Conflict and Human Rights: A Study of Principled Decision Making in Afghanistan," October 1998, CARE, Peshawar.

in the hope that they would gradually become more moderate. Over the course of several decades, this might lead them to a level of cultural behavior acceptable to the international community.

Alternatively, one could ignore them, concluding that their stance on women—given how backward Afghanistan had been even before, and how attractive fundamentalism seemed to be to many of that region's populations—was a regrettable but inevitable phase in the evolution of the region and the culture. Under this approach, one would develop a minimal list of demands concerning the drug trade and terrorism, and if the Taliban acceded to those, they would be seated at the UN and otherwise left alone.

Third, one could try to split the Taliban, encouraging the moderate elements to stage a coup d'état against the more radical, intransigent elements inside their own organization. The result would still be a fundamentalist government, but, it was hoped, a more reasonable one that oppressed women less and was easier to deal with.

There was a fourth choice: to get rid of the Taliban. This one was considered so unrealistic as not to deserve inclusion. Ironically, that was the one that, in the space of only a few weeks, was realized.

Major policy institutes such as the Council on Foreign Relations and the Peace Institute held repeated seminars and meetings and conferences at which these choices were heatedly discussed. For those of us political scientists and regional experts who were concerned about Afghan women, these meetings could be hard to take.* When the humani-

---

* This group can best be described as "a lot of women and Mr. T. Kumar," the wonderful Washington representative of Amnesty International.

tarian aid organizations decided that it might be best to live with the Taliban, it was a choice they made with pain, and you could respect their reasons. The policy community, by contrast, had no such honorable motives. It was infuriating to hear their self-serving calculations about how "harping on" the women's issue would spoil Western policy makers' and academics' burgeoning rapport with their Taliban counterparts, who were just starting to trust them and open up to them. It was exhausting to maintain constant vigilance lest the issue of women slip quietly off the agenda, awful to hear oneself like a broken record shrewishly bringing the matter up in every meeting, frustrating to raise one's hand again and again with the same remarks while one's colleagues fiddled with their pens and thought, "Oh no, not her again!"

And sometimes they would invite Leili Helms to these meetings, to "liven things up." An Afghan who had married the son of a former CIA director, she now served as a one-woman Taliban fan club and self-appointed spokesperson without portfolio. Journalists found her colorful because of the CIA connection and were amused that a modern Afghan woman was championing the Taliban. I witnessed the effect of this "liven things up" method at a Peace Institute conference. The meeting got off to a promising start, with a large number of regional experts present, including the group Physicians for Human Rights, who had just completed a difficult survey inside Afghanistan. Then Leili Helms rose to speak. Wearing a pin-striped suit with trousers, she asserted that life under the Taliban was bliss and any reports to the contrary were lies, that the economy was booming, agriculture was thriving and Afghan women felt respected, happy and safe, and that while she had not yet seen all of these marvels for herself, she planned to visit this utopia soon. This was too much for even the apologists to stomach, and the meeting ended in pandemonium.

Oddly, this "liven things up" formula was unique to Afghanistan. Institutes did not generally apply it to other subjects. It is not common academic practice to put together a panel of professionals and then throw in an eccentric provocateur as a wild card. It revealed a disturbing inconsistency in the way we were looking at the world.

THE FAILURE OF VALUES

Sweeping cultural generalizations are rarely accepted in educated circles, nor are blatantly sexist observations. Both are subject to contemporary mores that forbid ethnocentrism and command tolerance and equality. But there's a loophole—a loophole called Afghanistan.*

For some reason, Afghanistan is widely regarded as the one global exception to political correctness. Statements that would be condemned as racist or ridiculed as orientalist stereotypes if someone applied them to any other country or culture are deemed acceptable when the Pashtuns are the topic.

Probably it's the country's remoteness. Before this current conflict made all of us conversant with such place names as Tora Bora and Mazar-i-Sharif, Afghanistan was practically a synonym for geographic obscurity. In a world all too explored, all too globalized, that alone accounts for its fascination. Here is a place where people still drink fer-

---

* It seems likely that a similar loophole would apply to some other countries in that region, and certainly to countries such as Iraq.

mented yogurt instead of Gatorade, wear blankets and baggy trousers, with not a single Nike wing or alligator embroidered on any of their surfaces, and travel by oxcart instead of Rollerblades.

But there's a fine line between fantasy and projection, and Afghanistan seems to blur the mark. That might not matter, except that some of the affected individuals are aid workers, desk officers, reporters and analysts—people whose perceptions help form our policy and our style of interacting with the Afghans, people who at this moment are determining what the future will hold for Afghan women and men and what their quality of life and their human rights will be. Fantasy, indulged in private, does no harm. Projection, on the other hand, can do a lot of damage.

The projections most frequently encountered, in relation to Afghanistan, revolve around two core ideas: that Pashtuns, the dominant ethnic group of Afghanistan, are a wild people fundamentally and refreshingly different from the effete, overcivilized humans who otherwise populate this planet; and that the relentless oppression of women is part of their gutsy, lusty approach to life.

I have personally heard these views, either stated just as crassly as they are above or in more nuanced form, expressed countless times in seminars, planning sessions and conferences. But for two recent and typical illustrations, we need look no further than *The New York Times*. One article is entitled "Afghan and Pakistani Tribe Lives by Its Guns and Honor," and it opens dramatically:* "When a male child is born in a Pashtun village, gunfire is the first sound

* Rich Bragg, "Afghan and Pakistani Tribe Lives by Its Guns and Honor," *The New York Times,* Sunday, Oct. 21, 2001.

he hears. Pashtun men celebrate the birth of a brand-new warrior by firing their rifles into the sky, and the lead falls back to the powdery earth like drops of hard rain.

"The Pashtun, who are the dominant tribe in Pakistan's Northwest Frontier Province and make up about half the entire population of Afghanistan, have done this since they first robbed British dead of their muskets two centuries ago. Muskets did not shoot very high and the bullets were tiny . . . so there was little risk from falling lead during the celebration.

"Then, generations later, Pashtun took Kalashnikov rifles from Soviet soldiers. . . .

"'But the Kalashnikov bullet was so big and heavy that, when we fired it in celebration, it dropped back down back out of the sky, and killed us,' said Sher Zaman Taizi, a writer, professor and elder in the village of Pabbi, just outside Peshawar. That does not mean the shooting stopped. Tradition, the elder said, holds firm here."

This use of distinctly literary descriptions—lead falling to the "powdery earth like drops of hard rain"—urges us to find these people romantic. If it were true that the Pashtuns continued their practice with Kalashnikovs, routinely killing celebrants, then this would not be a mark of great intelligence. "Colorful, but of course not as rational as we are"—that is how colonialism traditionally viewed the rest of the world. Those it disliked were denigrated, but even those it liked were not treated as intellectual or cultural equals. Their exploits ranked under the "silly, endearing foibles of those quaint, stubborn Arabs/Kurds/Pashtuns," an approach that insults even as it praises.

"This is a tribe that anthropologists consider one of the oldest on earth, bound by a common language, but also by millenniums of marriage, and by blood. . . . A proud, almost arrogant people who fought Alexander the Great, they have fought among themselves for centuries, as families do. Their lighter skins hint at Aryan blood. 'Handsome, well-built, powerful and strong,' intoned Raj Wali Shah Khattak, a professor of Pashtun studies at Pashtun Academy in Peshawar and a Pashtun himself."

This paragraph is troubling. What does the "lighter skin" refer to? Lighter than what? Not lighter than that of the other Afghan tribes, if we even want to get into this kind of a discussion. The Tajiks are definitely lighter than the Pashtuns, as are the Hazaras, who have oriental features and pale skin. And what does *Aryan* mean here? Historically freighted, this is not a scientific category or an established racial designation. Colloquially, *Aryan* is associated with the German racial ideal glorified by the Nazis. What "hint" could link the Pashtuns, with their brown skin, black hair and brown eyes, to the blond and blue-eyed Übermenschen of Hitlerian lore, and why would anyone want to make such a connection? Some Afghans consider themselves Aryans, true, but so do some fringe groups in the United States.

"Handsome, well-built, powerful and strong"—maybe we should send dating agencies instead of aid organizations to rebuild the Afghan economy. And recall the source of this description: "Raj Wali Shah Khattak, a professor of Pashtun studies at Pashtun Academy in Peshawar and a Pashtun himself." Wait—"professor of Pashtun studies at Pashtun Academy in Peshawar"—wasn't that a segment on *Saturday Night Live*?

The mix of assertion, romanticism and political fact creates problems of judgment that distort the story. For example, obviously at least half of the Pashtuns must be female, but nothing in the article suggests that. Women don't make an appearance until the last paragraph: "There is, in Pashtun law, an alternative to war. If one village or clan wrongs another by killing one of its members, the village of the killer can offer to the wronged village a girl, to be taken as a wife by one of the villagers. But the woman . . . is mistreated all her life. She is never regarded as an equal. 'She is persecuted. . . . It is tradition.'"

So, we learn next, is racism: "The Pashtun demand that, in a post-Taliban Afghanistan, the new government should . . . give a leading role to the Pashtun. . . . To the Pashtun, the Northern Alliance . . . represents Tajik, Uzbek, Hazara and other minorities. The Pashtun do not consider those groups as their equals. . . . If the Northern Alliance tries to rule, it will be only the beginning of another war for the Pashtun, said elders and historians here. And war is just one more tradition." That, tragically, has been true for large stretches of Afghan history, where Pashtun efforts to dominate the other ethnic groups have extended to the point of massacres and have prevented successful state building. Here, it's presented as mere folklore.

This article illustrates what happens when we romanticize culture. The Pashtuns, because they are colorful, archaic and good-looking, are given a kind of exemption from the current global consensus on values, a human rights carte blanche. Yes, they persecute minorities and abuse women, but they're so terribly picturesque.

In this book, we have heard from men—completely typical, average Afghan men—who are light-years removed from any of the traditions or attitudes described in this *New York Times* article. From traditional (including rural) families, only moderately educated, in lower-middle-class professions, having grown up in refugee camps, exposed to fundamentalist influence, these were ordinary Pashtuns. Recall their thoughtful responses, their way of grappling with the issues of life and politics and culture, and you begin to see how insulting articles such as the one just quoted really are. These are intelligent people caught in a difficult place and struggling to come to fundamental judgments about how they want to live. They deserve better than our clichés.

So, most definitely, do Afghanistan's women, Pashtun and otherwise. They are the victims of the second *New York Times* article. Entitled "The Veiled Resource," this article also romanticizes, but notice the difference in tone.* When tribal men are the topic, the tone is dramatic, sentimental; you can almost hear the drums. The second article, addressing the issue of Kabul's women, is coy and jocular.

"I was in a burka shop the other day, chatting with the male proprietor, when two women walked in to browse the latest fashions (powder blue, gold embroidery)." This is the classic opening for a comedy routine. "I was in a burqa shop the other day"—the lighthearted introduction cues us that the article will be amusing. Women—that's a recreational issue.

"They observed silently as the two of us men discussed whether women want to wear burkas. It seemed a bit ridiculous, so I asked the women: 'What do you think?'"

"Scandalized, they raced out of the shop." I find this image obnoxious: the relaxed, powerful American male,

* Nicholas Kristof, "The Veiled Resource," *The New York Times,* Dec. 11, 2001.

perfectly at home in a Kabul burqa shop, in companionable conversation with the local, and able to terrify and scatter women like chickens with just a casual word. And by the way, what language was that word in? Does he speak Pashtu? Dari? Did he address these women with a serious interest in their views, in a language they understood? Why is the undertone one of amusement?

Archly, the writer relates that he spent a week "accosting" random Afghan women on the street, intending to interview them about the burqa, the Taliban and their views on women's status. Time and time again, he was "rebuffed." An outcome easily circumvented, if the journalist was sincerely interested in meeting and speaking with Afghan women, not just in caricaturing their restricted freedom.

Investigative journalism gains access to interview partners far more challenging than a conventional-minded Afghan woman. A female colleague, for example, could stop women on the street and speak to them, the method Kristof seems to prefer. If he could not find such a colleague, he could hire a female translator, one of the many Afghan women professionals who worked for international organizations or NGOs and are quite accustomed to such assignments. If Kristof had been determined to speak to the women himself, he could have arranged this either by going through Afghan men and having them set up respectable chaperoned discussion groups in a setting acceptable to Afghans or by asking the abovementioned Afghan women professionals to organize such a meeting for him. Randomly accosting women on the street, in public, was not only ineffective but also very rude and disingenuous, the outcome known beforehand and conducted just to make a point.

But what is that point?*

The article is weirdly disjointed, mixing paragraphs that seem to mock Afghan women and make them seem incapable of change with almost radical paragraphs urging their liberation. It jumps from one extreme to another.

First, the author draws a parallel to Japan, a highly traditional, patriarchal society that had equal rights for women more or less forcibly written into its constitution by the postwar Allied administration. A similar emancipatory contribution could, he suggests, be a beneficial outcome of the U.S. presence in Afghanistan today. But then he promptly erases this good idea in his very next paragraph, which features his lone female Afghan interviewee. Wahida Kamily, a twenty-three-year-old high school graduate, was the only woman who spoke to him. "Through the mesh of her burqa," she informed him "primly" that women should obey their husbands and that it was "right" for a man to beat his wife if she didn't.

The article ends with six factual passages, in neutral lan-

---

* On January 5, 2002, ABC aired a report from Kabul by its correspondent Jim Wooten. He had met a group of Afghan women, former schoolteachers, and interviewed them about the burqa, their life under the Taliban and their expectations and plans for the future. One of the women had organized a home school during the Taliban years. Several of them had just gone to the new Ministry of Education, asking for their jobs back. The women explained to him why, when they went out on the street, and even though they despised it, they still wore the burqa: because they remembered the Northern Alliance from its earlier period of rule and weren't confident that the situation as yet was safe. Their remarks were eerily borne out, as the journalist reported. Northern Alliance soldiers arrived at the house where he was conducting the interview and arrested the family's father. Before releasing him, they warned him not to talk to, or allow any of the women in his family to talk to, any more foreign journalists on issues such as women, the burqa or politics.

guage, outlining the importance of women's participation to economic growth and social progress, citing a number of Asian nations where this has proven true and exhorting the United States to regard the uplifting of Afghan women's status as an essential part of our nation-building effort there. Then it concludes with another joke, citing an Afghan man who initially seems to support women's political participation, only to take it back with a quaintly backward statement.

What does this leave the reader with? An abstract bow to equal rights, and alongside it, erasing it, the vivid anecdotal message that Afghan people, including the women, are light-years removed from wanting that. Who is this randomly chosen Wahida Kamily? Can one speak "primly" while completely covered under a burqa? What were the circumstances of this interview? Is there any reason to suppose that she speaks for millions of her countrywomen? What about the hundreds of women who demonstrate every week in Kabul for women's political inclusion and against the burqa? How about an assessment of the situation from some of those educated, professional Afghan women who used to be doctors, lawyers or journalists but were forcibly housebound under the Taliban? Wouldn't any of those women make much more interesting interview partners for a motivated journalist?

We are left with the impression that Afghan women are frightened little chickens who think it's fine for their husbands to beat them and don't really expect things to change. Why, look, even a high school graduate holds these submissive views!

This portrayal is, as a true rendition of recent Afghan history would make clear, highly unfair and inaccurate. In this book we focus on RAWA, but RAWA is by no means the only instance of women's resistance. Many other women ran secret schools, provided clandestine health care and subverted the Taliban's rulings in any number of ways. They are not the meek, somewhat comical slaves described in this article. From the many Afghan men and women we have so far met in this book, what comes across to me is how closely they resemble us in their values and aspirations. It is not their curious exoticism that shines through but their interest in a new and better way to live.

There's not a lot of wilderness left in this world, a fact bemoaned by critics of globalization. Tourists are everywhere, stomping across the planet in their Nikes, slathered under layers of Banana Boat sunscreen and expecting to find a Pizza Hut.

Some yearn for a spot of earth as yet untouched by modernity and its bland, comfortable sameness, and believe that they have found it in Afghanistan. With its rugged landscape and its archaic features, it can entrance you, make you feel that you have been transported to another age entirely. But you haven't—there's only one planet and only one age. It's still the third millennium, and no one has given us the right to choose which bits and pieces of it we want to share with the Pashtuns. History has shown that their land experiences periodic droughts, but no one will argue that we should therefore let them starve. Warlordism may be a tradition there, but it's one they're going to have to give up, because under the auspices of international terrorism, the rest of the world can't afford to let them continue playing that kind of game. Even if oppressing women were their tradition, it would rightly fall in the category of droughts and other problems that the progress of history and civilization provide us with the means—and thus the obligation—to alleviate.

We need clarity of vision, about others and about ourselves. We need imagination but not fantasies, and certainly not romantic delusions. We don't need to all be the same, but we do need to look at everyone through an equal lens.

THE FAILURE OF DIPLOMACY

Diplomats, meanwhile, were not romanticizing the Taliban, but they were equally failing to make any notable progress with them. For five long years of Taliban rule, no formula for dealing with them emerged. What is astonishing—especially in retrospect—is the patient persistence with which the international community persevered in efforts that very manifestly were not going anywhere.

Occasionally, there would be a break in the façade of professional diplomacy. At one point, for example, it got to be too much even for the nonjudgmental, endlessly patient UN negotiator Francesc Vendrell. The Taliban, he bit out after yet another endless, fruitless negotiating session, had "lost touch with reality."

His exasperated, impulsive sentence contained an insight. Though no one chose to explore it further, the Taliban were indeed not behaving in a logical, consistent, rational fashion. They were not responding as other states and actors did, and that fact paralyzed the international community. Thrown off stride, it just kept trying its familiar approaches and formulas, even when they weren't working.

This is worth thinking about, because the Taliban are not likely to be the last case of this kind. Commentators speak of them as "hijacking Islam" and "holding their country hostage." These are apt characterizations, and it is alarming to think that, barring a massive terrorist provocation that occasions a full-scale superpower military effort, the world has no better way of dealing with such disturbances.

Instead, the machinery of international affairs cranked on. World-class diplomats traveled to Kabul to hold solemn negotiations with uneducated young men over bizarre points of protocol. Would foreign aid workers, to get visas, have to sign a statement agreeing that yes, the Taliban could stone them for adultery if they should indulge in that offense? Would the Taliban please release the staff of the Italian hospital, arrested for the offense of speaking to opposite-gender doctor colleagues in the hallway?

Even if they were able to rationalize the substance of these talks, didn't the diplomats notice that they weren't getting anywhere, that sensible agreement was not being reached? These negotiations would go on for weeks, sometimes months, over some detail that the Taliban had fixated on. Delegations would fly in repeatedly for a series of meetings, then leave without a result and schedule the next round. Then, at some mysterious point, the Taliban interlocutor would announce that the discussions were now concluded and he was ready to "refer the matter to Mullah Omar," who could never be directly spoken to, was never seen and did not explain his decisions.

In one way, the story of the Taliban is a tragedy. Products of war, trauma and destruction, a group of young people who themselves had never known a single day of normal life or lived in a peaceable, normal society seized power and attempted to set up a regime. In the end, they caused enormous suffering. Until the violent conclusion, no one seriously tried to stop them. Tens of thousands had to die, including thousands of Americans in faraway New York and Washington and Pennsylvania, before action was finally taken. And one can't fully blame the Taliban, or hold them accountable. Many young Talibs truly believed in the messages of their reclusive leader; now they lie dead in mass graves, their arms tied behind their backs, butchered by the Northern Alliance, reminding us of the followers of other cult leaders whose visions ended in death.

American military officers were confounded to note that most Taliban troops, when bombed, "did not react in a normal or expected way." They didn't even have the common sense to scatter and run. They just hunkered down, terrified, and waited to be blasted. And this was not the only example of counterintuitive conduct on the part of the Taliban.

It's a useful exercise to try and discover more about their internal logic, their way of making decisions. For that purpose, let's go back to the start of 2001 and attempt a simulation exercise.

This is the scenario: The Taliban are in charge of a small, impoverished, nearly destroyed country. Twenty years of war have left the cities and towns devastated and the farmland riddled with mines. Cripples, widows and orphaned street children abound, but the civil war continues, and the Taliban are unable to subdue their challengers, who hold 10 percent of the territory. Two major earthquakes have left substantial damage that remains unrepaired. Now, a severe drought is threatening up to three million Afghans with starvation. Almost one million are homeless, wandering aimlessly in search of food and shelter. Tired of these problems, neighboring countries have closed their borders to Afghan refugees. Several warlords have announced that they are joining the civil war—on the opposing side. The UN Security Council has imposed sanctions. When the Taliban had first marched into this devastated country five years earlier, the population welcomed them. Their piety led people to believe that they would impose law and order and end the corruption and anarchy. Unfortunately, little has been accomplished since then. Lacking the skills of government, they have no notion of how to establish an infrastructure, how to plan an economy, how to build an administration. They don't even know where to begin. Neighboring Pakistan is eager to help, but their motives can't be fully trusted; they have long wanted to annex Afghanistan and would love to gain control of the government.

There's a popular series of video games, SimCity, SimTown and SimTower, that confronts you with the tasks of running a city, a town and a large building complex. You are faced with the constraints of budget and limited resources and unforeseeable crises, and within those parameters you exercise your skill at choosing options and deciding on priorities.

Essentially, what a government does is to play a kind of SimCountry. It faces a set of tasks and problems and has financial and other constraints. There is a set of options for dealing with these problems; each option carries consequences, holds risks and demands a specific price.

If we visualize the Taliban in this context, then given the extreme constraints facing their country in the spring of 2001, there was really only one way for them to play the game. They could try to mend some fences, which people were eager to help them do in the interest of regional stability; seek advice, which countless experts were anxious to give and large institutions were prepared to pay for; call on the international community to help them survive the looming humanitarian disaster, which it was poised to do and had collected the necessary funding for; allow the NGOs to step in with the skills, knowledge and resources they themselves lacked and let them build infrastructure and institutions and train a corps of local experts to eventually take over; stabilize the domestic situation and bring living conditions up to at least a minimal standard, so some trained and educated expatriates would feel it was safe to return home; seek a political formula to end the civil war; and devote all available energies to rebuilding the country.

But that was not what the Taliban chose to do. Instead, they alienated the international community through a steady series of outrageously offensive acts; appeared combative and hostile whenever addressing the international community; created the maximum number of obstacles for NGOs and UN agencies, to the point of throwing some of them out of the country; destroyed priceless cultural monuments, thereby alienating one of the world's major religions and simultaneously ruining a potentially invaluable tourist site; and devoted their legislative efforts to such matters as drawing up new lists of import bans (wigs and eyeliner strictly prohibited) and thinking about what color socks women should be allowed to wear.

That the Taliban unhesitatingly chose the second path frustrated and perplexed the international community, analysts and policy makers. It should have tipped them off that classic diplomacy was probably not going to work here, that normal state-to-state relations were not a likely outcome with this particular partner.

Instead, many chose to believe that the Taliban were merely inexperienced, undereducated and unfamiliar with affairs of state. That was true as well and might have served to explain one or another random misjudgment, especially during the first years of their rule, but it could not explain the staggering entirety of the kind of system they were trying to impose or the fact that things were manifestly becoming more rather than less extreme.

The Taliban governed from a capital city that was little more than a heap of rubble, and did not undertake the slightest effort to repair things. They purchased a fleet of Datsuns and drove these through the streets of that battered city for five long years, apparently without ever feeling the impulse to clear away the mess and rebuild. The exhausted, war-weary and defeated citizens of Dresden and Berlin and Vienna were out on the streets as soon as possible, clearing the debris and trying to make their cities function again. The Taliban, by accounts now coming out of Kabul, did not even bother to put furniture in their offices or repair the holes in the walls of their ministries. They didn't try to conduct a public health survey. They didn't try to attract investors.

Here's what they did instead. Upon marching into the capital and being welcomed by a desperate citizenry, they immediately collected all televisions and smashed them. Next, they yanked the ribbons out of any cassettes they found, and strung them into giant wreaths with which to decorate intersections.

Otherwise averse to structure and organization, they set up two elaborate bureaucracies: a Ministry of Vice and Virtue to establish lists of forbidden offenses and collect the names of people suspected of committing them, and an odd kind of "marriage bureau" that attempted to register all unmarried girls and make the list available to interested bridegrooms for anonymous selection.

In the spring of 2001, the Taliban issued two new edicts notable even by their own standards. Henceforth, the first edict announced, veiling alone would not be sufficient. Any woman who was out in public would additionally have to ensure that her appearance did not "have a human form." Secondly, women were now forbidden to visit "parks, picnic areas or other places of leisure."

On the face of it, these were just two new building blocks in the system of gender apartheid the Taliban were installing. Still, something about these two edicts was new, crossed a new kind of line. No human form—that was almost chilling. To be banned from parks, meanwhile, was reminiscent of the world's most infamous racist systems.

Apartheid is unnatural enough when applied to races. Apply it to gender, and society fractures in an entirely new way. Men eat together, work together, go for a stroll in the park together on mellow spring evenings, picnic together on flowery meadows . . . meanwhile, the women are at home behind windowpanes painted black by government edict, to keep any man from accidentally catching so much as a glimpse of them.

There is nothing else left between men and women in that kind of a world except sex. They can't be anything else to each other—not colleagues, not friends, not neighbors, not partners. Take away everything but sex, and obviously sex becomes enormously magnified. The Taliban, ironically, were bringing about the exact opposite of what they claimed to want. Like the Victorians, who ended up having to cover their furniture because their radical ban on sex ended up making even piano legs seem sexual, Taliban puritanism backfired. Gender apartheid is artificial and profoundly unnatural; therefore, installing and maintaining it as a social system is difficult. It requires enormous social and psychological effort to keep men and women physically and mentally apart—and the outcome will not be a very balanced or healthy society. The radical prohibition of the feminine, its banishment from the culture and the resultant burst of nervous hypermasculinity is a formula for trouble.

"Parks, picnic areas and leisure facilities"—the group of locations designated by the abovementioned Taliban ban represented an interesting choice. These are not classically places of illicit assignation; they are much too public for that. Especially in the context of Persian culture, these are traditionally the places where extended families congregate, from great-grandmother to great-grandchild. These age-old, popular family outings were now banned. Instead, there was one new locale where the Taliban did allow joint attendance by men and women, and where families were encouraged to go: public executions. In the spring of 2001, public executions, public floggings and public amputations of hands and feet were the only destination for a family outing officially encouraged by the Taliban. In place of normal relations between men and women emerged a society organized around violence.

There is another feature worth noting. Many of the Taliban's rules had the direct or indirect consequence of bringing men into intimate physical contact with other men. The religious police were not supposed to touch women, at least not with their hands. Beating them with sticks or whips was all right, not just to punish infractions, but as a routine method of "female crowd control." Men were beaten, too, but they were also touched in multiple ways. The Taliban would raid the bazaar, for example, to check the length of men's hair. If the hair exceeded the permitted length, scissors were brought out on the spot, and the offending man's hair would deliberately be cut in an uneven and patchy way so as to expose him to ridicule. While head hair was supposed to be short, beards were expected to be long, as evidence that the man had not performed the forbidden act of shaving since the Taliban issued the order. Beard length was measured by having Taliban soldiers twine their fingers into the suspect's facial hair, a strangely intimate kind of contact that was understandably resented by the victims. At prayer time, Taliban teams patrolled the streets in search of slackers, who would be whipped. These are not usual forms of government-citizen interaction.

In June 2000, *New York Times* correspondent Jeffrey Goldberg visited Pakistan and Afghanistan and spent time in the Haqqania Madrassa in the northwest frontier province, one of the religious centers–cum–school instrumental in producing Talibs and other young fundamentalist foot soldiers.* Mullah Omar holds an honorary degree from this institution, its director claims a close personal friendship with bin Laden and the head preacher had authored one of the fatwas, or "religious opinions," instructing the faithful to kill Christians and Jews. This institution, in short, was part of the Taliban's heartland.

Many parents were delighted to send their sons to this school and to others like it. Not only was the education free,

* Jeffrey Goldberg, "Inside Jihad U.: The Education of a Holy Warrior," *The New York Times Magazine*, June 25, 2000.

the children were also provided with room and board. From elementary school through graduation and even beyond, that son was taken care of. Later, he could have a career in the Taliban or some other fundamentalist organization. Some parents valued the economic benefits most; others specifically hoped to give a son to the jihad, the holy war— that would bless their entire family.

Goldberg found the madrassa, the only home these boys would know once they were deposited there at the age of six or so, to be a grim and cheerless place. The dormitories were filthy and Spartan, bare of anything that might comfort or please a child. No sort of entertainment or diversion was allowed. At mealtimes, the children lined up at the kitchen door and a scoop of food was ladled into their bowl. There was no mothering; for that matter, there weren't any women. The teachers, the cafeteria staff, the cleaners, all were men. There was nothing like a family day or a parents' day, when the children might receive visits.

One of Goldberg's guides during his stay was seventeen-year-old Muhammad. The young man had never been exposed to math or science or a foreign language or history or computers. Instead, he had studied the Quran. Being a Pashtu speaker, he could recite but not comprehend the Arabic text he had spent years memorizing.

The only women he had ever spoken to were his two sisters and his mother. After puberty, it would not have been appropriate for him to hug any of them. Goldberg asked the students what they thought their parents might feel if their sons died in the holy war. Such an outcome, they replied, would make their parents "happy."

To no one's surprise except maybe Mullah Omar's, these young men were preoccupied with thoughts of sex. Goldberg and the accompanying photographer soon found themselves confronted with questions, discussions and even clear sexual advances on the part of the older students. "Meeting students out of class . . . made for a number of interesting moments. I had, for example, been asked for sex, as had Laurent Van Der Stockt, the photographer with me. Sometimes the propositions were intimated; sometimes they were unusually blunt, especially given the Taliban's official position on homosexuals, which is that they should be killed. Those few students who knew a bit of English seemed most interested in talking about sex. Many of them were convinced that all Americans are bisexual, and that Westerners engage in sex with anything, anywhere, all the time. I was asked to describe the dominant masturbation style of Americans, and whether American men were allowed by law to keep boyfriends and girlfriends at the same time."

Having banished women, the Taliban were left with a quasi-homosexual public realm, to which they reacted with additional repression. As Amnesty International's reports document, Taliban persecution of homosexuals was particularly brutal. They even invented a new execution method for them, which, unlike the punishments of stoning and flogging, had no basis whatsoever in Islamic tradition. They crushed them by placing them behind a brick wall and then running a tractor over them.*

In his book *The Taliban,* Ahmed Rashid notes the Taliban's proclivity to give their violence a sexual turn. In battle or when taking vengeance on a defeated city, they dispatched their victims with three shots: "one bullet in the

---

* Amnesty International. See their Afghanistan country reports on web. amnesty.org/ai.nsf.

head, one in the chest and one in the testicles."* Their initial attack on the Buddha statues of Bamiyan focused on the groin, which they specifically targeted with missiles. And in 1996, when they dragged Afghanistan's former president Najibullah from the UN compound in Kabul, where he had been promised sanctuary, they castrated him, then dragged him behind a Jeep around the presidential palace and finally shot him dead before delivering the same treatment to his brother. That the UN continued to show such extraordinary endurance in hoping to negotiate and engage in dialogue with the people who had so brutally violated the immunity of a UN compound is remarkable.

One of the women we interviewed for this book was Mariam, a participant in RAWA's literacy classes. She was a refugee, a rural woman from a traditional background, and her assessment of the Taliban was considerably less optimistic than that of the UN. All the men she knew, she assured us, disapproved of the Taliban, found their ideas concerning women to be contemptible and didn't want to live in their sort of a divided world. However, she went on, the Taliban did offer some advantages to men with certain inclinations. A Talib could get a wife who wasn't just half his age but a quarter of it. He could buy her from a starving family or just claim her by force. What kind of men were attracted to the Taliban? we had asked her. "Perverted ones" was her considered reply.

TRAGIC GAMES

"Taliban soldiers try to surrender in Kunduz, but the Arab fighters among them won't allow it, vowing to fight to the

---

* Ahmed Rashid, *The Taliban* (New Haven: Yale University Press, 2000), p. 73.

death." "Captured Taliban soldiers are taken through the city on trucks, children throw stones at them and mock them." In November 2001, newspapers and television carried reports of mass killings of Talibs and showed footage of angry civilians defiling the dead bodies of Taliban soldiers and of Northern Alliance troops beating and taunting Taliban prisoners. These reports remained confined to the margins of the news; there were other, larger stories, and no one felt much inclined to pity the Taliban. Still, I couldn't help remembering my first visits to the region, in the 1980s.

I had spent a lot of time in the camps then, desolate settlements in the no-man's-land along the border. There was nothing there for a child to take comfort in—no balls, no sports fields, no playgrounds, no toys, not even a tree or a random scrap of something that an inventive child could use as a plaything. There was just sand and rock and tents. Any stranger was a welcome diversion, and boys would follow you wherever you went, like stray puppies. Many were, by the Afghan official definition, orphans, which meant their father was dead—they might have a mother, but in the common view, a woman alone was so vulnerable and helpless that you could not count her as a parent.

The camps' men were not kind to these boys. They would suddenly reach out and smack one of them, or chase them away. Then the boys would run off, back to whatever nowhere they spent their endless days in.

Those boys grew up to be Talibs, and as awful as their rule of terror had been, I couldn't avoid a feeling of regret. No one cared about them, no one helped them, and no one taught them—until the extremist mullahs of Pakistan saw in them the promising raw material of their own grandiose fundamentalist vision. They rounded them up, fed them, dressed them, sat them in their classrooms, filled their heads with their own eccentric ideas of what Islam should be, then gave them guns and sent them home with orders to establish a new and pure Islamic order.

Finally, belatedly, these boys had something to play: Sim-Taliban.

Meeting little opposition, the young men marched into Kabul and then kept going. Intoxicated by power, terrified by a task they were completely and utterly unqualified for, they began to govern exactly as you would expect a group of ignorant young men to govern. Remember their "ministers" and their "ambassadors"? Extremely young, they specialized mainly in giving blustery speeches. At times you could get the impression that they were deliberately testing the limits.

No one set them limits. Instead, they were allowed to careen ever further into extremism. Western visitors talked to them but "didn't want to tell them what to do," thus leaving the door open for Arab radicals, who had no such qualms.

For years, experts and diplomats approached the Taliban gingerly. In the end, the provocation became too grave, and the world came down on them with massive force. One cannot help but wonder if there might not have been a better way. The thought is worth pursuing, because the Taliban are not unique. In various places, young men who have never known a single day of normal life are being psychologically misused for someone's dreams of glory. Not just their own populations but the rest of us, too, are likely to pay the price.

A Note on Methodology

The research for this book was done under unusual and extreme conditions.

It didn't start out that way. My original plan was to study RAWA as a women's organization making an effort to oppose fundamentalism. Edit Schlaffer, my longtime research partner, and I had planned to interview refugee women, teachers in refugee schools and political activists, including those engaged in underground activities against the Taliban, which at that point—the summer of 2001—seemed in regrettable but firm control of the country. Then came September 11, followed by the U.S. move against the Taliban.

After the war began, our desire to keep the plan going increased a hundredfold. But was it feasible? We discussed it with Asifa Homayoun. Asifa was a member of RAWA, with a scholarly bent and a keen interest in sociology. Interviewing and documenting were part of RAWA's daily work. Members of their organization traversed Afghanistan constantly as self-designated reporters and sociologists, speaking to witnesses of Taliban atrocities, to survivors of attacks and to ordinary people to get information and a sense of the public mind. The results were posted on their website or printed in their magazine. RAWA's agents thus became our interviewers. We designed a basic sequence of questions, and RAWA provided the kind of access no outsider could ever have obtained, especially once the war broke out. The border region of Pakistan is easily accessible, but only RAWA had a network throughout the different regions of Afghanistan and in the areas contiguous with Iran.

If we had set out to do it deliberately, we could not have chosen a more dramatic timeline for our research. The interviews fell during one of the most intense phases of military and political change in Afghanistan's admittedly turbulent history. When we started the interviews, the Taliban were still firmly in control, and their overturn seemed unlikely to refugees and activists alike—a distant dream. The Taliban were hated, and they inspired enormous fear. To criticize them out loud, even in Pakistan, required courage. The people we interviewed spoke freely but asked us not to use their names.

Then the World Trade Center fell. The chaotic first ten days or so after that terrorist attack represented the only hiatus in the interviews. Everyone in the border area and in Afghanistan was in a state of panic. What would the Americans do? Whatever it was and however understandable it seemed, would they, and those they loved, survive it?

Then the bombing began. Many of the people we interviewed understood its purpose and clung to the American military's promise of precision targeting, but that didn't make things easier to take. Besides the fact that many of its members were in the direct line of fire, RAWA was also busy with a flood of new refugees. Asifa, in Kabul at the time, not only was busy trying to steer her organization through this time of turmoil and help people made homeless by airstrikes but also had to deal with her own three frightened children.

They couldn't sleep at night, she told us, not with the constant noise of the bombs. "They keep asking me to take them to a place where there are airplanes but no bombs," she said.

Next, the cities started to fall. Mazar-i-Sharif. Kunduz. Kabul. Kandahar. At what point did people really start believing that the Taliban would be defeated? Our interviews show a clear turning point. When people started giving their names, that reflected a new confidence that one could now express an opinion and not expect instant retribution.

But the people interviewed now had a new worry—would the Taliban be removed only to be replaced by a new set of fundamentalists and tyrants? Recollections of the Northern Alliance and their earlier reign of terror began to claim more space in the interview, along with suggestions for what should happen instead.

Ordinarily, in conducting research, the goal is to control the "noise" so that your data can be standardized and quantified. That wasn't possible with the rapid and enormous change taking place in Afghanistan. You can't control in a war. On the other hand, an acute crisis presents the social scientist with unique access to information and above all to moods and reactions with an intensity and authenticity that cannot be duplicated later, once the outcome is known and people have processed the events. The interviews in this book, therefore, provide a unique time-lapse view of the fall of one of history's most bizarre regimes.

Using the method of action research, our interviewers were free, indeed encouraged, to expand on our basic core questions in whatever way seemed appropriate. The men interviewed were all under thirty-five and educated at least through grade school. The women from the literacy courses were between thirty and fifty, and none had any prior schooling except for one woman who had once been taught part of the alphabet by a mullah. The RAWA activists interviewed were diverse in terms of age, class background and educational history. Everyone interviewed in this book is an "ordinary Afghan"; none had lived or traveled outside the country or the camps, with the exception of the RAWA ambassadors.

In the past few years, there have been two major empirical studies conducted among Afghans. Both of them were weighted heavily toward educated, urban males—the kind of person that outside researchers walking into a traditional setting can most readily gain access to and can converse with at their own greatest comfort level. In that sense, we are very proud of our sample, which gives representation to the rural, the uneducated and the female members of the Afghan populace—voices seldom heard in sociology, to its great detriment.

Index

About the Author

Cheryl Benard is the director of research at the Boltzmann Institute in Austria and a consultant to the RAND Corporation in Washington, D.C. She is the author of several best-selling nonfiction books in German, primarily on women's issues, and has published two novels in the United States. She lives in Potomac, Maryland, with her husband, Zalmay Khalilzad, and their children, Alex and Max.